SILICON ALLEY

DATE DUE

BRODART, CO.   Cat. No. 23-221-003

Cultural Spaces series, edited by Sharon Zukin
Other titles in the series:

After the World Trade Center:
Rethinking New York City
Edited by Michael Sorkin and Sharon Zukin

Buyways:
Billboards, Automobiles, and the American Landscape
By Catherine Gudis

SILICON ALLEY
The Rise and Fall of a New Media District

Michael Indergaard

ROUTLEDGE
NEW YORK AND LONDON

A volume in the *Cultural Spaces* series, edited by Sharon Zukin

Published in 2004 by
Routledge
29 West 35th Street
New York, NY 10001
www.routledge-ny.com

Published in Great Britain by
Routledge
11 New Fetter Lane
London EC4P 4EE
www.routledge.co.uk

Routledge is an imprint of the Taylor & Francis Group.
Printed in the United States of America on acid-free paper.

10 9 8 7 6 5 4 3 2 1

Library of Congress Cataloging-in-Publication Data

Indergaard, Michael, 1956–
    Silicon Alley : the rise and fall of a new media district / by Michael Indergaard.
        p. cm.
Includes bibliographical references and index.
    ISBN 0–415–93570–9 (HC : alk. paper)—ISBN 0–415–93571–7 (PB : alk. paper)
    1. Internet industry—New York (State)—New York. 2. High technology industries—New York (State)—New York. 3. Internet. 4. Electronic commerce. I. Title.
    HD9696.8.U63N745 2003
    338.4'7004678'09747—dc21

                                                                    2003013134

FOR JOHN AND FUMIKO
who endured—and helped me
endure—the creative storm

CONTENTS

ILLUSTRATIONS

PREFACE

I was in the right place at the right "moment in time," as the new media people referred to the early Internet days. I had just arrived in New York City in 1994 and was wondering what kind of research I could do here that might fit with what I had done in the industrial Midwest. The key problems for cities there involved the decline of their manufacturing base and the rise of a postindustrial economy that seemed to promote more inequality and less security. In fact, the emergence of the new media in old industrial neighborhoods in cities such as Boston, San Francisco, and New York signalled that an important new chapter had begun in the troubled postindustrial transition of American cities. It initially appeared that the creative folks who inhabit our cities were developing commercial applications out of a potent mix of technology and culture—and that they were creating some kind of place-based form of industrial organization. This was welcome news not only for cities but also for the U.S. economy, which had stalled in the early 1990s. Like most everybody who witnessed it, I was startled when Lower Manhattan's technobomenians seemingly sprang out of nowhere in late 1995. The early accounts in local newspapers and magazines had an almost ethnographic flavor, as if the reporters were anthropologists who had uncovered the strange beliefs and rituals of a previously unknown people. The "new media," as it was called, intrigued me for two reasons. First, at the time in which it seemed that the media giants were extending their reach across just about everything, here was a feisty band of independents who were agressively anticorporate and committed to developing some sort of alternative media—a space for cultural production that would be free of hierarchical control. Second, the organization of the new media called to mind the "industrial district" model of industrial organization in that it featured networks of small, specialized firms concentrated in an enclave. In the late 1980s I, like many researchers (e.g., Charles Sabel, Allen Scott), had been drawn to the industrial district as an alternative model to mass production. Industrial districts seemed to be well suited to a new fragmentation of mass markets into a proliferation of niche markets— as evidenced by the flourishing regional economies in parts of Europe and Japan. The districts seemed a promising model for securing and perhaps even revitalizing cities that had been hardhit by industrial change. They were also appealing because they promoted a more open and democratic industrial politics. Thus, the first "story" I pursued about the new media was the formation of what seemed to be a new sort of industrial district— one that combined digital technology with the creativity of cultural producers. This new melding of technology and cultural production was reflected in the audacious name that was given to the district—"Silicon Alley."

By 1998 the story had changed. Large amounts of venture capital were flooding into Silicon Alley, and increasing numbers of its firms were becoming hits in the stock market due to their big initial public offerings (IPOs) of stock. The new media was being subsumed within a very different kind of development—one that was more financial in nature than creative. Most observers either focused on the irrational nature of Internet speculation or embraced the "New Economy" thesis about the wonders of unfettered technology and markets. To me, the core issue was the institutional forces involved: neoliberal policies that made the flood of cheap capital possible and made financial devices more accessible to entrepreneurs, the long-term financialization of the U.S. economy, the spread of new business doctrines about a New Economy, and, more specifically, the efforts to spread the institution of venture financing to emerging sites of new media production such as New York. Especially striking was the way in which New Economy entrepreneurs used images of new media creativity to alter the image of depressed real estate in Manhattan—and to help propel start-ups through the venture financing system and toward the stock market. Such developments resonated with another scholarly focus on cities: their symbolic economies. Of particular relevance was Sharon Zukin's pioneering work—especially her insights on the interaction between material and cultural forms of power. In order to deal with the prominent role of imagineering and speculation in the development of Silicon Alley—and in its impact on the city—I added Zukin's notions about "circuits" of capital and culture to my vocabulary. Then I sought a good vantage point from which to watch the inevitable train wreck that would follow the stock boom.

When the stock market crash came, its dire effects on Silicon Alley took some time to unfold, but ultimately were much worse than I had expected. In no small part, this was because New York's new media became swept up in yet another story—the World Trade Center attacks that helped usher Silicon Alley (as we knew it) to the dustbin of history and left behind a traumatized city. It might appear that New York was back at square one in its postindustrial travails. However, it seems important to make something of the Silicon Alley experience—to recombine the valuable resources that were created and to think through what might be a more desirable framework to use in that endeavor. In fact, strong echoes of the Silicon Alley experience can now be heard, as a broad range of actors look toward New York's creative economy to serve as an engine to pull it out of its latest crisis. Many of the elements of the new space of cultural production that the new media created in the 1990s—and some of the institutional actors that rose to prominence—are likely to come together in some new combination during the rebuilding of Lower Manhattan—perhaps under the rallying cry of building "the First City of the 21st Century."

I propose that the reconstruction should include an effort to create a foundation for a new kind of industrial district—one that supports an ill-defined industry cluster populated by shape-shifting creative types who thrive on account of their ability to cross boundaries. I suggest that what is needed is a new kind of framework for bringing things together—a matter in which government policy matters a great deal. Problems that Silicon Alley had in developing sustainable applications of digital technology during the 1990s revealed problems in the framework that underlay the New Economy: neoliberal policies that selectively withdrew government so as to open up various markets (and subordinate everyone else) to the most powerful entrepreneurs—particularly from finance and real estate. A more desirable alternative, in my view, is a framework where government promotes a more open and more local industrial politics, in part, by opening itself up to requests for support that are developed collectively by assorted district participants and stakeholders.

My acknowledgments should begin with the people who kindly agreed to talk to me. They represented the following organizations: Abstract Edge, Agency.com, Cybergrrl Inc., Electronic Sales Systems, Ericsson Cyberlab, Flatiron Partners, Hudson Williams, New Media, the New York New Media Association, New York University Taub Urban Research Center, Open World Interactive, Pixelpark, Polytechnic University, Pseudo, RareMedium, Razorfish, Razorfish Studios, Silicon Alley Reporter, 360hiphop.com, and Word. Since I wish to preserve their anonymity I cannot thank them individually. I would like to give special thanks to some individuals who helped me make arrangements for interviews, namely Jerry Colonna, Sherry Reisner, and S. Ron Butler. One of the people who gave me the most support in my research was Andy Pratt of the London School of Economics. Andy became an extraordinary friend, mentor, and role model. Our relationship began when he good-naturedly let me (then a total stranger) come along to do interviews with him in the summer of 1998. That it was one of the most intellectually stimulating adventures I ever had was due, in large part, to Andy. I would also like to note the special contribution of Bob Tillman, a colleague from St. John's University. Our conversations helped me develop my thinking on the IPO system and various other suspect aspects of the New Economy. Other people with whom I discussed Silicon Alley included Susan Christopherson, John Eade, Kuniko Fujita, Shinji Hara, Wolf Heydebrand, Richard Child Hill, Richard Lloyd, Paul-Brian McInerney, Chris Mele, Kenkichi Nagao, Ake Sandberg, and Allen J. Scott. My final acknowledgments on the academic side are to those who helped me write a "cross-over" book that would appeal to the general public as well as to academics. First, there are the two people who strongly encouraged me to undertake a book project—Sharon Zukin and David McBride. Besides offering critical intellectual inspiration, Sharon patiently pushed me to commit myself to writing a book that would have a broader appeal—a contribution to a "public" sociology—and helped me pull my ideas together. David McBride, my editor at Routledge, played the lead role in helping me develop the right voice for this project. I think back to my first attempt at writing a prospectus (the words marched woodenly across the page like toy soldiers). While I was deflated when David indicated this to me, he rehabilitated me by announcing cheerfully that the book had great potential and he advised usefully that I try to write a bit more metaphorically. I take full responsibility for the excesses that resulted. Both Sharon and David were amazingly restrained in letting me find my own way. Finally, two nonacademics provided important assistance in helping me find the right voice. There was Lenny Galper who read my first chapter and gave me an enthusiastic thumbs up. And there was Deanna Marx—my mother. At a critical juncture I asked her what it was that people most wanted to know about the dot-com episode. After our talk I wrote chapter 3 and never looked back.

The rest of my family gave other vital support, without which I could not have finished this work. Along with my mother, my stepfather Charles provided love and comfort when I came home for several "working vacations." And my sister Jill White and her husband Steve kindly allowed me to turn their magnificent house into my work studio. In fact, I wrote the core of the book at "the White house." Finally, the ones who deserve the most credit are my wife Fumiko and my son John. They had the love and patience to weather my all-too-frequent bouts of craziness, especially during my frenzied two-month effort to finish.

This book incorporates some of my work that was previously published: an article in *Research in Urban Sociology*, Vol. 6 (2001), pp. 107–46; an article in *Urban Studies*, 40 (2003): 379–401; and a chapter I wrote for *Understanding the City: Contemporary and Future Perspectives*, edited by John Eade and Chris Mele (London: Blackwell, 2002), pp. 339–62. Sections of chapter 2 draw heavily on these works while chapters 1 and 3 include a limited amount of material from these sources. I would also like to acknowledge those who granted me permission to use their copyrighted illustrations: Agency.com (Urban Desires), the Association for Downtown New York (The Plug 'N' Go program, 1998) Bernd Auers and Bryce Lankard. Finally, St. John's University provided substantial financial support at various stages of my project in the form of a summer research grant and a research leave.

CHAPTER 1

THE NEW MEDIA PEOPLE
Who Were They and Why Did They Believe?

In the early days of the World Wide Web few could match the cool graphics of Jaime Levy, self-professed "East Village chick" and "early true believer" in the power of the net. She also hosted some of the hippest "cyberslacker" parties on the Lower Manhattan circuit. While a DJ spun records web pioneers showed off their latest HTML tricks or performed skateboarding stunts in her roomy East Village loft. Most were liberal arts types rather than programmers—principled slackers, arty punk rockers, and deconstructionists from "good" families (several were grads of Brown's Modern Culture and Media department). Some turned their web pursuits into business ventures. Early Internet start-ups were cool because, like punk bands, they were garage projects. The last cyberslacker affair, held near the end of 1996, was marked by a musical farewell to the garage tradition by Nicholas Butterworth, founder of a promising start-up, SonicNet. Formerly, a bassist in a punk band, he screamed out a fifteen-minute rant via a live mike:

> It's the death of the Web as we knew it. It's over! And wasn't it good while it lasted? Who was there, who was there in 1995? Reaping it in—the money, the fame, the parties, all of it flowing in. They came to you—marketing directors, the executive vice-presidents, the general managers, they came to you and said "We don't know what the fuck we're doing." It was beautiful! Everyone here, all my friends, doing creative things with a capital C . . . the dream was to be a media assassin, to be a guerrilla—and to be paid. Well let me tell you something: Now you have a choice. You can be a guerrilla, or you can get paid. You cannot do both.[1]

1

Butterworth found his paycheck (and became a corporate VP) when Sonic-Net was acquired by MTV's parent, Viacom, and transformed into MTV's online unit (MTVi). Other members of Levy's clique have made their mark in disparate ways. Stefanie Syman and Steve Johnson founded *Feed*, a critically acclaimed "webzine" that never made it commercially. Rufus Griscom and Genvieve Field started up Nerve, a webzine whose commercial success shows that "literate smut" pays. Douglas Rushkoff, a professor of communications at NYU and an up-and-coming media critic, has authored books such as *Cyberia* and hosted a PBS documentary, "The Merchants of Cool," on the commercialization of youth culture (by companies such as MTV). Jason McCabe Calacanis created a popular trade magazine for New York's new media industry—the *Silicon Alley Reporter*. Josh Harris, another impressario on the party circuit, turned his cybergathering into an Internet TV studio—Pseudo.com—and announced on *Sixty Minutes II* that his goal was to put companies like CBS out of business. But taking on media giants hardly meant that the party was over. On six occasions Pseudo was raided by the NYPD and given citations for running an "illegal nightclub." Razorfish, a webshop started by Craig Kanarick and Jeff Dachis in 1995, competed with Pseudo to put on the most outrageous spectacles on the party circuit. At the end of 1999 it was a public company worth $1.8 billion and employed two thousand in a dozen offices worldwide. Jamie Levy, who turned down a chance to own one-third of Razorfish in 1995, started Electronic Hollywood, a modest venture that created an award-winning animation short (about an East Village slacker). But like many webshops, Electronic Hollywood "paid the rent" through designing ads, cartoons, and online games for corporate clients such as Tommy Hilfiger and MTV's new unit—SonicNet.

Something strange happened in New York City as the twentieth century drew to a close. Technology became hip. Stranger yet, the city that was the capital of the "old economy," became a "new economy" hot spot of sorts—a playground for wired entrepreneurs and venture capitalists. The shift in hip sensibilities began in a familiar place, the bohemian environs of Lower Manhattan, but the new trend-setters were "*techno*bohemians." These creative types, who had begun experimenting with the Internet in the early 1990s, claimed that the web offered new possibilities for creative expression: anybody could be a publisher and there would be no need to compromise to please corporations. The media would be born anew.

Their visions of how the Internet would change the world inspired new ways of thinking about culture and media. However, in the thoroughly neoliberal 1990s the ability to meld art and technology in the creative process depended on being able to create products and markets—and charm investors.[2] Despite the rebel rhectoric, it was the corporate establishment, including the media giants and the masters of the financial universe, that stoked the fires lit by the technobohemians. Identities and strategies fluctuated in the white heat fueled by easy money and high-octane hype. The technobohemians were among the first to change. By the end of the decade, many had become full-time entrepreneurs seeking methods to make the new media pay its way. And the vision of new kinds of cultural production had become a vision of new consumer "choices." Moreover, assorted business allies also reinvented themselves, hoping to use the Internet to change the world—or at least a profitable chunk of it: corporations eager to go online, Wall Street expatriates turned venture capitalists, developers of wired real estate, newly minted MBAs and veteran execs itching to try out "new" economy entrepreneurship, and a legion of would-be players hoping to position themselves in the "deal flow."

Set in motion by a creative impulse and then propelled by financial forces, this wired carnival wound its way back and forth along Broadway for five years—from SoHo's wild parties to the stock market orgies of Wall Street and finally to the corporate spectacle that is Times Square. The corridor became a space where the rules were suspended while participants, intoxicated with the possibilities of a new media, tried on new identities and roles. This carnival took over the wired lofts and office buildings of artists, entrepreneurs, and executives who explored boundaries between the real and virtual worlds, as well as between culture, technology, and business. As they struggled to establish a new media industry—or exploit its image—assorted interests forged new circuits of culture and capital. In the process they created a place named *Silicon Alley* and formed a particular conception of Internet business opportunity. In order to answer the questions, "Who were these people?" and "Why did they believe?," we need to place them in a distinctive urban milieu that formed in the 1990s.

A PLACE

The Silicon Alley moniker identified both a place in New York City and a concept about the Internet industry. The terms "place" and "industry" usually imply a durability or continuity in sociocultural arrangements. But in Silicon Alley's brief but dynamic history, place and industry were works in progress. Telling the story of Silicon Alley requires an account of both place-making and industry-building—and nearly as many frames of reference as a postmodern novel. For starters, Silicon Alley's development was boosted by larger economic and political conditions that prevailed in the latter half of the 1990s—the heyday of neoliberal policy. Yet, its development drew on, and reassembled in unique fashion, distinctive elements of Lower Manhattan's physical and sociocultural environment. Moreover, bouts of place-making and industry-building that produced Silicon Alley were anchored in New York's uneasy postindustrial transformation. The aim of this book is to show how these forces came together to create this new space of cultural production.

Originally, the geography of Silicon Alley was rather well defined, the name designating a corridor in Lower Manhattan that followed Broadway south from the Flatiron District through Greenwich Village and SoHo. But over time the enclave's boundaries became ambiguous. Major offshoots sprang up in the Financial District and elsewhere in Manhattan; the city government tried to encourage the formation of new satellites in the other boroughs. And, at the high point, there were nearly as many new media firms and workers in the rest of the metropolitan region as there were in the city. However, there was something about the way that the dense mass in Manhattan marshaled energy that made it the clear center.

The district incorporated many elements of a setting that had long supported the making and mixing of creative culture and commercial enterprise. Segments of Manhattan's best-known cultural and commercial thoroughfares (Broadway and Fifth Avenue) ran through its midst, featuring landmarks such as the Flatiron Building (an elegantly strange, antique skyscraper) and New York University (a major research university that is wide open to its funky surroundings). A tangle of idiosyncratic side streets is endowed with thousands of small specialty shops and creative enterprises—many of them housed in old factory lofts (some with the cast-iron fronts revered as emblems of authenticity by yuppies). The warren of lofts, coffee shops, and restaurants allows the kinds of social encounters, both intended and accidental, that nurture creative subcultures. Of course, this terrain could not serve such a purpose if not for the presence of the various kinds of people that contribute to the cultural creativity and diversity of Lower Manhattan: college students, new immigrants, "old" minorities, gays, yuppie gentrifiers, and assorted creative types ranging from established professionals to burnouts and dropouts, with an army of struggling artists somewhere in between.

Much of this environment was incorporated by the new media with spectacular speed. Digital age imagery and infrastructure (e.g., high-speed Internet lines) seemed to bring a new liquidity to place. In part, the built environment was transformed as it was reimagined and reinterpreted. Two notable examples can be found on opposite ends of the enclave. The Flatiron Building, formerly a testament to the pioneering age of skyscrapers, was recoded as Silicon Alley's preeminent landmark—its gateway for those approaching from Midtown to the north. The new media's Downtown anchor was a modern office building that formerly housed Drexel, Burnham, and Lambert—the notorious junk bond firm that was an icon of fast capitalism in the 1980s. In 1996, the building was transformed into the New

York Information Technology Center—a new media hub and instant land-mark signalling that Silicon Alley had reached the Financial District. The physical task of turning large swathes of Lower Manhattan into new media production spaces seemed to be accomplished with similar ease, requiring only the stringing of a bit of wire through buildings—not the large-scale demolition and construction projects that accompanied commercial rede-velopment in the past. In reality, powerful social forces underlay this trans-formation. The rise of the new district was abetted by a larger postindustrial transformation that had left the area's physical and human assets unat-tached or underutilized as of the early 1990s. More directly, networks of or-ganized interests, singularly and in combination, mustered a new array of power relations that helped Silicon Alley materialize.

In part, Silicon Alley was the latest round in the long struggle to reinvent New York as a postindustrial city—a process that elite property interests began to promote while factories still dominated Lower Manhattan. In fact, the large-scale deindustrialization of Lower Manhattan over the last four decades was not only the result of changes within industrial sectors, but also the product of commercial redevelopment (and related rises in real estate prices) that dislodged manufacturers.[3] Consequently, New York, like many cities, has become increasingly dependent on cultural industries and producer services that produce or manipulate symbols. In New York, the traditional media industries (publishing, advertising, broadcasting, motion pictures) accounted for over 137,000 jobs in 1997; business ser-vices and securities employed 245,000 and 150,000 workers, respectively.[4] The most important of the producer services is the financial sector, al-though the real estate industry has a special role in mediating ties between postindustrial sectors and the city. Real estate interests, in alliance with public sector allies, have often tried to repackage and remake Manhattan real estate as a site for high value uses. This has sometimes given rise to grand designs and massive public support for big complexes that help lock-in the city's dependence on the office market. The contested con-struction of the World Trade Center, which swept away a district of small firms and ethnic neighorhoods, was the preeminent example. More often, ad hoc collaborations have pushed redevelopment through. These endeav-ors often involve public-private partnerships—institutionalized as the template for development during the crises of the mid-1970s. At a time when the city was in the process of losing 600,000 jobs and in danger of de-faulting on its bonds, political and business elites agreed that "the city's survival depended on a shared mission."[5] The new media's rise provided yet another opportunity for making over Lower Manhattan.

However, increasing dependence on the media, advertising, financial, and real estate sectors has made the city more vulnerable to business cycles, accentuated by the boom-bust rhythms of speculation; during downturns the city is burdened with surplus office space, especially in the Financial District. This was the case in the early 1990s when Lower Manhattan was pitted with empty space; in addition to factory lofts abandoned by a shrinking garment industry, the deserted space included downtown office buildings vacated by Wall Street firms in the wake of the 1987 crash and the subsequent recession.[6] Importantly, the rhythms of postindustrial expansion and retraction have become linked to the formation of creative communities. For some time, abandoned factory lofts had appealed to artists because they provided large, affordable spaces to work (and live). In fact, the colonization of lofts by artists that began in the 1960s and 1970s led landlords to boost rents, which further contributed to the displacement of manufacturers.[7] This pattern, in part, figured in the rise of the new media enclave. Yet, hundreds of new media firms also ended up in Wall Street office buildings—far outside the traditional terrain of artistic types. To understand this curiosity, and the formation of this new cultural production space more generally, one has to examine how social relationships formed to support the new media—a story that begins with the technobohemian social circuit.

As artists began to experiment with CD-ROMs in the late 1980s and with website design in the early 1990s, a distinctive subculture began to form. Their ranks included college-age young people who felt that opportunities for their generation were limited or mundane (hence, the birth of the cyberslacker). In contrast to the common view that digital technology reduces the need for people to meet face-to-face, many web pioneers sought out such opportunities. The cyberslacker party circuit that convened in the lofts of web notables was one important example. Such gatherings were important both for learning about the latest technical developments in web graphics and for reaffirming the sense that what they were pioneering was of special importance. They also provided spaces for the creation of a special set of sensibilities and ideals.

Initially, the web pioneers were driven by an artistic ethic: Use new digital tools to produce work that was "cool," that is, work that creatively explored the limits of the medium. But, they soon sought ties with business interests so as to be able to sustain their creative work materially, especially as the computer infrastructure and tools for doing the "coolest" things became more expensive. And in truth, for those who hoped to become known for their creative prowess, it became increasingly clear during the 1990s that fame awaited those who used technology to make money. Many approached corporations with evangelical zeal, spreading the word that a new media age was at hand. At any rate, the web pioneers gained powerful allies who not only helped "wire" the spaces of Lower Manhattan, but also made them accessible to creative types of modest means.

Two sets of organized interests played roles in helping a new media community materialize in Lower Manhattan. The first could be termed "new media industry-builders." Their ranks included a handful of venture capitalists initially, and then a number of major corporations whom they drew into the new media adventure. These early industry-builders focused on creating spaces—social as well as physical—wherein connections could be woven between the web pioneers and various business interests. Their success in creating a new commercially oriented circuit for the new media, including the formation of the New York New Media Association (NYNMA), shifted the center of gravity in the new media community. NYNMA proved to be a powerful device for linking diverse elements to the new media (and to the core group of venture capitalists). Its membership—over eight thousand individuals from some four thousand firms at the peak in 2000—included lawyers, accountants, and corporate executives as well as assorted digital entrepreneurs and workers.

When these industry-builders tried to secure a major property to redevelop as a new media center (the future New York Information Technology Center), they found that they needed the cooperation of real estate interests. Though most new media start-ups were located originally well north of the Financial District, the new media was first embraced by a Downtown real estate coalition that included the Rudin family (a major real estate developer), the Alliance for Downtown New York (a quasi-public entity for the Financial District), and the Economic Development Corporation of New York (a quasi-public entity for the city). This group had its own agenda regarding the new media: fill empty office buildings in the Financial District, where vacancy rates exceeded 20 percent in the early 1990s, by linking them with the new media. This strategy was all the more attractive when the new media was becoming identified as the first new industry to form in the city in half a century. Their provision of subsidized wired space in fourteen buildings played a major role in causing some seven hundred tech firms to settle Downtown. Another consequence was to reinforce the Silicon Alley identity while extending its perceived boundaries. When the bull market for Internet stock fueled an explosive expansion of the new media into new parts of Manhattan, other real estate interests similarly used the image of the new media to redefine their territories—further strengthening and extending the sense of Silicon Alley as a place.

A CONCEPT

A new vision of Internet business evolved with the development of Silicon Alley. As web pioneers struggled to connect with corporations, investors, and online users, their sensibilities about the Internet took a marked commercial turn. The commercial idea behind Silicon Alley was that the core problem (and opportunity) for Internet business was not developing technology per se, but creating and distributing new modes of expression that use Internet techology. The Internet economy was said to be a new media and communications business where the main avenue for creating value was developing creative business applications. This view of the Internet defined the enclave's identity vis-à-vis rival centers such as Silicon Valley. It also resonated with New York firms. The "new media" label indicated that its raison d'être was different from that of a computer enclave. New York assets lay in the media industries and business services, not computers.

Recent studies suggest that the power of a technology scheme depends on the networks of support that can be assembled.[8] Likewise, the viability of the Silicon Alley commercial concept has pivoted on the ability of new media actors, collectively and individually, to create ties with business partners, consumers, and investors. The provision of wired facilities by the Downtown real estate coalition was the most successful collective effort to organize material support for the new media. NYNMA's main contribution was to provide arenas where new media firms, job seekers, suppliers, and investors could meet one another and to host forums where new media interests could discuss collective issues.

Individual firms struggled in their efforts to gain leverage vis-à-vis web users and business customers. Most web designers, many of whom had hoped to become strategic partners for corporations, found themselves relegated to the status of subcontractors or modest service providers. Several thousand small computer firms who were able to earn a profit (usually modest) provided the bedrock for the enclave. Yet, they were overshadowed by the attention directed to several dozen start-ups that took more ambitious courses of action, gambling that they could become national contenders in an emerging sector. The gambits of the would-be national contenders usually involved some sort of network-building. Leading web design shops (e.g., Razorfish, Agency.com, and Rare Medium) added a broad array of services, and opened up offices in other cities (and countries), hoping to create extended service networks that would make them indispensable to corporate customers. Online communities (e.g., iVillage and StarMedia) created networks of websites and users organized around a theme (e.g., identities related to women or Hispanics). Some Silicon Alley providers of advertising services (e.g., DoubleClick and 24/7) set up networks of websites that they marketed to advertisers based on the latter's demographic targets. Finally, e-commerce firms, the segment made notorious in the dot-com frenzy, were marketing networks: they tried to use rapid growth and extensive advertising in order to make themselves into entities whose presence (and "brand") would overshadow rivals.

Most of Silicon Alley's would-be national contenders came to see the bull market for Internet stocks as a means of achieving rapid growth—and an instant extension of their networks and reputations. To this end they sought to connect with the financing networks of venture capitalists that fed into the initial public offerings (IPOs) on the stock market. Between 1998 and 2000 over four dozen Silicon Alley firms launched IPOs. As the stock market climbed and peaked, great riches and fame spilled into Silicon Alley. After a run of spectacular IPOs in 1999, twenty-nine Silicon Alley start-ups ended up with combined stock values that exceeded $29 billion. Founders of start-ups such as DoubleClick, Razorfish, Agency.com, StarMedia and iVillage became not only rich (on paper), but also celebrities. Their firms hired large numbers of employees as did firms that were positioning themselves to launch IPOs. The new media's rapid expansion boosted demand for other business services and overheated the real estate market to the extent that it seemed that the entire landscape of Manhattan was being made over.

The local media and leaders hailed the new media as New York's new economic engine—a sector that had lessened the city's dependence on Wall Street,while providing a path for taking New York into a "New Economy." But in fact, the lure of the stock market diverted, and even discouraged, leading firms from trying to turn users into paying consumers or from developing other forms of revenue.

ANOTHER "NEW ECONOMY"

Of course, the party's long over. The economy is indeed entering uncharted territory, but it conforms neither to the alternative media vision celebrated by the web pioneers nor the "new economy" mantra that enthralled stock analysts, entrepreneurs, politicians, and pundits at the end of the 1990s.

Early on, the dreams of an alternative media were relegated back to the subcultural margins as web pioneers sought credibility as entrepreneurs. Yet, the image of the new media as a transformative force burned even more brightly. New media visions and pioneers morphed to become part of a short-lived, but potent whirlwind that caught up investors and American cities. A tidal wave of capital and hype seemed to lift all boats or at least those firms that could tap into Internet-related wealth and images; when the stock bubble burst it was just as indiscriminate in capsizing Internet enterprises. The crash and ensuing slide in stock values smashed the hopes of Silicon Alley's would-be national contenders.

After the crash, Silicon Alley firms continued to work on the problem of making online enterprise pay, but hope faded that they would be part of an autonomous sector. It seemed more likely that most would take the role of producer services and assist corporate giants in weaving the Internet into their oligopolistic webs. Due to their myriad ties with subsidiaries and partners—and their ability to control intellectual property—the media corporations seemed poised to act as "financial shells within which all media can be merged and re-purposed."[9] Some firms that grew rapidly after going public still hoped to get big (and reduce competition) through mergering with, or acquiring, rivals. But the best that most of Silicon Alley's deflated champions could hope for was to follow the route taken earlier by Butterworth's SonicNet: become a subsidiary under the umbrella of a major firm such as MTV. Thus, despite Silicon Alley's anticorporate origins, its raison d'être became ever-more-wedded to New York's standing as a global corporate center.

However, Silicon Alley's ability to leverage New York's corporate base became problematic after September 11, 2001, when the shocking terrorist assault brought down the twin towers of the World Trade Center, killing nearly three thousand persons, and inflicting tens of billions of dollars in economic damage. The utter destruction of the World Trade Center and the staggering blow it delivered to the New York economy signalled that the old order was being challenged, although from a very different direction than had been anticipated. The new liabilities of global economic centers changed the context for Silicon Alley.[10] Symbols of global centrality and agglomerations of specialized workers and firms—once a dependable beacon for talent and money—may now invite targeting and mass destruction. The New Economy isn't what it used to be. Neither is New York (nor the world).

The astonishing reversals of fortune, for Silicon Alley and for New York, raise questions about the relationship between cities and economies that are increasingly digital and global. These issues are of more than academic interest. In rebuilding Lower Manhattan, New York will have to rethink its role and identity vis-à-vis the world economy and its needs and possibilities given the rise of new digital technologies. As the stench of the martyred towers faded, a whiff of desperation became evident. In a *BusinessWeek* issue devoted to "The Future of New York," the headline of the feature story declared, "The Center Must Hold." Even suburban real estate interests who prosper by wooing firms away from the city were quoted as saying that their fortunes depended on New York retaining a "white-hot center."[11] A section under the subtitle, "Silicon Alley," suggested that the magic of digital technology might keep the center "hot." Its author advised, rather hopefully, that an "Information City" complex of advanced business services, featuring a large "communications and computer-services workforce," was now bolstered by a "network of New York venture capital" that had been created during "the Silicon Alley boom." Moreover, the president of the New York

Software Association, discerning a glimpse of New York's future in the recent past, proclaimed that, "Silicon Alley can be a motor of rebuilding, just like we were a motor for the city's growth during the 1990s."[12]

But, what is one to make of the Silicon Alley that turned New York into a boom town during the 1990s? Was the enclave a Potemkim Village set up to snare a share of the not-so-smart money—a show put on to steal the spotlight from "real" centers of technology such as Silicon Valley? To be sure, it was showtime in New York, but at the beginning of the twenty-first century the studied making of symbolic gestures (e.g., entertainment, marketing, financial maneuvers) is a most serious business. Increasingly, it is a business that pivots on the interactions of media, computers, and capital. But what exactly is the role of cities here?

At first glance, one does not have to refer to the city to understand how the Internet and New Economy visions were joined. Even before the stock collapse, writers such as Robert Shiller and Thomas Frank sketched the mechanisms through which various intellectual and institutional threads had come together to promote Internet stock speculation and New Economy thought.[13] Some of the ideals that fired the imagination of web pioneers were embraced by right-wing libertarians and free market fundamentalists who argued that technology would reduce the restrictions faced by individuals and firms. Prominent Internet entrepreneurs such as Jeff Bebos of Amazon.com proclaimed that the new technology had "changed the rules" for starting up firms. The view that Internet technology meant that old rules and limitations could be transcended was given credibilty by financial analysts, business writers, business schools, and even by the Federal Reserve chairman and the treasury secretary.

Yet, these accounts do not explain how new media entrepreneurs and financiers made digital visions more "real" by weaving them into material arrangments—a process centered in the hothouse environments that cities supplied in the 1990s.

Creative Cities and Cyberspace

It is often said that cities no longer make sense in a digital age—that the ease of communication makes it unnecessary for people to cluster together. But, in fact, various kinds of Internet-related firms and workers have clustered in a new kind of urban place—the "new media" district—so as to influence how firms and consumers make sense of the Internet as a commercial domain. Why did these firms concentrate in urban enclaves such as Silicon Alley, the "Digital Coast" (Los Angeles), and "Multimedia Gulch" (San Francisco)? The answer in the case of Silicon Alley is twofold.

New media industry-builders sought the kind of resources that cities are uniquely equipped to supply, while Lower Manhattan real estate interests, seeing in the new media a reason for tenants to believe in the centrality of their properties, embraced new media firms (and visions).

It wasn't supposed to happen like this according to leading oracles of the digital age; "being digital" was being free of material world complexities; the processes of digitalization were "out of control"—beyond the reach of organized social action; digital technology would make economic exchange "frictionless."[14] Digital technology would provide a novel sphere of creative self-invention free from social and material constraints, especially those linked with urban life.

Yet, new media districts were very involved in the actual experience many people had in "becoming digital." A growing literature shows that cities that are centers for creating commercial applications of culture also take prominent roles in digital industries. The increased importance of creative places stems, in large part, from the restructuring of corporations. In *The Cultural Economy of Cities,* Allen J. Scott notes that many media giants seeking to develop distinctive products often "insert themselves into regional cultural-economic systems" where they can create "close linkages and working relations with a variety of other firms, and tap into the specialized skills and aptitudes of the local labor force."[15] Other accounts claim that creative places are taking the place of corporations in coordinating economic activities. Of special note are two books—*The New Geography* by Joel Kotkin and *The Rise of the Creative Class* by Richard Florida—whose celebratory accounts of the rise of "hot spots" in the 1990s directed attention to creative places and workers. Their thesis is that some types of cities are taking broad roles in making commercial use of ideas produced by a growing knowledge economy. As the symbolic attributes of products or services become more important, so too do places that host firms that are "adept at incorporating cultural knowledge, design distinctiveness, and fashionability into products or services."[16] The key claim is that the most critical endowment of such places is lifestyles that draw creative workers—such as the "black-clad artists, video producers, hip advertising executives, and designers" who perform "the artful manipulation of images and concepts."[17] The main attraction is place amenities that support "experiential" life styles; the openness of these places "to all forms of creativity" also energizes efforts to develop products and services that tap into—or evoke— particular lifestyles.[18]

Kotkin provides a useful comparison of new media districts to various kinds of computer industry centers. The latter include powerhouses such as Silicon Valley as well as software clusters that are springing up in peripheral cities and rural areas (respectively, "nerdistans" and "valhallas"). New media centers possess different roles and distinctive social profiles. While computer industry centers rely on science and engineering workers to devise technological infrastructure for the Internet (e.g., computer network systems, operating software), new media districts use an assortment of creative workers in areas such as graphic design, marketing, and advertising to create "content" for the Internet.[19]

Industry-building

I propose that the production of content falls within a larger role that new media districts play: prototyping commercial applications of Internet technology for broader segments of users. This endeavor includes creating new kinds of expression, consumption and exchange—the invention not only of Internet products and services but also Internet consumers.[20] The role in developing visions of wired commercial life meshes well with the creative place thesis. But that thesis pays scant attention to the problematic nature of technology applications, especially the material problems entailed. It is said that if creative types are present in a city, an economic base will soon develop to sustain their activities (if it does not already exist). The new media is depicted as part of a "cultural industrial complex" composed of "increasingly intertwined industries" such as "publishing, movies, advertising, television. . . ."[21] But, in fact, the new media's standing here was uncertain, subject to its success in linking up with assorted industry networks that serve to select, cultivate, and distribute products.[22] Silicon Alley's efforts at commercial applications show that new media districts have to muster various material supports needed to put new notions in motion.

That commercialization of the Internet poses material problems fits a basic finding in technology studies: Extending the reach of a technology pivots on an expenditure of material resources. Bruno Latour, a researcher of technology "networks," uses railroads as an illustration. Though we think of a railroad as connecting regions, in fact, only a limited number of points are linked up, not entire territories. A railroad connects particular places only to the extent that "branch lines are paid for."[23] The same is true for telecommunications systems. Electromagnetic waves are everywhere, but, in order to get CNN, a consumer must pay for material elements that complete the network, namely a satellite dish, or cable hook-up, "a subscription, and a decoder." And CNN, being a for-profit enterprise, must garner enough revenue from subscriptions and advertisements to be able to sustain the infrastruture, as well as the programming—and to make a profit.

The U.S. government created and maintained the early Internet for military and scientific purposes. The question now is, who will pay to develop the "branch lines" of a commercial version. Determining which products can entice customers to pay enough to sustain the enterprise is complicated by the broad changes that digital technology abets—a restructuring and cross-penetration of industries in the computer, media, and telecommunications sectors, previously kept separate by regulations and independent delivery systems. New media entrepreneurs have ventured into this unsettled terrain in search of the "killer application." Given the high stakes, they have had to contend with powerful firms from various sectors, such as Microsoft and Time Warner. Establishing a dominant application would likely "stabilize" some path of technological development, while closing off other possibilities.[24] Thus, the quest for a "killer application" might well determine which sectors and infrastructures would prevail in the digital age.

Accepting now that the problem has a material dimension, let us return to the issue of why cities gained roles in making commercial applications of Internet technology. To start with, cities are rich reservoirs of physical and human resources that can be used in assembling business networks. Just as important, they also provide social arenas and ties that aid in mobilizing these resouces.

Foremost among physical resources are buildings and premium telecommunications infrastructures, such as computer servers and high-speed Internet lines, which are concentrated in large business centers. These centers have the premium human assets discussed above—namely, battalions of creative firms and workers. They also host clusters of large corporations that are potential clients, partners, or investors for small creative firms. Finally, these places are blessed with venues for casual interactions and the webs of social ties they abet: It is the use of existing ties, and even more so the making of new ones, that allows social actors to turn a rich environment into more than a haphazard collection of objects.

Local social networks provide creative enterprises with links to potential clients, workers, support services, and investors. A classic example was Lower Manhattan's old garment district, once the world's greatest center of apparel manufacturers. A combination of collaboration and specialization allowed firms to exploit fashion-oriented segments of the market. Manufacturers focused on design and marketing while subcontracting various stages of manufacture—the cutting, sewing, pleating, button holing, and hem stitching. Specialization advanced to the point where dozens of kinds of services supported the enclave: "design, display and selling of textiles, sponging (cloth shrinking); factoring (textile banking); trucking, agencies that provide . . . models; the supplying of thread and trimming; embroidering; the manufacturers of belts; and repairing of machinery."[25] Add to this providers of marketing, showrooms, and press coverage. Clustering of firms allowed the face-to-face interactions needed to negotiate flexible subcontracting arrangements, enabling manufacturers to monitor markets until the last moment before committing to particular designs and volumes.

My introduction to Silicon Alley as a "place" hinted at some additional roles that localized networks play in spaces of cultural production. Ties rooted in face-to-face interaction (e.g., the cyberslacker party circuit) help establish and reaffirm the worth of novel activities and sensibilities. As new creative communities emerge, their social circuits connect with a city's larger media networks, which results in the reinforcement (and modification) of new creative identities as they are circulated in a broader circuit of institutions and publics.[26] Face-to-face interactions also provide rich forms of information which, along with shared cultural understandings, help cultural producers proceed under conditions of uncertainty that are endemic to design-intensive and innovative industries.[27] Indeed, the degree of uncertainty is striking in the case of the new media. There has been "no 'definitive' new media product."[28] This leaves a firm with few solid clues as to which products and services it should focus on, what skills or capabilities it should cultivate, or what steps in the production process it should do in-house rather than obtaining from other firms.[29] Andy Pratt, a leading new media researcher, remarks that it is also unclear how one should go about combining "software coding skills" with various skills related to "artistic and artisanal expression," for example, "writing and narration skills, visual ad layout, animation and directoral expertise."[30] Here, as in many aspects of the new media production process, *new arrangements tend to be a function of the types of networks that form*—for example, the kinds of skill sets and business sectors that emerging networks bring together in a particular district. In such unsettled conditions, network-building helps create working understandings across occupational groupings and across firm boundaries.

A final role of networks is providing forms of financing that allow firms and investors to minimize or spread out risk. In many cultural production districts, rotating credit associations support firm start-ups or expansions. Less formally, enterprises often rely on "friends and family" to raise money to start-up firms. In fact, this was the source of funding for most Silicon Alley firms. What was unique about new media districts was the adoption of forms of risk capital that were pioneered in Silicon Valley's computer industries—"angel" investing by rich individuals and venture capital funds. It is thought that the insider ties and expertise of venture capitalists reduces the odds for high risk ventures.[31]

Place-making

A new media district is also an epicenter for the reconstruction of place—a matter only partially decided by industrial development. While computer industry enclaves typically begin as *greenfield* developments, new media districts emerge in densely developed central city settings layered by the rise and fall of past industries. The making of new media districts requires urban redevelopment—and thus the cooperation of interests that control the built environment, namely real estate developers and local government. Besides supplying redeveloped properties, they provided institutions (quasi-public bodies, public-private partnerships) that helped market the district. The involvement of real estate interests was central to the extension of the new media across Manhattan, and it produced its own trajectory of economic impacts: a boosting of property values for areas that became associated with the new media and the extension of a sense of centrality to marginal places within Manhattan and even to other boroughs where the new media had established beachheads, such as Long Island City in Queens.

Making a New Media District (The New Economy Way)

In the ecstasy of its rise and the agony of its fall, the story of Silicon Alley has much to tell us about the nature of the new cultural spaces that burst into the limelight in the late 1990s and the New Economy that propelled them. Running accounts at the time depicted sweeping transformations as if change proceeded in a categorical fashion—old arrangements were pushed aside as the economy became "digital," "global," "weightless," or "creative." In contrast, my telling of the Silicon Alley experience shows the change process to be much more messy and to entail many continuities. Applications of technology entail a relentless tapping of, building on, connecting with, and incorporating of existing infrastructures, materials, symbols, and actors. This book also examines issues that deserve additional scrutiny: how venture capital came to new sites such as New York and how it ended up supporting speculation, how power was exercised in the making of districts, and how districts were enmeshed in their historical and national contexts.

Attack of the Changelings (Episodes I and II)

New York web pioneers believed that the Internet could smash the hierarchical power and cultural dominance of a major modern authority—the media giants. Their challenge to authority systems based on knowledge monopolies—and their propensity to cross boundaries and embrace new identities—calls to mind the "deconstructionist" perspective that originated in French literary circles.

Leave it to the era that brought us sockpuppets selling dog food to create the impression that life imitates French literary theory. Yet, new media researchers did find a blurring of boundaries and identities—and a rethinking of hierarchy that extended far beyond the media. Matthew Zook claims that the Internet industry is really "a method for the reorganization of existing systems of production and redistribution" around the "intensive use of information."[32] Wolf Heydebrand and Annalisa Miron declare the Silicon Alley "spirit" to be one of "transcending boundaries"; the new media production process spurred a process of reorganization that is "potentially unlimited"—a continuous "deconstruction and reconstruction" of production organization.[33] From this point of view, *the driving force in the making of new media spaces was the creative impulses of a district production system*; clusters of firms and workers developed innovative orientations and practices—and engaged in ongoing reinvention—as they responded to challenges.

However, my study shows that a second force also drove Silicon Alley's rise (and fall): *a social mobilization of a broader set of actors to connect with the bull market for tech stocks.* This impulse emerged out of encounters with the New Economy movement—a nationwide mobilization whose members announced, interpreted, or promoted the rise of a New Economy. Nigel Thrift remarks that this cultural movement was spurred by a circuit of business experts (consultants, business schools, management gurus)—a group that produces and disseminates business knowledge through engaging in "a process of endless, relentless and continuous critique of the status quo."[34] In the 1990s they advised executives to, in essence, deconstruct organizational hierarchies, and related practices so as to unlock creativity, productivity, and profits. Other interests became stakeholders in the movement; most important was the media, including a new business media, that helped publicize and distribute New Economy "knowledge" about a new version of capitalism. The doctrine touted projects, teams, and "expressive organization" as means for spurring managers and workers to be "passionate," to "do more," and to be more adaptable. The "adaptable" worker seemed a new media type—a worker who engages in "continuous learning," participates playfully in "practices that are only vaguely defined," and performs "constant cultural prototyping."[35]

The New Economy was as much about financialization of the U.S. economy as it was about digitalization. Financial interests led the way in turning elements of New Economy doctrine—a loose association of themes, principles, and practices—into a material framework for evaluating and promoting entrepreneurs.[36] Even before the New Economy era, Silicon Valley's venture capital had, at times, seemed part of a "casino economy" wherein "firm start-ups themselves become commodities."[37] I show that certain features of the New Economy eroded the ability or inclination of venture capitalists to assess risk, turning an infrastructure for innovation into an institutional support for speculation. Such conditions arose during the New Economy mobilization when platoons of venture capitalists—and a horde of wannabes—tried to transplant the institution from its bastion in Silicon Valley to new sites across the United States. In New York, an untested venture capital system became a springboard for Silicon Alley's development and its extension into the larger city economy. Through the venture capital nexus the new media's development became integrated into a system for cultivating start-ups as IPO candidates. In a quest for credibility as New Economy concerns (as well as capital), leading Silicon Alley start-ups hooked up with venture capitalists. And a flock of Manhattan business services and professionals—heeding a call to become New Economy players—swarmed to serve new media firms and to get in the "deal flow."

The Morph Masters

The insurgent ideals and district structure of new media enclaves conjured up images of freewheeling entrepreneurs and small firms that were unconstrained by hierarchy. However, the rise of the new media depended heavily on the publicity and resources provided by the old media, while many Old Economy powers in the corporate and financial sectors were eager participants. Moreover, the new order made no break with social hierarchy: though they navigated a more diverse terrain the new media people were, like the code-writing heroes of Kotkin's valhallas and nerdistans, predominately white males from (at least) middle-class families. The New Economy insurgency was a movement of advantaged segments whose diversity was occupational and generational in nature—a Rainbow Coalition of the "haves" and "should-haves" (children of the middle class hoping to salvage or renegotiate their occupational inheritance). And even then, not all New Economy changelings were created equal—or on a fast track to become new Masters of the Universe.

Three types of elite actors held positions that allowed them to dominate the making and mobilizing of Silicon Alley networks. Venture capitalists were the most important. They provided information, connections, and advice as well as capital, in exchange for equity stakes and managerial influence in firms. Moreover, by making themselves into network hubs, venture capitalists were able to play a leading role in creating Silicon Alley institutions. Second were corporations, who—ironically—had been morphing with gusto for over two decades. Their participation in Silicon Alley business ventures and its social circuits suggests that we should not interpret their ongoing restructuring as a retreat. Rather, the nature of their strategic power is changing as they use various kinds of networks to supplement organizational hierarchies in coordinating activities. Media giants, for instance, use their global distribution systems to mediate between clusters of cultural producers and consumers located elsewhere.[38] Third were real estate interests who control the morphing of the built environment—in symbolic as well as material respects. One device through which they wielded power was their control over building. Another was their control over development networks (quasi-public bodies, public-private partnerships).

Nested Spaces

The moniker "Silicon Alley" is sometimes used in other parts of the world as a generic term for new media districts. My study suggests some tentative points about how New York's Silicon Alley compares to other districts. With regard to districts within the United States, the key factor is the economic base provided by a city: While San Francisco's Multimedia Gulch drew on the computer industry of Silicon Valley, and Hollywood was the base for LA's Digital Coast, New York's Silicon Alley served Wall Street and corporate Midtown. Moreover, Silicon Alley benefited from New York's position as America's leading "Global City"—the complex of financial and producer services being a means for global business coordination.[39]

With regard to international comparisons, one is struck by the imprint of some thoroughly American trends on Silicon Alley: the New Economy movement, neoliberal policies, and financialization. It seems that a nation's institutional framework exerts a strong influence in the development of new media districts.

A good starting point in understanding how national differences matter is the thesis of Richard Child Hill and Kuniko Fujita that cities are "nested" (or embedded) in their national institutional settings. At one end of a continuum are *market-centered systems* under neoliberal states (e.g., the United States) that rely on equity markets for industrial financing; at the other end are *state-centered systems* under "developmental" states (e.g., Japan) that guide investment and the formation of entrepreneurial groupings so as to transform strategic sectors.[40]

Observers of new media districts in the United States have stressed the role of neoliberal policies in unleashing the financial sector and in allowing employers a free hand in making "flexible" use of labor.[41] In contrast, in Japan there is no freewheeling financial sector to support Tokyo's multimedia cluster; from the start, these firms were tied to traditional media firms. The national government, which has shifted the focus of development policy to science and technology, actively supports this cluster and other information technology (IT) clusters in Tokyo's central wards (which contain some six thousand IT firms). Fujita comments that Tokyo is like "a huge industrial district that transforms itself, under state policy, according to technological and market needs, but also according to Japan's future social needs."[42]

The majority of nations fall somewhere in between the market-centered and state-centered models. A number of societies whose national policies are more market centered have regional governments that are more interventionist. Within Great Britain, development agencies in Wales and Scotland actively support new media clusters; within Australia, the Victoria state government supports a new media district in Melbourne.[43] The Netherlands is a hybrid system that combines new market-oriented principles with the industrial planning tradition associated with European social democracies. The Ministry of Economic Affairs has supported a "cluster monitoring" program for new media firms that are concentrated in cities such as Amsterdam, Rotterdam, and Eindhoven. The program gives the government a prominent role in the social construction of the enclaves, as it gathers data to make the clusters more visible and encourages firms to develop collectively an agenda for the government.[44] Another type of hybrid can be found in East Asia. A number of Japan's neighbors that had long emulated its state-centered model, began to experiment with neoliberal measures in the 1980s and 1990s. The case of Malaysia is instructive. In the early 1990s its developmental state began to build the Multimedia Super Corridor—a massive IT enclave on the outskirts of Kuala Lumpur. A state agency in charge of the project wooed venture capitalists, and the government set up a NASDAQ-style stock exchange in the hope of generating IPOs. On the surface, these measures seemed to mark a neoliberal turn. Yet, my study found that the government wielded strategic control over these financial devices, suggesting that the neoliberal elements "were enmeshed in a framework where the state—and developmental agendas—remain at the center."[45]

Neoliberal regimes use sovereign power to influence digital development, but in different institutional locations. Whereas many societies boost national technological development through supporting innovative *places*, neoliberal policy in the United States boosts *sectors*—the financial as well as technological—by increasing the availability of venture capital and stock options nationwide. As a result, financial entrepreneurs were able to step into an institutional vacuum to wield power in the making of American new media districts.

What to Make of Silicon Alley?

This book uses the case of Silicon Alley to tell the story of how a place in New York City developed a distinctive vision of the Internet as a "new media" domain and how, in turn, efforts to enact this vision changed the city. That story necessarily highlights the interplay between local developments and larger forces. The enclave's development began with the creative impulse of local web pioneers; its later explosive growth was caused by financial forces that were rooted in broader economic and political trends.

Thus, efforts to create commercial applications of technology set in motion a complex mixture of changes in the creative communities and economic sectors, and urban spaces evolved. New media visionaries became linked to networks for industrial development and urban redevelopment—and then to a fuel-injected system for generating IPOs (and a small army of New Economy camp followers). As webs of material support were extended, the visionaries were exposed to new powers, pressures, and constraints.

It is misleading to distinguish either individuals or ideas from the networks to which they were joined. The Silicon Alley case supports two claims of network theorists like Latour: The identities and roles of social actors are changed when they join networks to support a technology scheme; and it is the mustering of networks of support that gives technology schemes their credibility. These insights help answer central questions raised earlier in this chapter.

Who Were These People?

The people who participated in Silicon Alley in the last half of the 1990s came from diverse backgrounds and became linked to the new media through a variety of relationships and agendas. After they joined New York's new media networks they became "different" people than they had been previously; and many of them are not likely to remain who they were during the late 1990s. For a four- or five-year period they collectively harnessed and cultivated their talents, energies, and imaginations for the cause of producing new Internet-related products and markets that they thought could change the economic order.

Why Did They Believe?

A fair number of entrepreneurs and financiers exploited the stock market bubble without any illusions that new media firms would be able to achieve revenues that justified their valuations. Yet, for a great many, the new media visions seemed increasingly plausible as the 1990s drew to a close. They were not merely caught up in some general irrational exuberance. Silicon Alley participants were intoxicated by the vision of a new media that emerged organically out of the creative commercial milieu of Manhattan. Even as the vision morphed it was made "more real" over time by rather impressive material developments: The growing participation by thousands of talented individuals and dozens of powerful organizations, the creation of new media artifacts and organizational devices, and a rising tide of speculative investment were developments that the local media generally interpreted along the lines of the New Economy storyline.

What Is the Role of Cities in a Digital World?

The explosive rise of new media districts seemed to confirm the advent of a New Economy and a renaissance for major cities—and to supply another set of prime exhibits for those promoting American-style neoliberalism as the template for globalization. One is tempted to ask whether the illusions of an era have ever been swept so quickly into the dustbin of history. The stock crash was followed by endless revelations of fraud by New Economy champions. More important, the destruction of the World Trade Center and ensuing war on terrorism have shown that the decade of the 1990s was only the opening act in the making of a post–Cold War world. But, in fact, the seamless transition the United States is making from a technoeconomy mobilization to one based on technowar, suggests that there is a resilient faith in the underlying ideological package of technologies, markets, and nationalism. As the world stage turns into a mosh pit for fundamentalists of all stripes, we should remember that societies confronted with unsettling or frustrating transformations are apt to turn to old ideals. It is imperative then that we make a reckoning with the illusions of the recent past: U.S. cities still confront many of the same problems and possibilities as well as new perils. The starting point is to consider the neoliberal parentage of the New Economy.

Like a great comet, the New Economy put on a spectacular show for a brief time. While Silicon Alley now seems part of the showy tail—especially its ill-fated national contenders—most of its firms were closer to the nucleus: a body of corporations (including the financial firms) that had been in motion for a quarter of a century. The forces behind this heavenly apparition—and a more fundamental transformation of U.S. capitalism—included globalization, digital technology, and a sustained neoliberal project. Since 1980, that project has sought to create frameworks for markets by setting in motion participants in strategic markets—namely, the markets for labor, capital, and technology. However, with the New Economy debacle and the overt shift to a contested, state-centered global order, the neoliberal project may have reached its limits.

Certainly we should lose faith in the claims that either unrestrained markets or technology are solutions for critical problems of economic insecurity. The New Economy experience left unanswered New York's postindustrial question. The making of Silicon Alley neither created an alternative foundation for the media nor for the economy. The superheated expansion of the new media during the stock market bubble actually reduced the diversity of Manhattan's business base, while reinforcing its role as a global center of corporate media and business services. Moreover, rising property values ended up driving out small firms and creative types from the heart of this new cultural production space, underscoring the contradictory underpinnings and fragility of this union of culture, technology, and business. One wonders if Manhattan's deepening role as a floodplain for speculative capital will erode away eventually the rich resource base that supports creativity and specialization. The new world that has emerged in the aftermath of September 11, 2001, raises further doubts.

In large part, the significance of Silicon Alley depends on what organized social interests will make of it in the future—that is, with what identities, relationships, and sensibilities that survive. There are reasons to believe that this new place of cultural production—and the commercial concept that animated it—will endure in some form. Though their ranks are diminishing, there are tens of thousands of specialized workers and thousands of specialized firms as well as community institutions such as the NYNMA and New York Software Industry Association and myriad networks connecting workers, firms, and these institutions. However, it is not clear how the resources that were created or mobilized in the 1990s—a time of triumphalism for the United States and the neoliberal project—should be recombined in productive and creative enterprise under very different conditions. The key question remains, What economic base can sustain the efforts of creative firms and workers? What this book hopes to make clear, in telling the story of the district's rise and fall, is that the combining and recombining of creative and commercial resources is a thoroughly social process rather than some sort of natural process as is often implied in the fantasies of technoprophets and mainstream economics.

CHAPTER 2

MAKING AND SELLING A
NEW MEDIA DISTRICT

*Before there was commerce on the Net, there were thousands of . . . Netheads . . .
experimenting to find its uses. It's always the pioneers, the poets and the prophets
who show the way for the rest of us.*
—Founder of P.O.V. and Web Lab, 1998[1]

*We were all a pain in the ass. . . . It was all about being brash and being different and . . .
independent and being punk rock . . . and . . . loud and being, "Fuck you,
Mr. Big Company, you don't know what you're doing."*
—Former Chief Scientist of Razorfish, 2001[2]

*With companies springing up all over "Silicon Alley" . . . the struggle between old and new
media is a constant topic of conversation. . . . New Media's partisans are legion: not just
the militantly nonconformist employees of the start-up companies themselves but their
whole support network of venture capital, lawyers, landlords, consultants, accountants,
and even the media conglomerate personnel who are helping them grow.*
—City Journal, 1977[3]

I encountered many strange worlds while exploring Silicon Alley. During a
visit to the SoHo loft of the financier who had coined the name "Silicon
Alley," I was waylaid by a two-hour rant about cyberspace and various
literary genres, leaving me in mental knots (I got lost somewhere around
H. G. Wells). Two young managers at Pseudo (a hip webcaster) barely con-
cealed their contempt for those who did not "get it" (i.e., me) amidst a
squalor that resembled a frat house after a Saturday night party. I humbly
ventured into the pricey offices of the Flatiron Partners (Silicon Alley's
flagship venture capitalists) to talk to a partner who, clad in a plaid flannel
shirt, looked like a lumberjack (the *New York Times* said he was worth $300
million). At a New York New Media Association event about online games
held for its "special interest group" on law, I sat elbow-to-elbow with fifty

sweaty lawyers in a 30 × 15 foot conference room in an "incubator" (for start-ups). And when I showed up to see the founder of the *Silicon Alley Reporter* (*SAR*)—the district's head cheerleader—he let me sit and watch him "work" a *New York Times* reporter.

What held this all this together? A hint was provided at yet another strange world I strayed into—the "Silicon Alley Uptown" Conference hosted by Columbia University's Business School. It was late in the year (November) and, as the year was 2000, it was late in the life of Silicon Alley. The stock market had crashed in the spring and even an Ivy League venue couldn't cover up the decomposition. An occasional speaker strained to resurrect the spirit of revolution, but they might as well have peddled the *Daily Worker* on a corner in Wall Street. Most everybody was honing their take on a new idea: corporations, not start-ups, would control the commercialization of the Internet. At lunch I sat with a table of MBA students and a young Arthur Anderson consultant. After we finished the small talk and the broiled salmon, they gently tested me (an interloper on their turf). They asked what I thought were promising ways of nurturing careers or businesses. Not being privy to the latest biz school "buzz" I flunked, as evidenced by their light chuckles and the comment that, I "had dated myself" (Jurassic, it seemed).

I redeemed myself when the talk turned to the late, great dot-com bubble. I argued that venture capitalists were able to manage impressions held about new media firms because of their intermediary positions in the networks that linked start-ups to the IPO system: In a situation where most people possessed little information on the prospects of new media firms they relied on the cues provided by the "smart" money. This went over well with the newly minted experts; despite their fresh faces, they had a healthy stock of cynicism—nourished by the war stories of friends and family members who had worked for plummeting dot-coms.

In truth, my account hardly did justice to the matter. Venture capitalists were only one contingent in an army of intermediaries who entered Silicon Alley to become New Economy players—including business consultants and newly minted MBAs. Their interest in serving up "buzz" on behalf of start-ups was curious, given that big consultancies could charge corporations a small fortune.[4] More important, my little spiel left unanswered a more basic question: How did the land of Internet "true believers" become a kingdom of "false profits"?

The story of how the new media "buzz" circuit took shape involved a broader process: the formation of a new space of cultural production. The birth of this space began with efforts to weave social ties around the creative use of digital technology; as new creative clusters and spaces became linked with the Internet it attracted the notice of various entrepreneurial types who drew from them to muster support for their own schemes. This sort of building on—and folding in—of previous arrangements was repeated until many features of the social world that formed during the enclave's rise became less visible (or recognizable). Efforts to make creative applications and build an industry were overshadowed (and neglected) as organized efforts to spur and exploit stock speculation grew. Silicon Alley's uneven record in applying Internet technology sheds light on the broader problems firms had in trying to commercialize a new wave of computer technologies in the 1990s. The case also highlights the social and cultural nature of technology cycles—especially the processes wherein organized interests promote new norms and sensibilities so as to discredit and displace old ones.[5]

THE UNBEARABLE LIGHTNESS OF BEING (DIGITAL)

A new sort of rebel yell echoed through Lower Manhattan in the 1990s as new media partisans vowed to unseat the media giants. Though their progressive credentials soon became suspect, for several years those who entered New York's new media space felt free to do new things—and to become people they could not be before.

TECH-PHILES (THE TRUTH IS OUT THERE)

We often associate revolutions and other social mobilizations with some signature ideal, but they usually involve ideological cross-currents and contradictory types of collective action. So it was with the technology-induced "revolution" of the 1990s. By the end of the decade the dominant view was that there had been something akin to a civil war, pitting the New Economy against the Old—the former being distinguished by its incorporation of "bohemian" elements while the latter supposedly stayed true to "bourgeois" values. Yet, some of the most fundamental of bourgeois values drove the New Economy. And views varied about whom the revolution was against (i.e., who it was that controlled "the system").

Technopundits with strong ties to the West Coast–computer culture offered the best-known early accounts of the purported revolution. They touted the magic of unrestrained technologies and markets—weaving together elements of the hacker culture (and 1960s counterculture) with right-wing libertarian philosophy. In their view, technology allowed individuals to free themselves from hierarchies based on corporations and even more so, government—and constraints of place. Though New York's digital revolutionaries embraced some of these ideas, they had their own take on the strife: They located the civil war within the media domain specifically. New digital technology would create an opening for a "new media" to challenge the old—a view reflecting New York's standing as a media city.

In fact, Mark Stahlman—the financier who coined the term "Silicon Alley" in 1993—had come up with the term "new media" in 1989. As an investment banker Stahlman had been the first to recommend Sun Microsystems. Later, he helped AOL go public. His earnings allowed him to quit his $500,000 job on Wall Street and to become a venture capitalist and a sort of free-floating intellectual. He combined his Forrest Gump–like presence in defining moments of recent computer history with a mad professor's single-minded intensity. No one individual served as the official theorist for New York's new media, but Stahlman's version of the new media captured the core notion: Digital technology had opened the door for an alternative to the mass media, which was a system of cultural control and manipulation. But, whereas most new media rebels cited media corporations as the powers behind the system, Stahlman argued that it was "technocrats" who used the mass media as an tool of "social engineering" and "psychological therapy" to dominate the population. The technocratic movement, he claimed, could be traced back to the likes of H. G. Wells and Alvin Toffler; moreover, he asserted that their heirs were none other than the West Coast "digital mafia" (and politicians such as Newt Gingrich).[6] Whatever else we are to make of his theory, it does reflect a new reality: an inclination of New York financiers to contest Silicon Valley's dominance as a center for innovation (and risk capital).

The notion that the Internet would allow cultural producers to bypass the media giants resonated with the sensibilities of Lower Manhattan's creatives. The web pioneers embraced the imagery of "the rebel" or "the underground" as they mixed an artistic ethos with utopian ideals of computer hackers. A generational factor contributed. Many in the so-called "Generation X" developed critical sensibilities about the opportunities "the system" offered them (the system in New York revolving around the media and finance). Those who were liberal arts grads were especially media savvy in a generation that was media savvy to begin with. For example, Rufus Griscom—a graduate of Brown's cultural studies program (and a cofounder of Nerve.com) remarked, "Continental philosophy, semiotics . . . prepared us well for the digital economy. We were comfortable with the lexicon . . . and we were naturally suspicious of systems of power commonly assumed to be irreplaceable."[7]

One institutional base for this ethos was NYU's Interactive Telecommunications program. The film professor who founded the program in 1979—Red Burns—was later lionized as the "godmother" of Silicon Alley. Her view, that computers could abet free communication and expression, helped create a cadre of computer-literate young people and an idealistic

Fig. 2.1 Mark Stahlman, portrait of the financier as a philosopher (Photo by Bernd Auers)

creed: Anyone could become an online publisher, and media giants were held in disdain. Many of her students, hoping to change society or remake culture, helped build the enclave's early culture and first firms.[8]

The cyber counterculture motivated creative types to experiment with CD-ROMs, online services, and the nascent World Wide Web before visions of commercial riches appeared. The early scene in New York was

Fig. 2.2 Urban Desires, September/October 1995

dominated by an "electronic arts movement" and by edgy "webzines." The arts were featured in early sites such as Echo, The Thing, Ada Web, The Blue Dot, and Rhizome. One of the most notable was Urban Desires, founded in the fall of 1994 by Kyle Shannon—an unemployed actor who did desktop publishing to pay the rent. He recalled that he wanted to do an erotic zine, but decided to extend its scope—while keeping the "sexual undertone." "The idea was that in the city so much is desirable. Food is desirable, and movies are desirable, and books and toys. . . . So we created this culture magazine that explored the dark side of all these things."[9]

Andrew Ross (an NYU media observer) reported that by mid-1995 Silicon Alley zines such as Word, FEED, Urban Desires, Total New York, Stim, and NY@work had formed "an independent sector of original content publishing" that was "distinct in feel and opinion" from corporate-backed sites (e.g., Time Warner's Pathfinder, Microsoft's Slate). He also noted that when the "zines" started up, supporters hoped that "native New York creativity would steal a march on the West Coast and launch a more democratic wing of the hi-tech community, drawing an audience and advertisers to a new media where no one controlled distribution."[10] Most of the web pioneers started out creating websites for friends and small firms. They

Fig. 2.3 Urban Desires, January/March 1996

became adept at putting together rather motley "web teams" to serve market niches or to do customized work. A flurry of corporate interest in getting on the Internet that began in late 1995 bankrolled more elaborate arrangements; some online versions of magazines or marketing sites ran hundreds of pages long. Even as corporations began to set up in-house web teams, start-ups claimed they would be able to produce sites that were as popular as corporate sites (or more so)—and more sustainable costwise. One zine editor noted that many leading publications on the web (e.g., FEED, Word, Urban Desires) were small operations that took advantage of ease of access and "insanely cheap" production costs:

> With no distribution costs, dramatically shortened production cycles, and a relatively simple programming environment, creating a Web site would cost a fraction of what it took to lauch a print magazine. You could put out a professional-looking daily publication with only a handful of staffers: an editor or two, an HTML jockey, maybe a UNIX geek . . .[11]

New media partisans claimed that the ability of small firms to "morph" and "serve their customers in real time" would be a decisive advantage over corporations.[12]

"Tattoos" and "Suits" (The Party Circuit)

A defining trait of Silicon Alley—an interest in breaking barriers between the virtual and real worlds—had its roots in the technobohemian community. The formation of this community was, in part, accidental, but also the result of attempts by early Internet users and digital artists to create real-world venues where they could meet face-to-face. The ties and ethos of these technobohemians produced the original new media circuit—a social circuit of parties and other gatherings that would serve as a foundation for everything that followed.

One of Red Burn's disciples, Stacy Horn, had a key role in linking New York's virtual communities with real-world venues. In 1990 she launched Echo (East Coast Hang Out), an electronic bulletin board modeled on "The Well" (the West Coast's pioneer online community). Operating out of her living room, Horn nurtured a virtual community that grew to 3,500 members. She was the first to organize face-to-face meetings and events for New York web pioneers. Horn recalled, "I wanted it to be a community, a social space where people would be able to tell the stories of their lives. . . . I recognized the importance of the face-to-face element."[13]

An @NY editor proclaimed, "without Stacy Horn, there probably would be no Silicon Alley. . . . Echo is the bedrock of Silicon Alley." Few originally expected a career in computers, but the editor reported (as of 1996), "Echoids populate the staffs of every important Silicon Alley venture. . . . Ask any hotshot Web designer where he met his partners and he's likely to tell you it was on Echo."[14] The interest in face-to-face interactions was behind the founding of many groups, including the World Wide Web Artists Consortium (WWWAC)—also started by Kyle Shannon. His motive was "to surround myself with people who knew more than I knew" so as to be able to keep up with rapid changes in Internet technology. The meetings also ended by promoting a special spirit—a sense of progressive possibilities. "There was a real comaraderie of invention. It felt like what I imagine the early days of the '60s protest movement must have felt like—all that hope. We can change the world, for everyone's sake . . . it was really free-flowing." The group also reveled in subjecting corporate agendas to savage critiques. "Very early on, we got senior-level people from Microsoft, AOL, and Prodigy to come in and say what they were up to. And if we didn't like what they had to say, we would just blast them for half an hour. We would just yell at them."[15]

Fig. 2.4 Urban Desires, June/July 1996

Another basic purpose of such groups was mutual support. For instance, the director of Webgrrls (an association for women in the new media) reported that the guiding rule for the group was that one needs "to say what you need and what you can give back"; this "sets up an exchange."[16] In fact, informal exchange was the main "currency" in the early days and such ties often led to spin-offs. For example, Shannon asked a "regular" on Echo for technical help when Urban Desires had trouble in getting its pictures to show up. He later helped the regular, who turned out to be Chan Suh, with "some design stuff."[17] Within a matter of months the two founded Agency.com—an early web design shop that later became a global firm with nearly two thousand employees and offices worldwide.

Silicon Alley's notorious parties were also key sites for weaving together web pioneer relationships and sensibilities into distinctive networks. They provided an occasion for one to reaffirm his or her identity as someone who "got it"—meaning they believed that the Internet would change the world (at a time when few people knew what it was). In 1995 Douglas Rushkoff (an NYU media critic) noted, New York had been "the most Internet-resistant city in the world. I'd be at cocktail parties with publishing people who would laugh me out of the room when I told them they would be using e-mail in the near future." Similarly, a website developer remarked, "I don't think there's any major player based in New York who really understands what's going on."[18] At their own parties the web pioneers reinforced the idea that breaking the barriers between the real and virtual world was a worthwhile endeavor: It produced new forms of expression. One entrepreneur who hosted these events—Josh Harris—started Pseudo as a venture that was part party and part company. It began by operating a "chat community" for Prodigy and evolved into an Internet TV studio (or webcaster). Harris relished comparisons of Pseudo to Andy Warhol's Factory and liked to say that he left the equipment on for the parties and waited to see what would happen. An insider recalls that Pseudo's first party in 1994 was an epic affair filled with "club kids, techno-music, drugs, models, cross-dressers, computers" and "the geeks who would eventually become the CEOs of Silicon Alley."[19]

The enclave began to change as a wider range of groups formed to explore the boundaries between the online and real worlds. The Silicon Alley Jewish Center, for example, billed itself as a nonprofit entity "dedicated to the interpretation of traditional Jewish culture and our evolving Internet-enabled lifestyle." Of special importance, was increased involvement by various business interests. The center of gravity on the party scene shifted to CyberSuds—a monthly beer bash organized by venture capitalists where corporate executives and business professionals could meet new media entrepreneurs. As the "suits" joined the "tattoos" the *Village Voice* suggested that the technobohemians were morphing into "cyberyuppies."[20] As the new entrepreneurs became more focused on business, they began to exit the old party scene. Groups continued to form to support face-to-face meetings, but increasingly there was some kind of business angle. A Kellogg Silicon Alley Group was created for one hundred or so graduates of Northwestern's Kellogg School of Management, a New York chapter formed for the Indus Entrepreneurs (an Indian network headquartered in Silicon Valley), and a group of Silicon Alley "elders" that styled itself after Dorothy Parker's Algonquin Roundtable regularly met at the Flatiron Diner to discuss issues such as what kind of metaphors best explained cyberspace to the average person (the agenda being to find out how to help consumers make sense of the Internet). The "Whatever Group" formed to provide a monthly dose of the kind of intellectual discussions they had before they became so busy (group therapy might include assigned readings of Foucault).[21] A 1997 tribute by @NY showed commercialism to permeate the culture.

> There's a new culture, a new society, a new lifestyle growing up here around Internet media. First and foremost, it's entrepreneurial . . . denizens of New York's new digital society are . . . constantly looking for the new—new ways of doing things, expressing themselves . . . new markets to conquer.[22]

The commercial turn led a FEED editor to joke, "It used to be I'd go to parties and meet my friend's friends and we'd start sleeping together. Now my friends introduce their friends to each other and we go into business together."[23]

EVERYTHING THAT IS SOLID MORPHS

Silicon Alley firms engaged in endless organizational shifts as they interacted with new partners, explored new markets, or chased new investors. Web design shops reinvented themselves into consultants or e-commerce firms. Much the same was true of individual participants—people who moved to New York to join the new media as well as hobbyists who became entrepreneurs or workers. Veteran new media people reinvented themselves as they crossed disciplinary, firm, or industry boundaries to join work teams or to take new positions. A vivid example of the kind of setting that promoted morphing in the early days was Music Pen. It used teams of workers from diverse backgrounds to produce CD-ROMs for firms such as Viacom and Scholastic. Its work force of fifty included designers, writers, animators, producers, composers, and "technologists." Their equipment included sound studios and a baby grand piano as well as computer terminals.[24] Music Pen's founder, Yee-Ping Wu, was herself a prime example of morphing. Before starting the firm she had studied classical music at the Julliard Academy; as a child prodigy in China she had performed for the likes of Mao and Khrushchev. Indeed, liberal arts majors proved to be adept changelings. The founder of a computer services firm who was a music major observes that she hires through an "MIT network" and her "own network of arts, theatre and music people." She remarked, "I have a Columbia grad who is a bassoonist. He does sales for me but I will see if I can train him up. My senior tech person is a MIT grad with degrees in chemistry and theatre. She came to New York and realized she wouldn't get a theatre job. . . . I trained her . . . and bill her work out at $120."[25] A manager at Razorfish Studios with a music degree and computer skills noted, "My job changes every 3 to 4 months, I find myself with an entirely different array of responsibilities. Right now I am compressing video for

Fig. 2.5 Heidi Dangelmaier, online game developer, who moved from San Francisco to Tribeca and started up Hi-D (Photo by Bernd Auers)

Internet streaming, maintaining an e-commerce site, and producing . . . [a] TV program."[26]

The production process increasingly required "hybrid" workers who could work across disciplines. The CEO of Agency.com noted, "We had to get employees who could talk tech to a client's technology group, talk business to the corporate executive and talk creativity to the marketing and communications people."[27] The boundary-crossing produced unique work opportunities. These, in turn, attracted creative types from around the United States. For instance, the unique work opportunities drew a West Coast native who became one of New York's hottest creatives—Jaime Levy. She recalled, "In LA we'd be limited to film, in San Francisco to technology . . . in New York, we've got the perfect combination of content providers— there are just so many bands, artists, and filmmakers."[28]

As time passed the shape-shifting of new media participants became more and more oriented to corporations than an alternative media. Ironi- cally, the web pioneers themselves drew corporations to the Internet hop- ing to become valued as guides or partners or "sponsored." Jaime Levy, for example, morphed from freelancer to the founder of Electronic Holly- wood after Arthur Anderson and Flatiron Partners helped her write a busi- ness plan—and she received financial support from a friend who had sold a firm to Microsoft for $400 million.[29] But most firms found themselves relegated to the status of disposable subcontractors. Some tried to upgrade their prospects by remaking themselves into comprehensive services or consultants. One executive stated that his firm, which started as "five guys in a room," was now "building long term relationships with Fortune 500 companies"; to do this, a firm has "to morph into a business with a global strategy and growth."[30] A webshop owner noted that the new media was being redefined, "not by artists or graphics but by how you solve business problems."[31]

Indeed, large numbers of corporate executives, lawyers, accountants, and financiers came to recast themselves as new media people. One factor behind the migration of executives to Silicon Alley was that start-ups, which received venture funding, faced pressure from their venture capital- ists to take on professional managers. The other side of the coin was that many business veterans were attracted to what seemed to be a special op- portunity for entrepreneurship. The founder of an online game site recalled that when he worked for Sony, "I had a bright idea every day but I didn't have time to pursue anything. . . . I sometimes wonder what I might have been able to do in the corporate world. But you only get a couple of chances in your life to do something special."[32] Robert Lessin gave much the same rationale when he resigned as vice-chairman of Salomon Smith Barney in 1998 to devote himself to his second life as an "*uber*-consultant and investor" to Internet firms; since 1997 he had invested his own money (in sums ranging from $100,000 to $1 million) in thirty-five Silicon Alley firms. Lessin thought his special opportunity was to connect his wealthy Wall Street friends to Silicon Alley—destined for glory on account of its role in applying technology: "The West is the creator of technology and the

Fig. 2.6 Jaime Levy, founder of Electronic Hollywood (Photo by Bryce Lankard)

East is a user of that technology and the world is shifting from the former to the latter."[33]

"THE DINOSAURS ARE COMING"

At a conference in late 1996, the CEO of iVillage remarked on a new interest of corporate giants in Silicon Alley: "There is this glass of water going 'thump, thump, thump' because the dinosaurs are coming."[34] Some of the most powerful corporations in the world were starting to enter Silicon Alley to draw on its resources or, in some cases, to expose their own units to the new media work milieu. The invasion came at a critical point as many content producers—zines and nonprofits for example—were either sinking into financial crisis or closing.

The corporate giants pursued a variety of strategies in trying to penetrate Silicon Alley. Most of the initial efforts proved to be awkward and ineffectual. Some media giants such as News Corp. and Time Warner set up their own new media units. News Corp. and MCI made a $2 billion investment in the Delphi online service. Though Stacy Horn commented that the service "has been hiring all the smartest and funniest people on Echo,"[35] it was not long before News Corp. pulled the plug on the star-crossed effort. Time Warner made a large investment in its Pathfinder unit, but drew criticism for relying on "shovelware" (content crudely pulled online from the company's movies and magazines). When Pathfinder tried to capture an edgier vibe in a "cybersoap" entitled "Theeastvillage.com," the graphic intensive site was difficult to download—and fizzled as a creative effort (as did the whole venture). By 1998 Time Warner—beset by squabbling and turf wars between internal units—was in full retreat from Pathfinder, as was evidenced by its sale of *People* magazine's online rights to AOL for a modest amount.[36] Another strategy several corporations used was creating Silicon Alley centers that they touted as gateways to their global networks. In 1997 Ericsson (the Swedish telecommunications giant) created a cyberlab where start-ups could make use of its equipment and technical assistance—if their agendas were compatible with Ericsson's. A staff member reported that New York start-ups

> will gain access to our extranet which includes not only Ericsson but also Ericsson's partners. . . . Silicon Alley will have access to the resources of the whole corporation and to the 130 countries Ericsson services . . . they will be able to contribute to Ericsson products that are sold in many . . . markets.[37]

A final strategy was to launch high-profile scouting/shopping expeditions. The most noteworthy was Microsoft's dispatch of an executive to scout for Silicon Alley content producers who might contribute to the new Microsoft Network (MSN). Though dozens of firms appeared to deliver pitches to the MSN representative, the enterprise soon turned rocky. For instance, after Stacy Horn met with MSN she reported, "It was like a clash of cultures, big time."[38] Free-spirited creative types began to criticize Microsoft for trying to get start-ups to sign away their digital rights while others complained that the software giant was merely in town to get new media firms to use its software (and PCs instead of MACs). In the end, Microsoft beat a retreat from its plan to become a power in the realm of Internet content. AOL fared better, as its Digital City unit bought two of Silicon Alley's most popular websites—Ada Web and Total New York. AOL also delivered a high-profile bashing to New York's alternative media stance (already under duress). At a Silicon Alley conference, AOL CEO Ted Leonsis scolded New York content developers for designing content to please themselves instead of the mass of Internet users: "You are not the audience.

You're drinking your own bathwater." He remarked that he saw a lot of the "Hipper than thou" attitude . . . in Silicon Alley." He added, "It's better to be successful than to be right."[39]

The bumbling efforts of the older corporate giants—and AOL's continuing march—suggested that maybe new kinds of media firms might be able to develop (and dominate) new Internet markets after all—if they went "mainstream."

FRAMING AN INDUSTRY ("IT TAKES A TOWN")

The lack of government involvement in Silicon Alley opened the door for diverse kinds of institutional entrepreneurs, but government policies privileged particular kinds of entrepreneurs. Neoliberal policy at the federal level favored financial entrepreneurs while local policy favored those from real estate.

Institutional Entrepreneurs

Silicon Alley's financiers, real estate developers, and media organs played key roles in helping the new media extend itself as they created new spaces and institutional frameworks for exchanging ideas and building relationships. While the web pioneers struggled to convert cultural creativity into business leverage, these powerbrokers were able to organize means for translating the enclave's sense of cultural vitality into images of economic vitality. They became major nodes in the Silicon Alley buzz circuit.

Three Silicon Alley trade publications played key roles in framing the enclave's commercial turn: two—*Silicon Alley Reporter* (*SAR*) and *AlleyCat News* were print magzines while *@NY* was an online newletter. A venture capitalist notes they "are part of the fabric" and "give people a common language."[40] Their influence pointed to the general importance of having central positions in district networks. The founder of the *Silicon Alley Reporter*, for instance, commented: "I have personal relationships with every CEO in Silicon Alley. They ask me for contacts, advice. Its very social. I helped lots of firms get funded. A lot of financiers in New York call me for my opinions on firms."[41] He remarked that firms, great and small, which wanted to navigate successfully the district depended on ties that extend across industry boundaries: "I don't know anyone who is successful who doesn't have an amazing network. There is starting to be an overlap in networks with media and industries such as publishing, lawyers, Wall Street. Big companies that participate in Silicon Alley do better instead of trying to do it all by themselves." Ties that provided access to capital became increasingly important. A co-owner of one start-up noted that he depends on his ties to local financiers: "Being in New York is very important—We'll never leave. New York City has a network of potential investors. This is my playground. We'll always have our headquarters here. A company like this always has to be looking for money—new rounds of investment."[42]

Early on, a number of financiers who sought to become local venture capitalists made themselves into network hubs in Silicon Alley; they also used their position as district financial brokers to become institutional entrepreneurs. Of special importance was their role in founding (and operating) an industry association for the district—the New York New Media Association (NYNMA). One of the lead actors recalls being motivated by a sense of rivalry with Silicon Valley: "I spent much of my time going to Silicon Valley. From the beginning there was a sense that what was being done here was different from what was being done in San Francisco. But the only ones that were setting themselves up as leaders of the revolution were these assholes in Silicon Valley."[43] After leaving Wall Street he set up a "cybersalon" as a means to bring together his Wall Street friends and his new acquaintances in the new media. He and another venture capitalist had an idea to start a larger, public organization. In essence, they created their own node on the party circuit—CyberSalon—which became a social space for nurturing new sorts of networks in the enclave. As they enrolled more participants, they turned CyberSalon into a Silicon Valley–type beer bash—CyberSuds. At the same time, he notes that they recruited corporate and state sponsors.

> We recruited companies as sponsors for $100,000. I got the State to provide $50,000. Some of it went to pay for the new media study; some went to support a venture capitalist conference. . . . We wanted it to be more like a community. . . . Our main activity was to throw a party, which made CyberSalon into a public event. There were only 15 people at first. It grew to as many as two to three thousand.[44]

NYNMA became the prime institutional actor in Silicon Alley. The association, which had only eight members when it formed in the fall of 1994, had increased one thousand–fold by the year 2000—its membership comprised a mix of financiers, graphic artists, firm owners, consultants, musicians, accountants, and lawyers. NYNMA played a critical role in bringing the new media industry into public view, especially by sponsoring surveys of the local industry. It also created services to help small firms access resources, with capital being first and foremost. NYNMA also created programs to help firms access labor—for example, an online job posting service and internship programs for high school and college students.

One of NYNMA's most critical contributions was to create forums where firms and support organizations could come together to discuss issues and agendas. NYNMA still sponsors meetings by special interest groups (e.g., marketing, business development), topical panels, and a yearly forum on the "State of the New York New Media." Such opportunities for exchanging views were (and are) also vital for the creation of novel business models and industry conventions. It was difficult for consumers, corporate customers, and investors to understand just what new media firms did. A *Silicon Alley Reporter* (*SAR*) editor noted, "When you are doing things that haven't been done before, you need a sounding board. You are making up the rules as you go."[45] Similarly, a partner at Flatiron Partners commented, "We are making it up as we go and making it up isn't a bad idea now."[46] And one of the venture capitalists who helped found the NYNMA remarked, "orginally, we were collectively thinking through business approaches and developing an ideological agenda . . . thousands have struggled to figure out how to make money at this. It takes a town to do this."[47]

Vision Thing: The Idea of Silicon Alley

At NYNMA events and in countless informal encounters in Lower Manhattan's warren of coffee shops, cafes, and nightspots, new media participants exchanged opinions on the problems of the district and individual firms. Such discussions produced some shared understandings about the nature of Internet business and the comparative advantages of New York as a new media center. Initially, two beliefs were central to district sensibilities: (1) The Internet economy is a media and communications business, not a technology business per se, and (2) Making content is how Internet firms add value. The "idea of Silicon Alley," an *@NY* editor reported, is that the main opportunity for Internet business will be "developing and distributing new modes of expression that use Internet technology—and then taking advantage of the audiences created."[48] Sensibilities about business opportunities were imprinted by one's view of how New York's economic (and cultural) base compared to that of other cities. A *Silicon Alley Reporter* (*SAR*) executive, expressing a common local sentiment, termed New York "the capital of everything."

> In Silicon Valley all the wealth and power exist solely to support a place like Silicon Alley. New York is the publishing capital of the world. In arts its on par with Paris. It is the financial capital of the world. Also in music. . . . San Francisco thought they could do content ventures because they could do the technology. . . . It didn't work . . . [most of] Europe is one to five years behind . . . France will become like a Third World country.[49]

This notion evolved as most firms found a need to develop special applications and/or market positioning. The revised view was that the role of Silicon Alley was making "creative business applications"—an endeavor that often involved content. The idea became something of a district convention, as was evident in an exchange at a 1999 NYNMA panel. The CEO of Agency.com proposed, "The concentration of people who create ideas is very high here. We are reaching a point where we don't have 'tech envy.'

What's left to figure out now? The way people use technology. To assess this is something we can do. New York is the place where people are paying attention to this."[50]

A senior editor at *Newsweek* made the comparison with Silicon Valley explicit: "I feel like I am in a technology bubble in Silicon Valley. New York is the media capital of the world. . . . It is also a creative center for the country and the world. That creativity will end up on the Internet. New York will apply the technology tools created elsewhere."[51]

A partner at Flatiron Partners then completed the Silicon Alley "party line":

> For people interested in technology New York is not the place . . . Silicon Valley is. . . . People here are more implementers. . . . But . . . technology is becoming a commodity. Services is where the value is. That's very good for New York. It's building services on top of technology. That is where the value is.[52]

PLACING SILICON ALLEY (AND REFRAMING WALL STREET)

In 1995 several powerful groups were exploring ways of boosting Manhattan's new media industry. One group, composed of Time Warner, McGraw-Hill, and Forbes, began discussing ways to start a Midtown facility for new media firms— a hub that strategically would focus resources, interactions, and attention on the new sector. They envisioned a center offering subsidized office space, equipment, and research facilities for 150 new firms.[53] However, they had difficulty finding a landlord who was willing to supply a major building for the project—until real estate interests from Downtown (i.e., the financial district) stepped forward.

Keeping Downtown office space occupied had been a chronic problem ever since the 1970s when the construction of the World Trade Center and other speculative office buildings added nearly 54 million square feet to the supply of office space.[54] During the go-go 1980s, new construction further swelled the supply of office stock by nearly 46 million square feet. In the aftermath of the 1987 stock market crash, and the ensuing recession that hammered New York, the commercial real estate market fell into a deep slump. Downtown vacancy rates jumped to 23 percent while rents plummeted. The Trade Center itself was fast becoming a hollow anchor; its vacancy rate hit 32 percent in 1996. The Port Authority was so desperate to get tenants that it relocated its real estate unit (two hundred in staff) from the 35th floor of Tower One to the 88th floor so that an insurance company could have an office one elevator ride from the lobby.[55]

When the head of the Alliance for Downtown New York approached the owner of an empty Wall Street office building in mid-June 1995 about hosting the new media center a deal quickly ensued. William Rudin, the grandson of a Manhattan real estate tycoon, agreed to convert 55 Broad

Street into a wired facility for new media start-ups. The 30-plus story building had been closed since the bankruptcy of Drexel Burnham Lambert at the end of the last Wall Street boom; moreover, the Rudin family controlled buildings in the vicinity that had some 2.5 million square feet of vacant space. City Hall, which had committed itself to revitalizing the Financial District's real estate market, agreed to provide a tax-credit plan to lower real estate costs for the center, which was christened the New York Information Technology Center (NYITC).[56]

Rudin spent $41 million outfitting the building with satellite hook-ups, high-speed video conferencing, fiber optics for local area networks, and high-speed Internet connections. Moreover, a number of features were added to signal the building's high tech nature. Upon entering the door (which had a computer mouse painted over it), visitors encountered a 14-foot video wall in the lobby that displayed feeds from the web, news, images from the Hubble Telescope, a virtual reality tour of the building, and material from tenant web pages. The Alliance and the Rudin company also framed the building as the nucleus for a high tech community. One Rudin executive stated, "Community is the most important thing we are selling here. It is the opportunity for chance encounters."[57] By late 1997 the building was full—of small firms, corporate new media units, and various services: NYNMA was one of the first tenants though its leaders expressed reservations about the site being so far from Silicon Alley's Midtown clients.

This success lead some of the participants to engage in a bit of reinvention. Rudin, whose family already owned sixteen office buildings and twenty-two apartment buildings, was said to see an opportunity to make his own mark. He reframed his business as creating wired tech centers and exporting the model to other cities around the world. Indeed, thereafter, he helped redevelop an old Grumman facility as the Long Island Technology Center and participated in developing a new wired headquarters for Reuters in Times Square. And in an effort to export his wired building concept, he formed ties with developers in London, Munich, and Singapore. For its part, the Alliance began to market itself as a technology district. With the city's backing, the Alliance extended the wired space concept with a "Plug 'N' Go program." It assisted thirteen more Downtown buildings in making available prewired office spaces with low rents and short leases. The pitch was that flexible wired space fit the needs of small firms that did not know whether they would grow, fail, or be acquired.[58] Plug 'N' Go buildings ultimately signed up 250 tenants. The wiring effort was accompanied by aggressive imagineering: The Alliance suggested the area would become iconic—a "Levittown for cyberspace."[59] Plug 'N' Go ads depicted entrepreneurship as a sort of extreme sport (see figure 2.7): They featured

Fig. 2.7 Plug 'N' Go ad, Alliance for Downtown New York, Plug 'N' Go Program, 1998

a yuppie type with sunglasses and a tie whipping over his shoulder, in a surfer's crouch on a surfboard (a computer keyboard) skimming the surface of the Hudson River—with the World Trade Center as a backdrop. The ad proclaimed that the "network of buildings" was located in "Downtown New York's new Information Technology District—the heart of Silicon Alley" while a breezy banner noted, "It's workplace and lifestyle joined at the hip."

Promotion of Downtown's wired spaces boosted recognition for the name "Silicon Alley" and created a sense that its boundaries extended far beyond the original corridor. Of signal importance was the PR campaign that Rudin and his allies waged for the NYITC in New York's magazines and newspapers. As one of Rudin's close associates noted, "Say it enough times, and people begin to believe."[60]

Buzz Club (The Medium Is the Story)

A major reason New York's new media became a force during the late 1990s was that it became a reliable source of "good" Internet stories in a period in which the Internet (and New Economy) became preoccupations of the old media. The rise of Silicon Alley's own media helped get the district's firms into the loop. Many observers credited Jason Calacanis—a young man from Brooklyn who started up *Silicon Alley Reporter* (*SAR*)—with doing the most to introduce the district to the world. Calacanis had done some web design and written a column on the digital scene for a hip magazine before he made his big move. He maxed out his credit card ($10,000) in 1996 to put out the first edition of *SAR* (a photocopy full of misspellings and typos) and personally delivered four hundred copies to Silicon Alley offices, using a luggage cart to make the rounds. The modest-looking newsletter drew attention with some bold stories, including one that criticized NYNMA for being out of touch and a major scoop that blasted Microsoft for trying to acquire the digital rights of ventures with its local partners.[61] Before long, *SAR* was a glossy magazine of some eighty or more pages. It soon became well known, but much more for its coverage of new media parties and personalities than for business analysis. *SAR* became an institution largely on the basis of "Silicon Alley 100"—a "must read" annual issue that served to bestow celebrity status on honorees. One insider recalled that part of the attraction was to see how many of the people one knew, as "a kind of measure" of your "connectivity."[62] Calacanis, himself, became a network hub. An entrepreneur observed that Calacanis—like the founder of Club 54—wielded power as the guardian of a hot spot: "Jason was the Steve Rubell of Silicon Alley. It was like a really hot club for a couple of years, and he was the guy at the rope."[63] A Flatiron Partner noted that "talking with Jason is like talking to a focus group . . . I . . . ask him what's hot."[64]

The district's own media were important for helping to establish the credibility of Silicon Alley firms—and the district itself—with external audiences. A *SAR* editor recalled, "We wrote about the firms when they were small. This made them real, validated in the eyes of others." He noted, "The people we put on the cover wanted to be on the cover of *Red Herring* or *Upside* or *Wired*. But those publications hate New York, disdain it. They are mostly about San Francisco. . . . Before we existed Silicon Alley didn't get much attention."[65] However, giving any of the district publications sole credit for putting Silicon Alley on the map is like gushing over a touchdown dive by a 160-pound halfback while ignoring his 300-pound linemen. The heavyweights that helped break the Silicon Alley story into the larger media circuit included the Downtown real estate coalition and NYNMA. The key event was the PR campaign by the Downtown Coalition that highlighted the conversion of 55 Broad Street. It was followed by a flurry of articles in local newspapers and magazines, including the *New York Times*, *Wall Street Journal*, and *Crain's New York Business*. A watershed moment was a November 13, 1995, cover story in *New York Magazine*. The cover made a district icon out of the Flatiron Building, which appeared to be ploughing up the street so as to push the title, "High Tech Boom Town," into the reader's face.

A founder of *AlleyCat News* noted that the press blitz seemed to make Silicon Alley more real: "The term 'Silicon Alley' appeared in the *New York Times* and the *Wall Street Journal*—so therefore it existed."[66] A second seminal event was the release of NYNMA's first industry survey in 1996. The fact that NYNMA's partner in the survey was one of the big consulting firms—Coopers Lybrand—gave the "numbers" special force. The kind of media reverberations that resulted were evident in the *New York Times* coverage that day. Aside from a regular story ("New York Area Is Forging Ahead in New Media") and a major article in its digital edition ("Report Gives City's New Media New Credibility"),[67] it also offered an editorial entitled "New York's Dynamic New Media," which enthused that, "new-media companies are clearly becoming a dynamic core of the regional economy."[68]

Silicon Alley media organs, local publications such as *Crain's New York Business*, and various new media business interests kept the stories about Silicon Alley rolling for several years. Though this circuit provided intense doses of Silicon Alley buzz, it is important to note that it reached a narrow audience—new media firm owners, financiers, and various segments of the larger New York business community—corporations, real estate interests, business professionals, and institutional investors. The general public in New York was oblivious to the existence of Silicon Alley (it only became quite aware of dot-coms at the peak of the stock market bubble).[69] Moreover, the new media rank and file tended to be engrossed in their own subcultures—and cynical about hype. Several new media workers I interviewed noted that they did not embrace the Silicon Alley identity. A veteran of new media ventures going back to 1995 remarked, "I don't think a lot of people identified with the name Silicon Alley. . . . Basically, it was a media term. It was the brainwashing of the media and companies like Razorfish. It was propaganda."[70] A former Razorfish worker commented,

"I didn't feel like I could tell people I was part of Silicon Alley. I didn't think people would recognize the name."[71] However, for entrepreneurial types the name Silicon Alley was a critical asset—especially if they aspired to be players in the deal flow of financiers or the stock market. As a frenzy of Internet stories built up, founders of start-ups took note that they were becoming "content." They soon realized that if their firm became part of the Internet story, it would get a flurry of free marketing that might create a "self-fufilling prophecy." Rufus Griscom recalled that when he launched Nerve in June 1997, it made it into the national media circuit:

> The day that we launched I was on CNNfn; a week later we were in *Newsweek*; a month after that there was a page on us in *Time*; and off we went. . . . What happened . . . was that tens of thousands of column mentions in newspaper, and just as many minutes of television time, had to be filled on a weekly basis with Internet-related stories. . . . And if you could position yourself as an Internet story worth writing about, there was a huge upside.[72]

CNNfn was one of a bevy of new financial media that sprang up in the late 1990s to cover the market for tech stocks. Silicon Alley's Buzz Club did its part to supply stories of Internet start-ups for this national circuit.

BECOMING A NATIONAL CONTENDER

Most Silicon Alley firms were small subcontractors or service firms that earned modest profits; over half of them engaged in content-related work. But increasing numbers explored new paths of business development. Some hoped to become something more than subcontractors doing project work—perhaps even national contenders in some major market segment.

The fortunes of start-ups following the idealistic, alternative media model steadily worsened as corporate customers imposed less desirable terms or started in-house units. Some tried to target demographic niches. One noteworthy example was Pseudo, which survived into the new millennium as an unrepentant purveyor of "edgy" urban content. Pseudo became something of an American Bandstand for the alternative music set. A Pseudo manager recalled, "We had this huge loft, had big parties that brought together artists, creative types. We had this idea of mirroring in real space what goes on in a chat room."[73] Many observers panned its business acumen, but Pseudo brought in $30 million in investment with its spin on Internet TV: The Internet would, like cable TV before it, cause the TV market to become fragmented into even more niches. By providing "authentic, credible, quality programing . . . and original content," the manager remarked, Pseudo webcasts could appeal to advertisers (soft drink, clothing, auto companies) who wanted to hit a segment of the 15- to 25-year-old market—a group that was put off by conventional mediums, but that was embracing the Internet as their own.

Unlike Pseudo, most of Silicon Alley's would-be national contenders abandoned the alternative media model. However, like Pseudo many firms tried to develop a position that would allow them to serve, or otherwise exploit, New York's mighty advertising sector. Many firms tried to take some kind of intermediary role in channeling Internet surfers to ads (or links to retailers) or the related role of tracking where Internet surfers went (and what they did). A fair number tried to become service intermediaries who could assist corporations with their online activities (or internal computer systems). Some major business models were:

1. *Web services* (e.g., Agency.com, RareMedium, Razorfish): Many web design shops came to call themselves "agencies"—a model derived from the advertising industry. They typically did contract work for corporations, such as designing splashy websites, developing banner ads, and planning online ad campaigns. A number sought to further boost their standing with corporations by remaking themselves into comprehensive web services or computer consultants.

2. *Advertising networks* (e.g., 24/7, DoubleClick): These firms assembled and profiled groups of websites so as to offer advertisers a selection of sites by their demographic profiles. They also tracked users and profiled them so as to be able to match them to different types of ads.

3. *Community networks* (e.g., about.com, iVillage, StarMedia): online communities organized networks of sites according to some theme such as ethnic or women's interests. The aim was to bring together large numbers of users, allowing the firm to receive premium rates for ads and for links to online retailers.

4. *E-commerce firms* (e.g., Alloy, Barnesandnoble.com, Bluefly): Online retailers sold goods to consumers (e.g., books, CDs, or clothing) and typically tried to get themselves linked to clusters of websites such as online communities or "portals" where large numbers of users entered the web (e.g., browsers).

THE SEARCH FOR THE KILLER APP'

Silicon Alley produced several dozen national contenders that made their way into the stock market. This book will follow four of the most prominent cases—firms who were among the leaders in their categories: Razorfish (web services), DoubleClick (advertising networks), iVillage (women's online community), and StarMedia (Hispanic online community).

The Jeff n' Craig Show: Razorfish

To many, Razorfish—one of the enclave's most notorious firms—seemed emblematic of the whole New York approach to new media. But, it became more of an anomaly as national contenders distanced themselves from the nose-ring set. Razorfish was founded in 1995 by a colorful odd couple: Jeff Dachis—a dance major who reinvented himself as a hard-nosed business-man and Craig Kanarick—a graduate of the MIT Media Lab. Some shared experience often underlay such partnerships: In this case, the two had met each other at Hebrew School in Minneapolis.

Razorfish joined a parade of ambitious webshops that sought to remake themselves into comprehensive service providers or consultants. Razorfish termed its focus "digital change management," which meant that like other IT professional services it provided "a mix of technology, consulting and design."[74] However, Razorfish was still generally considered to be an "edgy design shop"[75]—a view that reflected the manner in which it went about distinguishing itself from rivals. For one thing, the decor of its headquar-ters was studied "over-the-top." The stainless steel tables and desks were matched with a 6-foot-long felt-covered coffin that was actually a mobile turntable (Dachis was a DJ on the side). The walls were honeysuckle yellow and displayed art that was "well-hung" (several photos of nudes and a painting of what might be called the moment of truth in the sex act). The aura emanating from the founders was equally startling. Kanarick—Razor-fish's chief scientist—complemented his blue hair with business attire that matched blue suits with orange shirts or grape purple suits with black shirts (and purple socks); Silicon Alley insiders coined the term "Dachismo" for CEO Dachis in tribute to his self-conscious performance as a "brutal capi-talist"—and his romps around town on his Harley Davidson 883 Sportster or Ducati Monster 900 SEI motorcycles (with a bright mustard yellow hel-met and army pants). In work and play the "Jeff n' Craig Show" projected an unblinking, in-your-face confidence in themselves that transfixed the media and allowed them to enroll terrified corporate clients. The latter seemed to fear that they were members of an archaic culture that faced ex-tinction as digital technology fast-forwarded the evolution of business in the direction of blue hair and pornographic office decor.[76]

Despite (or maybe because of) its over-the-top imagery, Razorfish drew the monetary backing of Ominicon, a holding company in the advertising industry. In late 1996 Ominicom purchased 20 percent of Razorfish for $3.6 million up front and an equal amount contingent on performance; it also provided a line of credit to be used for making acquisitions. The deal al-lowed Dachis and Kanarick to become some of Silicon Alley's first twenty-something millionaires and (for four years) the owners of a global firm: After a year's buying spree in which it acquired other firms, Razorfish ended up with over one thousand employees and offices in cities across the United States and Europe. For its part, Ominicom sold 25 percent of its stake in Razorfish for $141 million in February 2000, making 80 times its investment.[77]

Counting Cliques: DoubleClick

The two software engineers who founded DoubleClick in 1996—Kevin O'Connor and Dwight Merriman—worked together at the same Atlanta corporation before retiring to a basement to devise an Internet start-up. O'Connor noted DoubleClick's hybrid nature, remarking that they considered California but moved to New York because, "we're a tech company and a media company, but mostly a media company."[78] The firm developed ad tracking and measuring services that it claimed could help make advertising the Internet's killer application. It stated that it could "get the right advertisement to the right person at the right time."[79] There were three parts to DoubleClick's business. It (1) did direct marketing, (2) assembled a network of websites that it packaged as distinctive demographic groups for advertisers who wanted to reach particular audiences, and (3) devised a tracking technology to profile users so they could be matched with ads. The system gleaned information from the user's Internet address and the "cookies" (bits of software) that are stored in their hard drive every time they visit a website. This allowed DoubleClick to measure how often a user had seen an ad, their clicking habits, and how long they used certain areas of a website. A DoubleClick executive explained, "An advertiser could say, 'I want to reach business people in the financial industry who live in New York City and ski, and I only want to reach them between 9 and 5' and we can target exactly such people and only them."[80]

DoubleClick aspired to someday being able to "judge exactly which advertisements are causing what actions among consumers."[81] To this end it sought to develop more sophisticated ways to use cookies and to link online users with data about their offline behavior—or even their identity. DoubleClick swapped $1 billion in stock for Abacus Direct—an IT company that tracks the catalog-buying habits of 88 million households in the United States. Its plans to marry online users with offline data brought a storm of protest from privacy advocates. DoubleClick's position had been that when consumers are online they are "making a rational choice—they are willing to give up info in exchange for value."[82] However, in response to a Federal Trade Commission investigation it promised to alter its plans. One commissioner advised firms "to establish with customers that for giving up information, they get something of value";[83] DoubleClick's answer was that ads provided users a "free" Internet.

DoubleClick's prowess at developing technology was matched by a knack at raising venture capital. In 1997 it raised $40 million from venture capitalists on the West Coast and Boston; this spurred venture capitalists in New York to become more assertive. It also allowed DoubleClick to expand its operations. It had been delivering 500 million ad impressions a month in 1997; by 1999 it was delivering that many a day. The cash also allowed DoubleClick to go global: In 1998 it opened up operations in fifteen countries.[84]

What (Yuppie) Women Want: iVillage

Several veterans of the media business started iVillage in 1995 under the rallying cry, "Internet for the rest of us"—based on the idea that the youth-oriented Internet ventures had left baby boomers unserved. iVillage soon shifted its focus to become an online community for women—particularly, the high-income, well-educated segment that advertisers cherished. iVillage's point woman was co-founder Candice Carpenter—previously CEO of Q2 (the upscale cable shopping channel) and president of Time-Life Video and Television. iVillage offered a network of over fifteen websites and shopping areas as "channels" that users could access, according to their needs or interests. These included "Diet & Fitness," "Working Diva," "Relationships," and "iBaby" (iVillage's own online store). One of its sites, "Parent Soup," provided parental guidance from child-rearing experts, medical advice, and news—and allowed users to exchange ideas in chat-groups on topics such as "Sex after Kids" and "Anger Management."[85] Carpenter proposed that the iVillage model was compelling because it was organized to meet the needs and sensibilities of women—particularly when it came to their roles as time-starved consumers who needed information. iVillage's network of sites contained myriad opportunities for gaining "product information" and for actually getting one's shopping done online; moreover, Carpenter claimed the network structure fit the more "integrated" nature of women.

> Pulling together different sites and categories under "women" turns out to be really positive. Women traditionally do not put up strong fences between the different parts of their lives. If you watch a group of women at work, they will go from [talking about] what kind of stockings they're wearing to talking about their company's strategy, to their investment portfolio in about ten minutes. . . . So when you create a women's network, you create a place where a woman can take all the things that are on her plate and deal with them all in that one spot.[86]

The business plan was to bring together "demographics" that online retailers, advertisers, and sponsors hoped to reach. But iVillage's rise seemed to stem more from Carpenter's ability to use her status as a media veteran to draw investors who wanted to try out the Internet—but not with a twenty-something whiz kid.

Viva la Revolucion! StarMedia

Fernando Espuelas and Jack Chen—who founded StarMedia in 1996—met in Greenwich, Connecticut, where, as children of recent immigrants, they ended up taking English classes together. Espuelas graduated from Harvard with a computer science degree and worked as a marketing director for AT&T Carribean and Latin America; Chen had worked as a securities analyst at Credit Suisse First Boston and an investment banker at Goldman Sachs.[87] StarMedia was a "Latin American" online community that claimed to have invented the category. Espuelas stated that its mission was "unifying Latin people around the world" by creating a "central plaza," a "place where people can find each other, can communicate, [and] can share ideas."[88] His vision suggested a blend of Simon Bolivar and George Gilder. StarMedia would "break a five hundred year pattern of monopolies in Latin America . . . of political, information, social, economic power by giving individuals the ultimate ability to share information and communication."[89] The liberation theme seemed, in part, a useful means of elevating StarMedia above its main rival—AOL's Latin American unit (vulnerable to the charge of cultural imperialism). In hopes of gaining revenue from ads and from selling subscriptions, StarMedia offered a dozen channels, including sports, news, personal finance as well as chat and e-mail. It tried to balance a panregional approach with localization; it used dozens of editors located in cities such as Mexico City, Buenas Aires, Santiago, São Paulo, and Bogota to localize its content while also running content that appealed to national and Latin American identities.

StarMedia made a splash through its ability to raise venture capital. In late 1997 it rasied $80 million in private funds from sources that included Intel, Chase Capital Partners, and Henry R. Kravis (the leverage-buy-out specialist); it was the largest investment that a private Internet company had ever received.[90]

Taking It to Another Level

By 1998 the character of New York's new media and its enclave had shifted. The alternative media movement had largely stalled (for want of financial sustenance) and many web pioneers had moved to more commercial ventures. Start-ups found themselves having to make peace with some "higher powers"—first and foremost, corporations whose business they needed—but also landlords who controlled affordable wired space, financiers who possessed risk capital and inside ties, or media brokers who could make them a glowing chapter in the Internet story.

While corporations were a force in their role as new media customers, their initial efforts to make themselves into commercial powers on the Internet fared poorly. Silicon Alley's institutional entrepreneurs interpreted this to mean that the Internet was still open for commercial conquest—for a new kind of firm that was willing to break the old rules and to make bold gestures. These institutional actors were not so much a base to help new media start-ups create sustainable markets for new Internet products or services as much as they were a foundation to help the start-ups cultivate and exploit the image of business "rebel."

So it was that the networks that were constructed around venture capital and a new media circuit became a springboard for taking the new media insurgency to another level—another domain, in fact. The rebels were positioned to take their campaign to the stock market—to reap the glories and spoils of their Bull Run.

CHAPTER **3**
Capital and Credibility
Hooking up with Wall Street

How do you put a value on a start-up? It's an acorn. What's an acorn worth?
—Founder of a Silicon Alley start-up[1]

*I need mentoring, contacts, exposure, along with $1 million. I'm looking
for someone to put me in front of their Rolodex so I can tell my story.*
—President of E-media[2]

*Just a few years ago, we were dance or literature majors, actors with day jobs. Now
we live in a strange world where it seems as if every 10th person has won the lottery.*
—Marisa Bowe, editor of Word[3]

Seeing the world to be on the brink of epochal changes Silicon Alley folks
often referred to their exploits as "a moment in time." In fact, their prover-
bial "fifteen minutes of fame" stretched out to some eighteen months between the start of the dot-com stock frenzy at the end of 1998 and the
spring 2000 crash. Yet, the jarring rise and fall of the dot-coms did give one
the feeling that time had indeed collapsed. Instant acceleration and then a
dead stop. How did something this big come together and then fall apart so
quickly? Why did so much support build up for a cause that, in hindsight,
looks to have been based on flimsy assumptions?

The dot-com episode, and the New Economy era in general, raise important questions about how technology, culture, and capital interact in
a "free market" setting. Yet, most discussions of the New Economy's dark
side—the speculation and the scandals—sidestep institutional issues,
stressing instead individual psychology and morality. Stock speculation is
attributed to the accumulated failings of individual investors—their "irrational exuberance," greed, irresponsibility or laziness—and their tendency
to engage in "herd" behavior (its not such a leap to blame Mother Nature if

you see markets to be governed by naturalistic forces). When the discussion moves to suspect behavior on the part of business actors it is usually said to be due to the "bad character" of a few individuals. But sermons about the desirability of individual prudence and honesty ignore the systemic nature of New Economy problems as well as the more ambiguous activities of a large cast of participants. Focusing on character as a fixed individual trait badly misses the mark; New York's new media people collectively underwent an extended bout of shape-shifting during the 1990s. In order to account for the actions of dot-com participants—both buyers and sellers—we need to identify the web of ties and shared understandings that infused New Economy calculations—a web in which new media districts had prominent positions.

It was a linking up of the new media with the financial sector and the old media in the late 1990s that led large numbers of people to believe that dot-com start-ups were carriers of revolutionary change—and worth $100 or more a share. The general public was hardly aware of the new media until the "old" media plugged in to cover the new media's stock market exploits, and dot-com start-ups used their venture capital and IPO money to launch a blizzard of ads. The media blitz celebrated the start-ups as leading characters in a *New Economy saga*. It was wondrous enough, though not very pretty. Idealistic technobohemians gave way to bratty conquistadors, smug in their certainty that it was their destiny to rule over a new New World. Some corporations also testified to the onset of new times as they offered studied portraits of their insurrectionary side. A TV commercial for IBM, for instance, featured street scenes from around the world where individuals would pop out of crowds holding up signs announcing, "I am somebody." On the surface the message was that "Big Blue" was a global liberator who could help energetic individuals use technology to transcend their social circumstances. But the essence of such ads was to present a firm's New Economy credentials; the message was really about the firm itself—"I am somebody because I am of the New Economy." What distinguished the dot-coms—and injected immense energy into the New Economy story—was their use of IPOs to say, "I am somebody."

During the late 1990s hundreds of Silicon Alley start-ups seeking not only capital, but also credibility as New Economy enterprises hooked up with venture capitalists. Of these, several dozen "national contenders" followed the financing networks all the way to Wall Street in the hope of launching spectacular IPOs of stock. Their efforts were complemented by a horde of financiers and other professional pumpsters who competed to shepherd start-ups to market. The IPO process itself depended on an image-making apparatus that connected new media start-ups with the old media as well with as with Wall Street. By 1999 Silicon Alley's big market connection was supplying well-scripted (and well-connected) candidates for IPOs. New York's new media district became part of a larger phenomenon—one revolving around the financial sector.

Totems of the New Economy

When visions of a New Economy flared in the twilight of the Second Millennium digital technology supplied the explosive imagery. However, it was a mobilization of financial forces that drove the idea of a New Economy—and the new media—into the public consciousness. As tech stocks rocketed to new heights the number of references to a "New Economy" in the business media soared from 1,000 in 1998 to 20,000 in 2000.[4] The rise to prominence of new media districts was as much about the financialization of the U.S. economy as it was about its digitalization.

A troika of forces is driving financialization. First and foremost, is neoliberalism. For some time development of the computer industry has been wedded to deregulation and promotion of the financial sector, which began in the 1970s and accelerated during the 1980s. Silicon Valley, which originally depended on defense industry subsidies, began to take advantage of favorable financial regulations in the 1980s—laws on taxation, bankruptcy, stock listings, options and financing that facilitated "risky investments."[5] The link between technology and finance was reinvigorated by Clinton policies that treated the sectors as twin engines of the economy. The Telecommunications Act (1996) aimed to spark restructuring across the telecommunications, computer, and media sectors to boost competition, investment and innovation, especially vis-à-vis the Internet. Clinton policies that aimed to increase firm access to capital added fuel to the mix. U.S. Treasury Secretary Paul Sommers and Federal Reserve Chairman Alan Greenspan took up the New Economy mantra that digital technology, in combination with free markets, was changing the rules of the economy. In one of the New Economy's oddest makeovers, Greenspan morphed into the Great Helmsman of the New Economy (or perhaps its Rain Man). He refrained from boosting interest rates as a boom stretched on and cut rates to carry the boom through rough spots (e.g., the Asian crisis)—actions that probably helped fuel stock speculation.

Two other developments became intertwined with the neoliberal surge: (1) the rise of a new model of firm governance stressing managers' duty to maximize "shareholder value" and (2) a massive shift of middle-class savings into mutual funds. The dominant interpretation of the new model is that shareholder value was being maximized if quarterly earnings statements showed high profit levels. As the United States came out of recession in the early 1990s corporations were hard-pressed to meet these expectations. By middecade mutual funds and pension funds began to turn to venture capital funds, which had reaped high rates of return in the past. From 1995 to 2000 they moved increasing amounts of middle-class savings from "blue chip" corporations into high-risk technology ventures. The total raised by U.S. venture capital funds more than doubled between 1995 and 1997, increasing from some $4.2 billion to $9 billion; subsequently, the totals more than doubled each year—rocketing to a mindboggling $102 billion in 2000.[6]

With numbers of this magnitude one is tempted to deem the new media firms and the New Economy mere by-products of surplus risk capital. I argue, however, that the flood of venture capital funds and a new wave of start-up firms helped give meaning and credibility to each other within the emerging New Economy paradigm. A key tenet of New Economy thought is that a new kind of firm was taking center stage—one that possessed relatively few material assets but was able to use its digital capabilities to transform segments of the economy. The model drew heavily from the example of West Coast tech giants that dominated the markets providing the infrastructure for the Internet—firms such as Microsoft (software), Sun Microsystems (workstations), and Cisco (switchers and routers). Neil Fligstein, a sociologist of markets, notes that these firms maintain their dominance in their respective markets through either buying up innovations in their area or by incorporating the insights in their own main products. This strategy has been an influential model for new firms. Many observers cite Cisco as the paradigmatic New Economy "business model." Cisco is something of a virtual firm as it makes extensive use of business networks and Internet systems to minimize its own physical operations. Cisco is also known for using its high-valued stock as a currency to acquire small companies with superior technology or talent.

Fligstein argues that the strategy of leaders such as Cisco leaves start-ups with several options. They can use niche strategies to avoid competition (the path taken by the majority of Silicon Alley firms). However, if they want to maximize their financial potential by being "innovators who take risks," several other paths stand out: They could "go 'public' and sell stock, sell the firm to one of the industry giants or try to become one of these giants themselves."[7] The payoff for playing second fiddle could be huge—Cisco used $6.9 billion of its own stock to acquire Cerent—a start-up with revenue of only $10 million.

The New Economy financial calculus might seem to suggest the eclipse of the shareholder model of the firm. However, I propose it actually represents a further evolution of the shareholder model. The New Economy version is that if you want to maximize investor value you have to be willing to "go for it"—to be the kind of risk-taking innovator who might become the next giant or to at least do well enough to receive a lucrative buyout. This calculus is embodied in the venture capital gambit: a few big hits and some decent buyouts should more than make up for a bunch of failed ventures, resulting in high returns for a fund.

The apparent fit of dot-com start-ups with the New Economy model of the firm gave investors a reason to believe that a large number of opportunities existed for high-return investments. It justified the extension of the venture capital model of risk financing to new sectors and places. Notice, for instance, how a Silicon Alley venture capitalist cited the rise of "real" Internet business as evidence that expectations (in 1997) had become more realistic:

> Two years ago there was no business on the Internet, so the only way people could get money or attention was hype. People are now buying on the Internet, advertising on the Internet and using it everyday. We're beginning to see the real emergence of a business as opposed to a concept . . . we're entering a period when expectations are . . . in line with reality.[8]

Investors—and various "experts"—did not subject New Economy firms to the same "make-or-break" expectations regarding quarterly performance that was held over the heads of Old Economy firms. The question then is, How did they know which firms were "New Economy" enterprises? New media participants in places such as Silicon Alley played a basic role here, as they testified to the New Economy status of particular firms or groups of firms. The key criteria was that a firm had the business model and financial support to become a "first-mover" in a new Internet market (and thus reap high returns); in practice, new media cultural traits were proxies hinting at a New Economy business model. The cultural mobilization of new media districts complimented the financial mobilization. The districts not only produced visions of epic forces, but also artifacts attesting to the material reality of a new kind of firm: loft workplaces, a distinctive social scene, and employees with quirky looks and attitudes. The role of middle-class savings largely went unrecognized by the public; dot-comers became the totems of the New Economy—its emblems embodied in tattooed and pierced flesh.

On the other hand, capital—especially, venture capital and IPOs—contributed a great deal to establishing the credibility of new media visionaries (as well as their operating funds). Thus, it came to pass that members of capitalism's lost tribe, which had only recently returned from the wired wilderness, translated prophecies for the new millennium into prospectuses for stock offerings.

THE NEW BOYS–OLD BOYS NETWORK

Silicon Valley norms and sensibilities about venture financing imprinted New Economy thinking—and efforts to make sense of new media firms and districts. In his book, *Bamboozled at the Revolution*, John Motavalli—an Internet business veteran—observed that a cadre of technology leaders and pundits (e.g., *Wired* magazine) zealously promoted "the credo that Silicon Valley and its values and innovation would completely change the face of the American economy."[9] However, we can hardly take for granted that this cultural project would be well received in New York (where the average chip-on-the-shoulder is the size of the Brooklyn Bridge). Leading Silicon Alley firms became interested in hooking up with Silicon Valley–style venture capitalists in particular, hoping to gain credibility as well as capital. Establishing the merits of new firms was a daunting problem in an emerging industry where few were making profits. The Silicon Valley model suggested that start-ups could gain credibility by getting the backing of the "smart money"—venture capitalists whose inside expertise and connections were thought to give them an advantage in assessing high-risk ventures.[10]

Though their numbers were small initially, Silicon Alley's venture capitalists were potent change agents. Capital did not flow into Lower Manhattan in a generic form as if a convoy of Brinks trucks had pulled up to the Flatiron Building and begun to disperse billions of dollars. Venture capitalists transformed pools of capital owned by rich individuals and elite institutions into something new—a circuit of exchange with its own set of understandings, obligations, and symbols as well as its own medium of exchange (venture capital itself).[11] They prepared the enclave to receive this new currency by creating understandings and ties that bridged the worlds of new media entrepreneurs and elite financial interests.

While Silicon Alley's venture capitalists argued that the enclave's role was different from that of Silicon Valley, they contended that Silicon Alley had a similar potential to generate innovations that were immensely profitable—and that it needed a Silicon Valley–style financing system to realize this potential. They spearheaded efforts to introduce elements of this financing system to New York, including norms about the virtues of risk taking in exchange for equity in a start-up, alternative criteria for assessing firms, and the need for a system of "angel" investing (an "angel investor" is a well-to-do individual who invests small amounts of capital in exchange for equity).

However, creating venture capital systems in new media districts entailed a "translation" of the Silicon Valley model rather than its replication. The districts represented a very different kind of setting than that in which the model originated. The development of the Silicon Valley computer industry was already underway when the venture financing system emerged (typically, the venture capitalists were successful entrepreneurs); moreover, the financing system formed at a time when Silicon Valley's innovative exploits were being subsidized by Cold War defense spending. In contrast, venture capitalists in new media enclaves were trying to create financing networks at the same time that initial attempts to commercialize Internet technology were taking place. As we saw in chapter 2, early venture capitalists in Silicon Alley actually played a role in organizing a commercially oriented ensemble. Their conception of Silicon Alley's unique role as a form of media paralleled their view of their own special role in the world of venture capital: New York's financiers understood the media business, Silicon Valley's didn't "get it." Though Silicon Alley's venture capitalists created an impressive set of insider ties, the sector's newness meant that their experience was rather shallow. Finally, pre-Internet Silicon Valley never handled the volume of venture capital that descended on fledgling new media districts. In January 2000 Silicon Alley received over $481 million in venture capital;[12] at that rate, Silicon Alley's total for the year would have been almost $6 billion—exceeding the $4.2 billion total received in the entire United States in 1995! *Extending the Silicon Valley model of financing to new places and sectors was one of the defining developments of the New Economy*—and a highly problematic project.

One had to go against the current to argue that New York had potential as a center of innovation and entrepreneurship. So how did Silicon Alley's fledgling corps of venture capitalists redefine the possiblities in an old city whose economic base was Old Economy corporations? We saw that they made themselves into network hubs in Silicon Alley; they also became hubs in the circuit of media coverage about the enclave—stories commonly quoted them, and their presence was cited as evidence of New York's viability as a center of innovation. The venture capitalists led the way in introducing New York to the Silicon Valley system of venture financing; their expositions on Silicon Valley's virtues were baselines for identifying New York's shortcomings. A Silicon Alley venture capitalist, for instance, touted Silicon Valley's culture of "serial entrepreneurialism": "Look at the classic Silicon Valley model where an entrepreneur starts a company and sells to Microsoft, then starts another and sells to Oracle, and so forth and so on. It's the culture, and its absolutely what we should expect. It's capitalism at its finest." In contrast, in New York, "there is no culture of technology . . . which means there aren't any role models or angels."[13] Silicon Valley risk culture also upheld a different set of criteria for evaluating the merits of potential recipients. For instance, a 1997 article in *Crain's New York Business* noted that financiers operating in the Silicon Valley mode were funding Silicon Alley start-ups that had virtually no histories. Instead, they evaluated their management, business models, and venture backing; in contrast, New York banks were doing little new media business because they demanded to see three years of financial reports and required that founders put up personal assets as collateral.[14]

Silicon Valley also had a "relational" advantage. The CEO of Rare-Medium noted that a web of ties allowed Silicon Valley venture capitalists to assemble the assets needed to turn business models into "self-fulfilling prophecies":

> New York is so . . . underdeveloped in terms of relationships. Those Claude Perkins guys, and Benchmark [Silicon Valley venture capital firms] . . . have it wired. It is a complete self-fulfilling prophecy. They have capital, they have all the corporate relationships, they have all the head hunting relationships. And the ideas that emanate from them . . . they get the best guys to run them.[15]

The key assumption underlying these expositions was that New York's new media start-ups would have to get venture capital if they wanted to make it big—to star in their segment. For example, one of the partners at Flatiron Partners proposed that the opening for his firm was that New York lacked "the venture capital to help firms grow to the point of becoming leading firms nationally."[16]

Silicon Alley entrepreneurs, who hoped to build large firms and big reputations quickly, learned to seek out the smart money in the district's burgeoning party circuit. A former employee of Time Warner's Pathfinder recalled: "To be involved in the new media world is to have to go to all these parties to try to raise money . . . they are all worried about who to talk to."[17] Of course, the point of all this compulsory socializing was to link up with venture capitalists, who had adroitly made themselves the life of the party—and powerbrokers. An article for *The Industry Standard*—a national New Economy magazine—observed that Silicon Alley's early venture capitalists were central figures in an emerging "new boys network" of entrepreneurs and financiers who were not only well connected in the new media community but also had links to major corporations and Wall Street.[18] Mark Stahlman, the financier who coined the name Silicon Alley, had retired from investment banking after having helped take AOL public. Robert Lessin was a former vice-chairman of Salomon Smith Barney who brought dozens of Wall Street employees with him after he bought out Wit Capital. Others were partners in venture capital firms based in New York who wanted to explore the innovative firms emerging in their own backyard. Bryan Horey, who worked with Stahlman in founding the NYNMA, was a partner in a New York venture capital firm when he helped organize New York's new media as was Fred Wilson when he joined a computer magazine editor—Jerry Colonna—to found Flatiron Partners.

The case of Flatiron Partners provides a good look at how venture capitalists positioned themselves to exercise cultural authority. Early on, the media annointed the firm as Silicon Alley's flagship venture capitalist. A 1997 article in *Crain's New York Business* credited Wilson with "helping to put Manhattan's Silicon Alley on the map with Silicon Valley" while the

1998 article in *The Industry Standard* stated that, "among Silicon Alley investors, all roads lead through Fred Wilson and Jerry Colonna."[19] Starting out in 1996 with $50 million contributed by Chase Manhattan and Softbank (Japan) Flatiron's early high profile in the media was largely the result of its intense networking. Although Flatiron later backed firms such as StarMedia, theStreetcom and Kozmo, its local investing was initially cautious. *The Industry Standard* stressed the duo's networking agenda while comparing their contacts with entrepreneurs to Hollywood auditions: "Wilson and Colonna have worked hard to insinuate themselves in the middle of Silicon Alley, fielding calls and answering questions for entrepreneurs they don't intend to fund, essentially making their office seem like a casting agency on the day of an open call."[20]

One partner recalled speaking "on the circuit to educate" firms on the ways of venture capital. At the start, "We had 1,200 business plans sent to us in the first three or four months." He said that he told most entrepreneurs that it was too early in their firm's development for them to be seeking venture capital: "A venture capitalist needs to put capital to work, to do deals that are in the two- to three-million-dollar range. New firms couldn't use that much. They needed seed capital—up to $500,000 tops. . . . We couldn't do $100,000 deals."[21] Instead, he advised new start-ups that the right funding source for them was an angel investor. In fact, Flatiron formed ties with angel investors to find out which firms were promising candidates for larger investments. It also took a proactive role in lining up firms with angels.

Most of Silicon Alley's financiers made strategic use of ties to rich individuals—and elite institutions. Mark Stahlman's financing firm touted its status as an "affiliate" of Accel Partners—a major venture capital fund. Robert Lessin pursued the vision that a Silicon Valley–type mindset could be cultivated if Silicon Alley was linked to New York's leverage buyout millionaires. He used his old Wall Street ties to found the Dawntreader Fund—a $20 million fund targeting Internet businesses. Lessin called the fund, "a portal to the Internet for the most intriguing group of individuals in the world"—a group of forty investors that included ten billionaires.[22] Flatiron Partners created its own bridge to old boy money—an arrangement with the New York Investment Fund whereby its members (elite individuals and institutions in the New York City Partnership) could buy into new media firms that Flatiron backed. Flatiron touted its usefulness as a bird dog for the old boys—including David Rockefeller who bought into StarMedia. Wilson gushed, "David Rockefeller is 82 years old. There's no way he could find that."[23] Moreover, Flatiron Partners took a similar role for Rockefeller's old bank—Chase Manhattan. Speaking of their role as a Chase Manhattan "affiliate," Wilson remarked, "We have separate offices, we're in the Flatiron district, we don't look like a bank and we don't act like a bank. Entrepreneurs are comfortable with us."[24] So was Chase Manhattan. In 1998 it upped its bet on Flatiron Partners, putting up an additional $300 million.

The venture capitalists joined broader efforts to organize angel investor networks and to educate entrepreneurs. For example, NYNMA worked with Horey, Lessin, David Horowitz (COO of Warner Communications and former MTV CEO)—and Esther Dyson (a nationally known Internet guru and venture capitalist) to form an Angel Investors Program. By May 1997 they had assembled a network of thirty investors and hosted a novel event—a public forum where start-ups could deliver a twenty-minute pitch to a group of investors. A month later a similar event—"Ready, Set, Pitch"—was held by the *Silicon Alley Reporter*. A panel of representatives of Microsoft, USA Networks, Sony Online World, William Morris Agency, and Flatiron Partners delivered biting critiques after six-minute pitches by a mix of hapless unknowns and "established" start-ups (RareMedium) and personalities (Jaime Levy). Media coverage of these events indicated that they had a bizarre air—reminiscent of a failed Broadway production (if not the "Gong Show"). Commenting on the novelty of a public airing of investment pitches—they usually take place behind doors—Jerry Colonna stated that an educational agenda was behind the amusing spectacle: "Is it staged? Certainly. But . . . the community needs this desperately. I think the goal is education, not just entertainment, and the education is for those pitching and people sitting in the audience."[25] Entrepreneurs who had formerly been "actors with day jobs" would have found the experience to be strangely familiar. The lessons to be learned seemed to be those of the theater. Entrepreneurs not only needed to develop a coherent story, but also, in the manner of actors, to make a convincing delivery of their lines. And venture capitalists were drama critics and coaches. However, new media thespians would hardly need to wait on tables to make ends meet if they gained a starring role in the defining spectacle of the New Economy—the IPO road show.

The Star-making Machinery Behind the Popular Stock

One of the keynote speeches at "Silicon Alley 1999" had a fiery "the end is near" tenor of a street preacher's sermon. Nobody laughed or walked out. A crowd of two thousand executives, entrepreneurs, and venture capitalists "hung on every word" of Jack Hidary, the young co-founder of EarthWeb. Hidary warned executives in the financial and media sectors that they had better embrace the Internet more aggressively or "risk becoming take-over candidates." He noted that Time Inc., worth some $70 billion, had passed on an opportunity to invest in Yahoo in 1995. Now Yahoo was worth $30 billion. If Time did not quickly establish itself in the new media, Yahoo might well buy it out within five years.[26]

Barely 30 years old, Jack Hidary had credibility. In fact, he was a star. Five years before he was a medical researcher at the National Institutes of Health when he joined his brother and a friend in founding a web services firm that evolved into EarthWeb—an online service for techies. Hidary's hard science background set him off from most of his Silicon Alley peers, but it was not the reason for his credibility or his celebrity. His rise to star status, and that of several dozen Silicon Alley entrepreneurs, provides an intimate look at the process through which New Economy reputations were made at the end of the 1990s.

Though the faithful avowed that the Internet "changed everything," it was hooking up with the stock market that changed everything for new media districts and firms. Extraordinary IPOs by a series of Internet firms and the rise in the stock values of firms such as Yahoo, AOL, and Amazon.com in 1998 propelled the Internet to prominence as a material and symbolic force. The market value of Amazon.com increased 638 percent (to $18.9 billion), Yahoo rose 452 percent (to $11.7 billion), and America Online increased 294 percent (to $40.9 billion).[27]

It has become fashionable to cite global "flows" of capital as forces that determine the fortunes of cities. However, it was not inevitable that the flow of capital would wash into Silicon Alley. For some time new media industry-builders as well as place-builders had worked to link New York's new media with its financial district. Likewise, the hooking up of several dozen Silicon Alley firms to an emerging bull market for Internet stocks was the result of active efforts by new media entrepreneurs, venture capitalists, and their collaborators on Wall Street. Moreover, the successes of two Silicon Alley IPOs altered the course of the market, helping propel the dot-com phenomenon toward its historic peak (and fatal excesses). The first IPO was that of EarthWeb—Jack Hidary's firm—on November 11, 1998. EarthWeb was initially listed at $14 a share for the IPO. On the first day of trading its share value opened at $40 and peaked at $89, before settling down to some $48.[28] This was the most spectacular opening day rise in Wall Street history. The record was short-lived, smashed thirty-six hours later by theglobe.com. Listed at $9 a share, theglobe.com opened at $87 a share as a "queue" of buyers placed orders; after the average share changed hands five times, the stock peaked at $97 a share. It ended the day at over $63 a share.[29]

Dozens of Silicon Alley's leading firms began to shift their priorities from getting established in some Internet market to positioning themselves vis-à-vis the financial markets. There were multiple motives. Certainly, some hoped to enrich themselves. For example, a co-owner recalled turning down a buyout offer from another firm: "You don't make money on a strategic buy—you make it on financial buys. That was the kind of money we were interested in."[30] Other founders seemed to be seeking a personal sort of validation at a time when the media limelight was focused on New Economy stock exploits. Those who were more interested in building a credible business, hoped that an IPO would provide publicity that allowed their firms to stand out. Relatedly, an IPO could also bring financial resources that could be used to push their firm ahead of the pack. Many owners wanted to raise large sums of money so that they could acquire other firms (in the process gaining capacities or eliminating competitors). In addition, owners and venture capitalists alike thought that IPOs would provide firms with the kind of resource that was needed to attract or retain skilled workers—stock options. The reason for going public given by one of EarthWeb's co-founders evoked the full spectrum of New Economy business sensibilities:

> We wanted to be first. Historically, the first-mover advantage is huge. We've seen the big get bigger. We're now at the stage where to win, we have to get as much market share as we can. And the only way to do that is through consolidation and really rapid growth. And you can't do that without some kind of currency, and what people really want is stock.[31]

We see here many of the elements of the Cisco model, including the idea that stock is a "currency." This suggests that the basis of the dot-com stock rush was more cultural and institutional in nature than psychological.

In contrast to accounts of dot-com stock that focus on "irrational exuberance," I propose to examine the roles of new media entrepreneurs, venture capitalists, and assorted other interests in organizing exuberance and in "minting" these new currencies. As the cultural and financial industries have become interwoven in a "symbolic" economy, the content of cultural industries increasingly concerns financial news and commentary while the financial sector has taken on the structure of certain cultural industries. I argue that the production of dot-com IPOs proceeded in a manner that was similar to that used to produce "hits" in cultural industries (e.g., pop records, books). Silicon Alley developed into a New Economy "hitsville" at the end of the decade.[32]

It might seem that we don't have to go to such lengths to account for the theatrics. After all, Silicon Alley entrepreneurs were always adept at putting on a good show. Consider the case of Seth Goldstein, the founder of Site Specific. Speaking of his own intimate circle he recalled: "We all came out of theater. . . . There was a sense of casting. You cast your technical person, you cast your creative person, then you show up for the client and everybody has to look their part. So much of it was about packaging and . . .

making people feel that you know more than they do."[33] However, Goldstein's later exploits—as an "entrepreneur in residence" at Flatiron Partners—bear witness to the rise of an *apparatus* for selling companies and their stories to the public. At the peak of the dot-com frenzy in 1999 he offered a portrait of the ideal entrepreneur, stressing the need to link one's story to a larger drama: "As a good entrepreneur, you're playing a role in a script that's bigger than you. You're part of a greater story and you need to know what that story is. And then you need to cast people in it. . . . It's about having a story and convincing others of the value of your vision." Furthermore, venture capitalists systematically selected, cultivated, and promoted certain types of entrepreneurs for the IPO track. Goldstein remarked, "You want an entrepreneur with a messianic vision—a script written in their mind that's waiting to be given legs. I look for passion. . . . "[34]

This intermediary role performed by venture capitalists was analogous to that of cultural industry brokers who select and cultivate raw cultural products. In the case of the dot-coms, the product was a start-up possessing a credible script with one or more "trained" executives to deliver the lines with gusto. Goldstein's comments imply that venture capitalists also acted as script doctors. Along with entrepreneurs, they helped create a new genre—the New Economy tale of a virtual firm that could unleash the forces of unfettered technology (and markets).

That it became the "greatest story ever sold" required the collaboration of the institutional gatekeepers of the IPO market. Here the IPO production process resembled the cultural industries in another basic respect—the organized effort to influence, or even co-opt, the institutional gatekeepers who evaluate products critically and at the same time influence consumption styles. Key gatekeepers in the case of dot-com stock included major accounting firms, Wall Street investment banks, and the financial media—"reputable" experts (until recently) whose endorsement of dot-com scripts and executives was essential for an IPO to succeed. Thus, a second role of venture capitalists was to create ties with these financial gatekeepers that would provide a start-up with a favorable entry into the stock market. This became easier as escalating IPOs gave financial gatekeepers a complementary interest in the New Economy "product line." Many of them endorsed the new genre (as well as individual firms) and helped cultivate a taste for a new style of investing and a new set of investment criteria.

What was unique about the dot-com IPO production process as a form of cultural production was that it was driven by escalating jackpots and hypercompetitions involving financial service providers: start-ups vying for venture capital and for slots in the IPO machine; venture capitalists competing both for start-ups to add to their stables and for top investment banks to underwrite IPOs by their start-ups; accounting firms competing to get the business of IPO candidates; and investment banks competing to be selected as underwriters for promising IPOs.

ORGANIZING EXUBERANCE—THE EARTHWEB IPO

The case of EarthWeb offers a glimpse at the machinery that propelled New Economy stories forward and made extraordinary IPOs possible. In late 1994 Jack Hidary, his brother Murray, and their friend Nova Spivack founded EarthWeb's predecessor—IdentiNet—a webshop that did consulting. The eureka moment that led to EarthWeb occurred as the firm struggled to catch up with the launch of a new software: They realized that ever-changing technologies burdened web workers such as themselves and IT professionals in general. Jack Hidary recalled, that on every project, one had to dig up "information about which vendor was appropriate—Oracle vs. Sybase, Netscape vs. Microsoft—which one was appropriate for the project, who's using this."[35] They started a site for IT professionals that collected information on technology that was submitted by the users themselves. They dropped consulting in mid-1997 to focus on the online service; after the firm acquired six content sites it became a network offering specialized information. Barely a year after they restructured the business, the trio began to look into an IPO.

The story that EarthWeb took to market, like many in Silicon Alley, touted its special ability to generate advertising revenue. EarthWeb's founders argued that their experience as web consultants gave them an intimate understanding of IT professionals, which, in turn, would enable them to give advertisers targeted access to a valued niche. The high-end niche would allow EarthWeb to charge higher advertising rates and to avoid the cyclical downturns that afflict advertising.

It was going to be a challenge to make the story compelling enough. By normal criteria, EarthWeb did not have much of a business going. It charted losses of $4.9 million on only $1.4 million in revenue in the nine months leading up to its IPO; moreover, two advertisers (IBM and Microsoft) accounted for a quarter of the revenue while "barters" with other firms (e.g., swapping ad space) accounted for another quarter.[36] In order for EarthWeb's story to compensate for the weak numbers—a common problem in Silicon Alley—it would have to be embraced by assorted financial concerns who would in turn pass it along to investors.

A successful IPO depends on a chain of interests lining up to provide serial vouching for the potential of the firm. To get out of the starting gate, one's venture capitalist had to be willing to promote you—and to have credibility with an investment bank. Venture capitalists often have ties to the investment banks that underwrite the IPO. The venture capitalist gives the firm credibility with investment banks, who in turn, give a firm credibility with prospective stock buyers. Buyers are themselves stratified between the investment bank's favored customers—institutional investors for whom stock orders are reserved at a set opening price—and subsequent waves of less-connected buyers who may pay four or five times as much during the course of the first day of trading. The key step is whipping up enthusiasm among a vanguard of institutional investors so that the stock explodes out of the gates with an accelerating price that draws buyers from the general public. In such circumstances, the involvement of the insiders (venture capitalists and institutional investors) is hardly irrational—they are the ones most likely to receive huge returns while being less exposed to risk. For their part, the investment banks get 6 percent of the total raised in the IPO. The way the process is organized, the risks of untested firms are largely borne by a mass of less-informed investors who join in at the later stages.

In the "informal schmoozing" stage of EarthWeb's IPO (see table 3.1) it met investment banks through the personal ties of its executives and through its venture capitalist—Warburg Pincus. In a "beauty contest" among banks interested in EarthWeb's IPO business, the firm chose four banks to act as underwriters with J. P. Morgan selected as the lead underwriter. The duty of the underwriters is to then perform "due diligence"—assess the firm's business record and its prospects in its market segment. The underwriters help the firm prepare a prospectus, which is a detailed analysis of the firm, its history, products, management structure, and financial data. It should also disclose any risks that come with investing in the IPO. After filing the prospectus with the Securities and Exchange Commission (SEC) the underwriters set the opening price at which the stock is to be sold and determine the number of shares to be sold. EarthWeb's stock was priced in the range of $12 to $14 a share.

In many dot-com IPOs the stock was purposely underpriced so as to draw in (and reward) the vanguard investors while the number of shares to be sold was set under the level of expected demand in the hope of creating a feeding frenzy on opening day. Following a "quiet" period there is a "road show"—an intense tour where company management seeks to stir up interest in the IPO among institutional investors. This is the time to make good on whatever drama coaching their venture capitalist has provided. Jack Hidary gave a vivid recollection of a grueling tour of thirteen cities that started on the West Coast and ended on the East Coast:

> You have seven meetings a day for ten days. On top of that you have lunch and sometimes a dinner where you speak to many investors at once, but the seven

Table 3.1 Steps in an Initial Public Offering

Step One: Informal Schmoozing
Make contacts among the investment banking community. When an investment bank underwrites a stock, it is essentially buying the stock from the company and reselling it to portfolio managers, who then sell it on the market on the first day of trading.

Step Two: Bankers' Beauty Contest
Banks make formal presentations explaining how they would underwrite the offering if they were selected.

Step Three: Due Diligence
The underwriters study the company's business record and prospects in its market segment. Then the company files with the SEC.

Step Four: Quiet Period
After the filing, company employees are prohibited from making public statements about the company until 25 days after the stock begins trading. The underwriters set the opening price for the stock offering based on a comparable group of companies.

Step Five: The Road Show
Company management goes on a whirlwind tour to get institutional investors interested in buying the stock.

Step Six: Taking Orders
The underwriters set the final price of the offering. Institutional investors then place their orders with the underwriting banks.

Step Seven: The Stock Is Traded
In the first day of public trading institutional investors can reap immediate profits from selling; company management must wait 180 days before selling its stock.

Source: Adapted from David Ball. 1999. "Unearthing an IPO Sucess." *Silicon Alley Reporter* 3,2: 44–49.

> meetings are all one-on-one. So you meet with seventy, eighty, ninety investors. . . . You tell the same story again and again, and you get the same questions again and again. Everytime you've got to make it fresh.[37]

After the road show the underwriters set the final price of the offering and institutional investors place their orders. On the first day of public trading the institutional investors could reap immediate profits from selling; senior management and pre-IPO investors (e.g., venture capital funds) had to wait 180 days before selling. Even then it was awkward for managers (but not the venture capital investors) to sell large amounts of stock because it suggested that they lacked confidence in the firm's prospects. In fact, manipulations of the IPO so as to create an opening day spectacle had mixed results for the firm. The amount of capital that the firm raised depended on the price and size of the offering *set by the underwriters before the opening*. Underpricing or undersupplying the stock cut into the amount that a firm raised. Even the publicity to be gained if the value of its stock skyrocketed on the opening day was a two-edged sword; if the stock started to plummet in value the firm could quickly lose credibility.

EarthWeb ended up raising $24 million—a war chest that could be used to boost its market share and revenues. The credibility of the new stock was reinforced by a favorable report from a financial analyst at J. P. Morgan—its underwriter. The analyst reaffirmed the EarthWeb storyline, proposing that the firm, "is able to deliver a very lucrative and attractive market to advertisers that is not easy to reach . . . advertisers are willing to pay much higher rates."[38] Despite the fact that EarthWeb's valuation of $300 million was over two hundred times its revenue—and two firms had similar websites—the analyst praised EarthWeb's good "concept story." In response to the rating, the *Silicon Alley Reporter* noted, "If enough people buy into the concept, the stock price will enable the company to execute it."

Every (Stock) Pitcher Tells a Story

As was the case in Silicon Valley, the New Economy version of the self-fulfilling prophecy depended on being able to assemble a diverse network of supporters. That is not to say that such networks resulted from some sort of conspiracy. The dot-com IPO apparatus emerged from an evolving ensemble of financing networks that developed new shared understandings about imperatives and possibilities in the New Economy. However, the participants came to possess overlapping interests when it came to revving up the production of IPOs. The IPO process and participant sensibilities changed as the stakes grew, competition heated up, and promotional webs thickened. Between 1998 and 2000, the apparatus became increasingly geared to initiate, sustain, and exploit waves of speculative investment.

Venture capitalists and financial analysts took the role of oracles in the media, proclaiming that "the market" was "sending a message" or that a particular IPO would be a "test" of the market. However, it was the oracles themselves who defined specific IPOs as being "tests" and who interpreted the results—if given half a chance, announcing an opening of the IPO "window" for particular firms or types of firms. Yet, one or two oracles did not an IPO make. A firm was set to exploit (or even initiate) a wave of investment when a chain of actors lined up to affirm its potential. It was said that they "bought" into the story, investing reputations and services in hopes of realizing a sizeable gain of some sort.

"Wired" Execs

The buying into a start-up's story often began with "professional" executives who came aboard sometime after the firm was founded. The weight that their opinion carried depended on how strategic their own ties were. A Morgan Stanley executive advised start-ups that having people "with relationships on Wall Street . . . helps establish your credibility with the underwriter even before that first meeting takes place."[39] Before an IPO, start-ups needing to find sources of funding often sought a Wall Street vet to serve as their chief financial officer (CFO). As competition for a CFO who was "wired" to investors escalated so did the pay offers, including size-able amounts of equity. The equity stake was key: Landing a seasoned CFO was said to be like winning the approval of a savvy investor because the CFO would not leave a higher salary on Wall Street in exchange for equity unless the firm's prospects were solid. *Crain's New York Business* noted, "Even eager candidates are being choosy about jobs, often demanding full disclosure of a company's finances. . . . They're grilling management as well as investors, bankers and accountants to get a fix on a company's prospects."[40] Two points are worthy of notice here. First, the concern of prospective CFOs was not as much about the long-term viability of a firm but "to make sure the company will make it to the IPO." Second, they, like most everyone else, looked to financial sector notables to vouch for the credibility of the firm.

New Economy Accountants

One of the first agents of the financial services sector a start-up encoun-tered was an accountant. The founder of i-Traffic, a Silicon Alley start-up, advised start-ups to select an accounting firm that had geared up for IPO business:

> A growing battery of opportunistic providers in the area are realizing the im-portance of grooming these start-ups effectively. . . . You definitely have to sell the vision to these guys as much as you would to a potential hire or investor . . . the level of attention and dedication that a firm will provide you with is di-rectly related to whether they buy into your vision.[41]

The *Silicon Alley Reporter* added that, what was at stake was not so much "sound accounting" but gaining an accountant who would "give credence to your cause."

In fact, *Crain's New York Business* reported (in 1998) that major ac-counting firms were "trolling" Silicon Alley. "Having identified new media as the industry of the future in New York, the big firms are pouring re-sources into Silicon Alley in a manner that belies their traditional conserva-tive images."[42] A partner at Arthur Anderson declared that being in Silicon Alley, "is like being in Detroit in 1905 and asking if you should go befriend that Henry Ford fellow." *Crain's* noted that for Silicon Alley firms, "having a first-class accountant on board is considered crucial to their credibility when they seek private backing or plunge into the public markets."[43] Thus, when the CFO of 24/7 announced that KMPG Peat Marwick "has learned our business inside out," it implied that his firm had been found IPO-worthy. For their part, accounting firms were interested in fees for SEC filings, venture capital deals, and IPOs—especially IPOs. KMPG's head partner for new media noted that, "IPOs are where everybody has placed their bets"—which implied that they were partners in the IPO exploits of companies such as 24/7. The accountants helped give credibility to the whole sector as they sought roles in certifying claims regarding user privacy, the security of online transactions, and the veracity of website user counts (a concern of advertisers). An Ernst and Young partner advised, "This is the Wild West. We're clearly trying to keep law and order"; his counterpart at KMPG remarked, "We're all trying to get . . . a collaborative business community where everybody is up-front and honest."[44]

Silicon Alley start-ups found accounting firms to be quite collaborative even when their assets amounted to little more than a fanciful story. Take, for example, the case of CyberShop, a virtual department store, that offered six hundred different brand products for sale on its own site and on AOL's Shopping Channel. Its business model stressed the enterprise's virtuality: It would fill orders, and the products would be shipped directly to the customers. Its founder bragged, "No inventories. No salespeople. No Store. Just bits and bytes."[45] However, he did have a blue chip accountant: "My philosophy from the start was that I needed to have triple A advisors, so it would be a triple A deal when it went public." At a time in which it had no office or employees CyberShop managed to land Arthur Anderson as its accounting firm. An Anderson partner involved admitted that, "My initial impression was that it was a great story but futuristic." Like many of the accounting giants Anderson only charged a fraction of its normal fee. After CyberShop had an IPO, Anderson received $150,000 for its IPO work. CyberShop's model proved to be a bit too lightweight. In the year following the market crash its stock dropped from $56.87 to 56 cents a share; it changed its name to Grove Strategic Ventures and its business model to "Internet business incubator."[46]

Blue Chip Banks

The most crucial step in preparing for an IPO was selecting an investment bank to act as the underwriter. The prospects for an IPO, *The Industry Standard* noted, are "determined mainly by the prestige and sales networks of the underwriters."[47] The most prestigious are Wall Street investment banks such as Morgan Stanley Dean Witter, Goldman Sachs, Merrill Lynch and J. P. Morgan. A Morgan Stanley executive advised that when a firm's profit and revenue numbers are weak it must present "other indicators of potential" to gain credibility.[48] Despite the sophisticated technologies and techniques wielded by the New Economy's financial engineers it was, once again, the story that mattered—the opportunities in your segment and your firm's positioning. It also paid to have executives that the bank knew. In turn, a bank's ability to pass the story along should be a key consideration in selecting an underwriter. The Morgan Stanley exec noted, "If I'm an entrepreneur, what I want is someone who will be able to articulate my story on my behalf to investors"—especially, the "capacity for high returns." The bank should be able to use its analysts to link your story favorably to larger developments: "I'm going to start my relationship with a firm that has a set of market professionals who know not just how to get deals done, but also are engaged in forecasting, aware of the greater picture. I want people who can position my company for high visibility beyond today or tomorrow."[49] In other words, you should be able to rely on the analysts to issue reports that make your stock look good after you go public. The CFO of 24/7 added that, "The confidence of the underwriter carries a lot of weight in the marketplace."[49]

Competition among investment banks to underwrite dot-com offerings became fierce as the IPO market heated up. The banks began to exploit the IPO market in 1996, expanding their technology units and adding new media and e-commerce specialists to their stables of analysts. Though the fees for IPOs were high, the banks were also interested in the prestige and publicity, hoping that spectacular IPOs would draw new investment banking clients. As the IPO tide fluctuated, they exercised restraint when market momentum declined, wanting to avoid anemic IPOs that would reduce their own credibility. By late 1998 they felt compelled to throw caution to the wind. Even the most prestigious banks competed to finance "concept deals"—offerings where a firm had "little to show but an idea."[50] Underwriting fees escalated into the hundreds of millions. At the peak in the first quarter of 2000, Goldman Sachs—the number one underwriter—backed fifteen IPOs raising a total of $4.5 billion: Its 6 percent cut amounted to $270 million.[51]

Ironically, the dot-com frenzy began to eclipse the Wall Street banks despite the banks' intimate involvement in producing IPOs. In December 1999—a time when Wall Street had set aside $13 billion for bonuses—the *New York Times* reported that "the Internet, like an electronic black hole, has stolen all the glory." The banks were losing personnel to start-ups because stock options promised quick riches. A Morgan Stanley executive claimed that the new mindset was, "I want to be a multi millionaire by the time I'm 30, but if I stay at Morgan Stanley, it may take me until I'm 50."[52] Banks that lagged in the IPO market found it difficult to prevent defections among their technology bankers and analysts who left to take positions with dot-coms (as CFOs or as strategic planners). Given the stakes, candidate firms were likely to pass muster on the way to the IPO and almost certain to receive support from the bank's analysts once the stock was listed.

The New Financial Media

Bank analysts became one of the gatekeepers for a new circuit of media coverage and commentary that firms yearned to enter—a system that *Business-Week* called the "Wall Street's Hype Machine." It reported, "Never before has Wall Street raised expectations quite so high—and never before have the media joined in quite so willingly as cheerleaders and stock-pushers."[53] It outlined several elements of a stock promotion apparatus. First, advertising by brokerage firms increased 95 percent in 1999, reaching $1.2 billion—three times the amount in 1995. Second, the role of analysts had changed from researchers to "celebrity pitchmen"—for their firm's clients as well as for their own establishments. Third, coverage of finance was being altered by the proliferation of cable TV outlets and personal finance sites on the Internet (and the celebrity status of some journalists). Fourth, finance was becoming a form of entertainment (as reflected in NASDAQ's "Disneyesque" efforts to make itself part of the show). Finally, a central theme in the financial media was the supposed "democratization of investing"—the idea that ordinary people were taking control over their financial destiny through active investing. For example, the president of CNBC declared, "In 1956, a select few on Wall Street would have gossiped about the information we give out. . . . We've democratized the whole process."[54] However, representatives of investment banks and money managers had ample opportunity to tout their own interests on the new media circuit— they were the main "content." For instance, CNBC's nonstop financial news programming hosted thirty or so guests a day; most were analysts and money managers (who were expected to provide viewers with stock tips). Thus, Henry Blodget, a Merrill Lynch analyst, appeared on TV seventy-seven and forty-six times in 1999 and 2000, respectively, often on CNBC and CNN.[55] Blodget, who gained fame for correctly predicting that the stock of Amazon.com would reach $400 a share, had also declared, "It is a mistake to be too conservative in projecting future performance. The real risk is not losing money—it is missing major upside."[56]

THE UPSIDE'S UNDERSIDE

Evidence is mounting that the accounting and financial analysis performed by many large establishments was compromised thoroughly during the New Economy gold rush. In 1999 "buy" recommendations by financial analysts outnumbered "sells" by seventy-two to one; ten years before the ratio was ten to one.[57] Celebrity analysts accumulated so much influence that firms would select their underwriters on the basis of whether they had a "star analyst" who could cover their company. Mary Meeker, a star analyst who covered Internet and e-commerce stock for Morgan Stanley Dean Witter reportedly earned $15 million in salary for 1999 while

Henry Blodget's compensation at Merrill Lynch increased from $3 million in 1999 to $12 million in 2001.[58]

In fact, Blodget's Internet analysis team at Merrill Lynch was a target of an investigation by the attorney general of New York State that resulted in a $100 million fine against the firm in 2002. The attorney general found that Merrill Lynch's analysts were involved actively in investment banking transactions and that their compensation was linked to their efforts in this area. Blodget's own reports stated that his analysts assisted the investment banking unit by wooing clients, marketing public offerings, and initiating "research coverage"—the analysis unit would begin coverage of investment banking clients that it would not otherwise cover, thus, sending their name into the financial media circuit. Most damning, the attorney general uncovered sensational evidence that public ratings assigned to client stock by the Internet analysts was often at odds with "the group's contemporaneous internal analysis or opinions."[59] Though the unit made disparaging comments about a number of stocks, it "never published a single reduce or sell rating on any stock covered by the internet group" between the spring of 1999 and the fall of 2001. The in-house comments about firms given favorable ratings included, "fundamentals horrible," "such a piece of crap," "a powder keg," and "a piece of junk." Another example concerned none other than 24/7—the Silicon Alley firm whose CFO spoke of the importance of having the analysts at one's underwriter express confidence in your firm. Merrill Lynch did its part, presenting 24/7 with the second highest rating— "accumulate"—with projections of a 10 to 20 percent price growth. Yet, internal correspondence at the same time the rating was released, deemed 24/7 stock "a piece of shit."[60]

The next section examines how Silicon Alley firms "made out like bandits" in the IPO market. Before that, let us consider whether they were crooks in a literal sense: Did anybody who helped organize dot-com IPOs really believe or were they all manipulators and predators? In thinking about this I propose, as a first step, that we cast aside the heroic portrait of the rational individual that lies entombed within mainstream economics (in much the same manner that Lenin's corpse is enshrined in Red Square). In contrast to the idea that individuals rationally calculate how to act so as to best serve their own interests, economic sociologists argue that people often are not sure how to act or even have a clear idea of what their "interests" are. Individually and collectively, they commonly act on the basis of norms or prevailing notions about what constitutes sensible behavior.

I propose that we study *the frameworks for thinking about IPOs* that prevailed in Silicon Alley at the end of the 1990s. Two ideas became salient as New Economy thought and dot-com IPOs made their appearance. The first was the idea that a new kind of firm had taken the scene that could dominate new markets (or at least be bought out by a dominant firm). The second was the idea that even a worthy firm had to go for an IPO if it wanted to score a major success. A third perception emerged later in the wake of startling IPOs by firms that were weak candidates: The IPO apparatus can propel forward firms of dubious merit. At the apex there was a widespread perception among insiders that a multitude of "greater fools" was out there who could be exploited. In this light, there were two possible motives for entrepreneurs seeking IPOs: They believed in their firm's potential to be a hit beyond the financial arena—or—they were willing to play along in the deceptions. The numbers of the latter surely blossomed in 1999. For example, a dot-com veteran recalled the sham enterprise that he went to work for: "They were supposed to be in e-publishing. In the four months I was there the business plan changed three or four times. They wanted to go public. They had an underwriter working with them. It was a take-the-money-and-run operation. They had nothing legitimate to offer to anyone."[61]

The motives of "serial" participants were even more questionable. They may have believed in the merits of particular firms and the industry as a whole. However, during the high tide many engaged in predatory behavior as they tried to sustain and exploit demand for start-ups that had little chance of becoming viable firms. Some participants from the financial services sector engaged in systematic predation (or fraud). Greed was not the only motive. There was an imperative to stay in the game so as to maintain one's credibility as a New Economy player. The misdeeds were enmeshed in *a subcultural fabric that emerged in a setting of unrestrained competition*. In fact, it was difficult to recognize that misdeeds were pervasive in the New Economy until its competitive fervor—and subculture—had weakened.

BULL RUN: DUMBING DOWN THE SMART MONEY

In the near term it seemed that the endings of dozens of Silicon Alley stories would be quite happy. In the spring of 1999 a string of seventeen successful Silicon Alley IPOs elevated the standing of firms such as Razorfish, iVillage, about.com, and theStreet.com; later in the year StarMedia, Agency.com, and others joined the crowd, resulting in a grand total of thirty-one Silicon Alley IPOs for 1999. Looking at the larger region, PricewaterhouseCoopers reported that forty-one new media IPOs were launched in the "New York area" raising a total of $3.5 billion.[62] The year also saw large increases in stock value for the new cohort of public firms; as a group their stock rose 116 percent in value by the end of 1999. The increase was even greater for the fourteen firms that had gone public before 1999 (e.g., DoubleClick and 24/7); their combined value rose 142 percent during 1999.[63] At the start of 2000, the combined market value of twenty-nine leading Silicon Alley firms was reported to total $29.5 billion.[64] Silicon Alley's Bull Run continued into the early part of 2000 as twenty firms filed for IPOs; seven firms went public before the April crash.

Most of the firms profiled in chapter 2 had big opening days or impressive run-ups in value after going public. On its opening day iVillage closed at just over $80 a share; it later climbed to $130 a share. Agency.com, which closed at $76 a share, was worth $98 a share by the end of the year; its rival Razorfish was close behind at $96. StarMedia hit just over $60. Some of the more suspect firms that had gone public before 1999 fell hard during the year. Theglobe.com plunged to $9 a share while CyberShop slipped to only $6. Other firms we have looked at had solid showings: EarthWeb's stock was up to $50 a share while 24/7 stock looked like a piece of gold—hitting $59 a share. DoubleClick, the most highly valued Silicon Alley firm, rocketed to $250 a share by the end of 1999.[65]

For a time the IPOs kept the wheel of fortune spinning, bringing a huge influx of venture capital into Silicon Alley. The enclave's venture capital totals had begun to build even before the IPOs, rising from $49.5 million in 1995 to $161 million in 1997.[66] But as the number of IPOs mounted, the floodgates were flung wide open and venture capital surged in. The amount for the second quarter in 1999—$536 million—was over ten times the amount Silicon Alley received for all of 1995.[67] In 1999 110 Silicon Alley firms received a total of $4.6 billion—a sum that exceeded the venture capital distributed across the entire United States in 1995 ($4.2 billion).[68]

For some time only two or three venture capital funds had focused on Silicon Alley: In 1999 a dozen new funds opened there. By 2001 there were eighty-six investment funds operating in Silicon Alley—sixty-three of which had offices in New York.[69] Boosters were emboldened to make favorable comparisons with Silicon Valley. At "Venture Downtown 2000," a NYNMA event where venture capitalists now paid $1,000 to hear start-up pitches, Alan Patricof—a top New York venture capitalist—reflected: "We didn't have the networks that existed in Silicon Valley. But now Silicon Alley is growing virally, like the Internet. The number of venture capital companies in New York has quadrupled. . . . We've reached critical mass." The head of the NYNMA similarly exulted, "At first new media entrepreneurs here didn't have the investment flywheel that existed on the West Coast. But thank God for lust and greed and competition. . . . We started getting venture capitalists in our own backyard."[70]

Not everyone was so sanguine. In mid-1998 Flatiron's Jerry Colonna wrote a column in the *New York Times* claiming that "illogical overbidding" for start-ups might threaten the Internet industry. Because of the stock frenzy, "Internet companies are going public that have no business going public."[71] He predicted that their eventual failures would tarnish the industry. Colonna proposed that the stock "mania" had, in part, been fueled by a series of "mindboggling stock-for-stock transactions." He cited Microsoft's use of its own stock in the $400 million purchase of Hotmail, a provider of free e-mail services. He advised that when a firm such as Hotmail—with little in the way of revenue or even a plan—could gain this kind of money, it could cause venture capitalists to "start outbidding each other to provide capital to what they hope will be the next Hotmail." Firm founders might feel they failed if they "walk away with 'only' $2 million to $3 million" while their investors would feel likewise about returns of "only" 200–300 percent. A month later, Colonna spoke of the "danger of a systemic problem from overvaluation of unsound businesses" and "young people with expectations out-of-whack." The easy money might "spoil a generation of entrepreneurs . . . and go up the food chain . . . impacting venture capitalists and other investors."[72] The action was even hotter in early 2000 when Colonna's partner, Fred Wilson, warned that an oversupply of capital was distorting the process of firm formation: "I would not be surprised if there were 20 or 30 new Internet companies a day being formed in New York. That's scary. People are forming companies for the wrong reason. They aren't passionate about their ideas . . . there is so much capital in New York anybody can start a company."[73]

But for venture captialists that got in early—like Flatiron—there was an element of crocodile tears to such lamentations. Take, for example, the case of Flatiron protégé StarMedia. StarMedia's stock, which made its debut on May 26, 1999, peaked at $67 a share in July 1999. Flatiron's investors, who had to wait six months after the IPO to cash in, could sell shares in December, a time when the stock traded at between $25 and $40 a share. They would have made out nicely, considering that Flatiron bought in at 50 cents and $1.50 per share before the IPO—and given that the stock crashed to less than $2 a share in late 2000.[74]

In fact, Flatiron continued to increase its own investment fund as did its competitors. Bear Stearns and Wit Capital each raised new funds of $200 million while General Atlantic and Capital Z Partners started a $300 million fund. The Rockefeller family's venture investing arm (Venrock Associates) embraced Internet deals. Silicon Valley funds increased their investment pools for Silicon Alley or set up affiliates there; a striking example of the latter was when Draper Fisher Jurvetson set up an affiliate office. It was not a token effort. Timothy Draper himself showed up for an elaborate debut party costumed as Batman (this being Silicon Alley a dark hero was appropriate). Trying to distinguish his firm from competitors, Draper touted this special benefit for start-ups—cocktail parties where they could meet two hundred other firms backed by Draper affiliates in Silicon Valley, Los Angeles, and Virginia and possibly form alliances.[75]

An assortment of nontraditional players tried to position themselves as Silicon Alley financiers. Kohlberg Kravis Roberts—a leverage buyout firm—began to invest in new media start-ups. So did corporate giants such as Time Warner and Anderson Consulting—the latter formed a $1 billion venture fund. Several growing Silicon Alley firms, including RareMedium and Concrete Media, set up "incubators" for start-ups as did a host of other entities. New Economy versions of incubators—once the province of public or nonprofit agencies—were for-profit ventures that provided office space and technical services in exchange for equity. Other examples included a local affiliate of California's Idealab and i-Hatch, a venture founded by the ex-head of Bertelsmann's online bookstore, the former head of CBS's Internet unit, and a former Lazard Freres venture capitalist. By the end of 1999 over thirty incubators were operating in Silicon Alley.[76]

The hypercompetition to line up start-ups, along with an unfettered tide of capital, quickly eroded the infrastructure for reasoned risk-taking that is the hallmark of venture capital. After the fact, this was admitted by Silicon Alley venture capitalists, who, in the manner of good revolutionaries, engaged in self-criticism. At a panel discussion in 2001 Alan Patricof confessed, "All of us have committed the sin of underpricing our capital over the last couple of years." He added, the "nature of the business changed from 1998 to the early part of 2001." In particular, "momentum investing" had caused them to lose their "discipline."[77]

The distortion in the venture financing system was especially evident in the acceleration of the investment cycle for start-ups. As Flatiron Partners stressed in its original outreach, venture capitalists usually forgo the initial "seed-round" investment in a start-up, waiting for them to mature. They typically come in during the second or third rounds of financing. However, the process accelerated during the dot-com IPO craze. Venture capitalists felt compelled to get involved much earlier in a company's life-cycle because stock investors had been willing to embrace IPOs from young start-ups. A comment by an i-Hatch partner captured the new mood: "We want to find the guy as he is just looking for the cocktail napkin to write his idea on."[78] The founder of another incubator bragged, "We streamlined the execution process to the point that we felt we could get a company from a scribble on a napkin to a launch in 90 to 180 days. As a result . . . companies are more efficient and burn less capital."[79]

Little more than a napkin—its development strictly a financial matter—the New Economy firm finally seemed to pull free from the tethers of the material world. However, virtuality came at a heavy cost. Venture capital backing usually signals that a firm has credible prospects in its product market; during the bull market the endorsement, in effect, was that a firm had credible prospects in the IPO market. Silicon Alley observers were torn between the impulse to cheer the stock successes and their concern that speculation was undermining efforts to create a sustainable industry. *@NY* warned that the "stock market chase" had diverted Silicon Alley firms from their real strength—"fearless creative thinking"; the *Silicon Alley Daily* advised firms to "focus on the business models that generate revenue and that inspire the market that really matters . . . customers" instead of "business models that the stock market is rewarding."[80]

ROLL OVER SGT. PEPPER

Despite some misgivings Silicon Alley notables interpreted stock market successes as validating the enclave's media orientation and the media conception of the Internet industry. To start with, the media sensibilities of New York firms about brands and image seemed to pay off in the stock market. After iVillage's big IPO helped spark a run of IPOs in March 1999, an investment bank executive called it: "a lesson that the companies with the highest profile in the media earn the highest valuations. . . . In the absence of any rational metric with which to value a company, investors are betting on the future . . . that means image and brand."[81] Moreover, stock market successes were interpreted as validating the media conception of Internet business—and Silicon Alley itself. Fred Wilson declared, "New York has become the center of the Internet content business. People said that all the technology plays have been done. Now it's time for what you can build on top of the technology." Robert Lessin added, "The West Coast creates technology and the East Coast creates brands. Now that technology is becoming off-the-shelf, companies need media companies as partners to build . . . brands."[82] Brian Horey proclaimed that stock wealth had put New York's new media "ecosystem" on a developmental path similar to that traveled by Silicon Valley: "This wealth is the . . . seed capital that will be reinvested in start-ups and will help strengthen the . . . ecosystem of new media in New York. Over the last 30 years, this has turned Silicon Valley into an enormous economic flywheel."[83] After the series of big IPOs, being rich *on paper* became the defining virtual experience in Silicon Alley. It was real and unreal at the same time. The *Silicon Alley Reporter* was quick to translate the Silicon Alley experience into pop culture terms: IPO riches not only validated New York's new media notables as entrepreneurs but also as cultural authorities. The alleged double-play in the culture-capital circuit was illustrated graphically in a January 2000 issue honoring the "top 100 Silicon Alley executives." The magazine cover was a take-off on the album cover of the Beatles *Sgt. Pepper's Lonely Hearts Club Band*. The *Sgt. Pepper's* cover is a classic piece of pop culture that enshrined the Beatles as the vanguard of a host of cultural icons—ranging from Edgar Allan Poe to Marlon Brando. In the *Silicon Alley Reporter* version, the "Silicon Alley 100" fill in for the original icons that once backed the fab four, and four digerati replace John, Paul, George, and Ringo. The source of the new fab four's cultural capital was clearly the value of the individual stakes they held as founders of firms that had spectacular market values (at the end of 1999). Three of the four executives were from start-ups profiled in chapter 2: iVillage's Candice Carpenter (worth $180 million), Fernando Espuelas of StarMedia ($191 million), and Kevin O'Connor of DoubleClick ($749 million); flanking them in the front row was a co-founder of a fourth featured firm: Razorfish's Jeff Dachis ($169 million).[84]

It seemed that Silicon Alley innovators might change the world after all—with stock options. In a *Silicon Alley Reporter* editorial Jason Calacanis cited stock options as allowing the new media to triumph over the old, adding that the battle was also about vindicating his generation—previously maligned by the old media:

> In the early '90s . . . the media was obsessed with a generation of indifferent teenagers and twenty-somethings who couldn't be bothered with social causes, careers, or the general state of humanity. . . . They branded us slackers. . . . Our generation wasn't filled with slackers, it was filled with such media-savvy, and media-saturated individuals that we knew that participating in the existing paradigm would . . . result in low pay and long hours for some old-school company. . . . Equity is the revolution of our generation.[85]

Moreover, Calacanis claimed that the drive for equity—"in the form of stock options"—had continuity with the fight for "equality" waged by the young in the 1960s. His effort to resurrect the progressive aura for the new media raises some basic issues to take into the next chapter: Were Silicon Alley entrepreneurs, circa 1999, either progressive change agents or cultural authorities?

CHAPTER 4

TAKING NEW YORK INTO A "NEW" ECONOMY?

In my world now, it's everybody looking for something
interesting regardless of what they are, who they are.
—Wall Street/Silicon Alley Lawyer[1]

It makes good sense for one of the world's leading high-tech companies
to locate its regional headquarters in the World Trade Center, which offers
excellent high-tech amenities. Sun Microsystems is a strong addition to the
complex's tenant mix. We are proud that the World Trade Center, already
a focal point of international business, is becoming part of Silicon Alley . . .
—Port Authority Executive Director, February 4, 1999[2]

All that is solid morphs. Or so it seemed as Silicon Alley's boundary-cross-ing carnival spilled into the rest of Manhattan in the late 1990s. Take, for instance, the creative fusion unleashed in the makeover of a sweatshop in Chinatown. The new landlord, Kushner Studios, was an architectural de-sign shop that planned to use the presence of new media firms in the build-ing to make its own crossover into cyberspace; Kushner hoped to create an online portfolio, build an online "brand," and make the design process "more interactive." Its remodeled office on the fifth floor included the usual Silicon Alley design elements such as hardwood floors, concrete ta-bles, pointed bricks, and exposed steel girders. It also featured a novel touch—a 1987 General Motors school bus planted in the middle of the office. Other tenants included Buzz (a new media PR firm), Fuel Factor (web design shop), and Internet Interactive Studios—a Hamburg-based streaming-video company whose clients included AOL and Der Spiegel. The edgy composition also retained a Chinatown accent—a Buddhist tem-ple, complete with sleeping quarters for the monks. Reflecting on the New Economy version of urban renewal the would-be cyberarchitect observed,

"We like the neighborhood because it is so sleazy. But people like us moving down here [is] going to make it not sleazy."[3]

As the decade came to a close many Manhattan business services embraced the new media storyline while real estate interests capitalized on the imagery to freshen up their properties—from the weathered districts of printers, warehousemen, garment makers, and flower peddlers to the shimmering money mills of Wall Street. So powerful was the impulse to reimagine Manhattan spaces as new media places that the operator of the World Trade Center—the planet's biggest and best-known ensemble of premium office space—used the arrival of Sun Microsystems in 1999 as an opportunity to link the complex to the Silicon Alley moniker. The breathless headline of the Port Authority press release trumpeted, "World Trade Center Is Hot New Address on Silicon Alley."[4]

The coupling of culture and capital that made new media spots white hot also began to change the larger city. Even as a historic bull market reached its peak, many notables declared that the new media was replacing Wall Street as New York's economic engine. Wielding billions of dollars in speculative investment, new media firms injected a tidal wave of wealth into New York and other cities such as Boston and San Francisco. The new media created a great many jobs, stimulated demand for business services, and spurred a huge rise in real estate prices. However, New York's embrace of the new media led it to absorb high levels of risk. It also fueled a transformation of city spaces that was more virtual than material in nature, but all-too-real in its effects. New place names and boundaries replaced old ones as the business district expanded to new corners of Manhattan and other boroughs. An array of businesses were displaced, eroding districts that provided the city with distinctive streets and less affluent residents with jobs.

BECOMING WIRED

The extension of the new media into the rest of New York offers another occasion to ask, Who were the people involved and why did they believe? The spread of new media networks and cultural sensibilities in New York can, in part, be attributed to the extension of a new digital production complex. As additional firms and workers encountered the challenges of this novel production realm—and of the shifting product markets it serves—they adopted (or developed) new means of organizing enterprises and careers (e.g., projects, networks). And they found that new sorts of ethics, norms, and identities helped them make sense of, and to manage or navigate, the novel situations they were experiencing.

A rich body of work on Silicon Alley[5] and other new media districts[6] suggests that new media producers are driven to link with—and alter—an ever-widening circle of workers and firms. Heydebrand and Miron propose that "boundary-transcending projects and networks" pervade client-based innovations in Silicon Alley. Relatedly, there is a hybridization of roles: The role of boss merges with those of sponsor, friend, colleague; lawyers, who provide legal and business advice, become "network partners." Moreover, they observe that the Silicon Alley "spirit" of "transcending boundaries" "animates a broad range of actors—from "hackers" to "young executives of start-ups" to "lawyers."[7]

Following authors such as Nigel Thrift[8] I argue that a second force also contributed to the new media's extension: the New Economy cultural mobilization. This broad movement was as much about the financialization of the economy as it was about digitalization. We saw that a swarm of business interests sought out start-ups as clients in the hope that they would share in stock market riches. This chapter picks up the further extension of this ring of faith as a growing crowd of business services joined the new media's forced march through Manhattan.

Economic sociologists provide a good starting place for understanding how New Economy networks and norms spread across New York City. Paul DiMaggio and Walter Powell[9] propose that intermediaries such as venture capitalists and consultants help distribute New Economy business "recipes." Similarly, studies of Silicon Valley report that business professionals—executive search firms, accountants, consultants, and lawyers—mediate networks, accept equity in clients, and help institutionalize new norms.[10] In fact, Manhattan business intermediaries played key roles in extending new networks and norms. Like other new media players they cited the Silicon Valley model as they sought to gain cultural authority as change agents. The motive was not to copy Silicon Valley per se but instead to persuade others that one could help them become part of something larger.

Thrift hits the mark in comparing the promotion of New Economy models to a social movement. Researchers report that movements are abetted by the making and extension of networks and narratives (stories). A narrative tells a story of "becoming"—of a nation, a people, a generation—that invites participation by projecting an attractive or irresistible future. Francesca Poletta[11] notes that the narratives that attract participants to movements often have an open quality. They are intriguing, but ambiguous, in the way in which they link events to larger trends—allowing people in different localities to fill in the gaps to fit their own situations. Such traits are evident in the narrative of Jason Calacanis reviewed in the last chapter: He portrayed the wielding of options as a historic blow against the old media—and as a vehicle for the redemption of Generation X.

As they put themselves at the center of the action new media firms, assorted business intermediaries, and the local media spurred change by weaving a tapestry out of new social ties and narratives—stories of various actors and spaces becoming part of Silicon Alley and of New York becoming part of a New Economy.

NEW YORK "GETS IT" (A NEW ENGINE)

The coming of the New Economy to New York, in the form of the new media, was reassuring news for many business interests. Having taken a beating in the early 1990s, they were looking for a reason to believe in the local economy. What could be better proof that New York's postindustrial course was finally settled than the rise of an "immaterial" economy powered by "virtual" firms?

The media credited Silicon Alley with helping ignite a wave of job creation (80,000 a year in 1998 and 1999) that brought job totals back to pre-1989 levels. A special issue of *Crain's New York Business* on "The Rebirth of New York" stated, "No story has been more integral to the rebirth of New York."[12] *Crain's* publisher claimed the new media was altering New York by giving it a new economic base:

> The most significant change in the economy's landscape is the emergence of the new media industry. . . . It is gobbling up space and talent at a furious pace, luring smart young people to the city and creating risk-taking entrepreneurs . . . the Internet is here to stay, and New York is uniquely positioned as a content provider and innovator.[13]

Similarly, another special issue of *Crain's*—entitled "Power Alley"—began, "New Media has revived and transformed the city's economy. It has accounted for nearly one-third of job growth in recent years, resuscitated neighborhoods and revived nightlife. In some ways, it has supplanted Wall Street as the City's premier industry."[14] Reporters claimed that the enclave helped New York renew its claim to centrality by allowing it to overcome the legacy of deindustrialization: "Saddled for years with a dying manufacturing sector, New York lagged [behind] other major U.S. cities in growth and was seen as a technological backwater." A Chase Manhattan economist remarked, "New York is at the forefront of an industry that is growing rapidly rather than being at the tail end, as it has been, of every other force in the last half of this century." Another *Crain's* story called the new media the leading edge of a "new economy" responsible for the city's comeback;[15] a third suggested that the new "rules" extended to the use of urban space: "Silicon Alley . . . has turned into an economic juggernaut that is reinventing the life and economy of the city. . . . New media companies are redrawing the physical landscape, rewriting the rules of business and eclipsing industries that have dominated the economy for decades."[16] Indeed, there was plenty of evidence of a remarkable expansion in the new media sector.

Table 4.1 New Media Employment in New York City, by Employment Status, 1995, 1997, and 1999

	Employment Status			Change	Percent
	1995	1997	1999	1997–99	Change
New York City					
Freelance	6,150	12,680	20,773	+8,093	+63.8%
Part Time	2,800	11,280	12,820	+1,540	+13.7
Full Time	18,350	32,013	104,665	+72,652	+226.9
Total	27,300	55,973	138,258	+82,285	+147.0%

Source: PricewaterhouseCoopers (2000, 29).

A PricewaterhouseCoopers study[17] estimated that the number of new media firms in the city grew from 2,601 in 1997 to 3,831 in 1999, an increase of 1,230 or 47.3 percent. The number of new media workers in the city surged from 55,973 in 1997 to 138,258 in 1999, an increase of 82,285 (147 percent) (see table 4.1).

Another sign of the enclave's vitality was the number of firms it drew from outside the region. As of 1997, 600 new media firms had moved or expanded to the region from another location; by 1999 the number had increased to 1,700 firms. An estimated 400 of these firms were from other countries while some 290 were from the Bay area (San Francisco/Silicon Valley).[18]

Crain's publisher linked the new media's rise in the city to Mayor Giuliani's neoliberal policies (e.g., privatization of services, tax cuts, and use of workfare clients to clean up parks). However, in her assessment, one of neoliberalism's champions—Wall Street—did not come off looking so good. The "surge in new media" she said, "lessens our dependence on the financial sector."[19] In fact, this sentiment infused most narratives of the new media presented above. A nagging anxiety was evident—the notion that New York *needs a economic engine* because *it cannot count on Wall Street.* This discomfort was, in certain respects, quite ironic. Wall Street had been white hot in the 1980s, and the heat was even more fierce in the latter 1990s. It was largely because of Wall Street's stoking of the FIRE ensemble of producer services that New York City could claim to be the economic capital of globalization. That Wall Street's growing role worried even conservative business boosters was testimony to just how devastating and dispiriting the 1987 crash had been. The local elite backed Wall Street's rabid advocacy of global financial liberalization during the 1990s—a bid to bolster its centrality, which was eroding in the United States.[20] The Asian financial crisis and the near meltdown of Long-Term Capital Management (a hedge fund) in the late 1990s raised fears that the wheels would fall off the bandwagon again.

Wall Street's role in the city's recovery was debated hotly. Mayor Giuliani and Governor George Pataki rejected claims that the financial sector was becoming more dominant. Pataki's chief economist argued, "It's Wall Street and new media, Wall Street and old media, Wall Street and a whole lot of services that cater to the corporate headquarters here." A real estate executive similarly remarked, "Wall Street's influence in the economy has steadily declined for the past half decade, mainly because of the growth of the new media. A huge part of the growth in employment is in all kinds of things related to the Internet."[21] Yet, the securities industry of Wall Street loomed large in the 1990s recovery. Wall Street revenues increased from just over $70 billion in 1994 to over $180 billion by 1999; its profits grew from $1 billion to $16 billion in the same span.[22] For a sense of perspective, the total revenue of the new media in the city in 1999—$9.2 billion—was about what Morgan Stanley Dean Witter earns in a quarter.[23] A study by the Federal Reserve Bank of New York concluded that New York had become much more dependent on Wall Street since the 1987 crash. The percentage of city income that Wall Street accounted for was 19.0 percent by 1999, in comparison to 11.0 percent in 1987—and 4.0 percent in 1980; moreover, Wall Street provided about one-third of the city's tax revenue. The financial sector's modest contribution to job growth underscored the uneven distribution of the income it generated. The percentage of the city work force accounted for by investment banks and brokerage firms only increased from 4.4 percent to 4.7 percent between 1987 and 1998: An increase of 24,000 in the number of securities and commodities brokers was offset by a decline of 21,000 in bank employment. The lead contributor to job growth was "business services," which grew by 80,700. The Federal Reserve asserted that much of this was also linked to Wall Street. The securities industry was a key source of revenue for a wide range of businesses, such as "publishing, accounting, marketing, legal, computer, and business services companies."[24] The Federal Reserve study estimated that about 14 percent of total employment in the city was linked to the securities industry.

Regarding the impact of the new media on employment, another Federal Reserve study offered a sobering conclusion: The new media probably did not represent the rise of a new sector but the digitalization of segments of the traditional media and business services.[25] Adding to this, Silicon Alley's debt to a new financial-media industry nexus (documented in chapter 4), makes it even harder to credit the new media with reducing New York's dependence on Wall Street.

THE CONTENDERS PUMP UP

Silicon Alley's national contenders were the New Economy's shock troops in New York; they bore big war chests filled with IPO cash ($1 billion in 1999 alone), a new business culture, and a new currency—options. They parleyed the cash and the options to acquire workers, services and office space, and other firms (there were 138 mergers among New York Internet and computer firms in 1999).

Of the fifty-plus new media firms in the New York area that went public between 1996 and April 2000, thirty-seven were located within the city. The total number of workers employed by this group grew from 5,980 to 19,718 after their stock was listed—with most of the increases coming between 1999 and 2000 (see appendix A). The rise in employment of 13,738 represented a 230 percent increase. The work forces in fourteen of the firms exceeded 500 employees: RareMedium (929), N2K (502), 24/7 Media (1,327), Multex.com (561), Globix (850), Applied Theory (642), Alloy Online (585), Jupiter (706), BarnesandNoble.com (1,752), Predictive Systems (652), Agency.com (1,700), StarMedia (779), DoubleClick (1,929), and Razorfish (1,994).

The rise in revenues was even sharper, growing from a total of $550 million to nearly $3.5 billion—an increase of almost $3 billion or some 526 percent (see appendix B). Ten firms had revenues of over $100 million: RareMedium ($110.1 million), N2K ($147.2 million), 24/7 Media ($146.1 million), BarnesandNoble.com ($320.1 million), Agency.com ($202.1 million), DoubleClick ($505.6 million), Razorfish ($267.9 million), iTurf ($138.7 million), Juno Online ($114.0 million) and Wit Capital Group ($375.5 million).

The cases of DoubleClick, iVillage, Razorfish, and StarMedia allow a closer look at how the national contenders used stock to pump up as they enacted the New Economy's prime directive: become the "first-mover" in a market by aggressively establishing one's "brand" and by boosting revenue growth. As of November 1999 the stock market value exceeded $1 billion at three of the firms. DoubleClick led the way with a value of $6.6 billion. The respective totals at Razorfish, StarMedia, and iVillage were $1.8 billion, $1.6 billion, and $585 million.[26]

Razorfish aimed to become a "leading edge provider of digital communications solutions" through "building a critical mass of . . . talent and establishing a multi-national presence through both acquisitions and internal growth."[27] After its IPO Razorfish used stock in four 1999 acquisitions:[28]

- April-June: buys out remaining interest in three subsidiaries in Finland, Germany, and Norway, for $1.4 million in cash and 200,000 stock options;

- September: used 1,312,000 shares of stock and $750,000 in cash to acquire Fuel and Tonga, Inc.—an LA firm that does graphic design and "branding";
- November: exchanged 36,069,224 shares of stock for outstanding shares of stock in i-Cube, a Boston-based provider of electronic business services with offices in Massachusetts, California, London, the Netherlands and Germany that employed 435 and had $57 million in revenue in 1998;
- December: issued 1,250,000 shares to acquire Lee Hunt Associates, a marketing firm in the entertainment industry known for "launching, positioning, designing and promoting media brands and television networks."

By the end of 1999 Razorfish had offices in four U.S. cities and seven cities in Europe. In 2000 it used stock to make three more acquisitions in Europe:[29]

- January: issued 399,000 shares and paid $3.1 million in cash to acquire Ob International Holding AB, a Swedish IT/strategic consulting firm;
- May: issued 141,000 shares to acquire Limage Dangereuse Rotterdam, a visual communications agency in Rotterdam that focused on "the creation of online-identities and interactive and graphic design";
- August: issued 446,000 and paid $1.4 million in cash to acquire Medialab AG, a Munich-based "e-business solution provider that specialised in strategic consulting, back end technology and advanced web design."

DoubleClick put an even greater emphasis on expanding its business globally. Its *Annual Report for Fiscal Year 1999*[30] announced that in order "to take advantage of the global reach of the Internet we have established and continue to establish networks in Europe, Asia and other international markets" and that it sought to offer advertisers "the ability to run global campaigns." The firm made five acquisitions in the fall and winter of 1999. In January 2000 it exchanged stock worth $75.7 million and $10 million in cash for a 30 percent share of ValueClick, a provider of cost-per-click Internet advertising solutions. As of the fourth quarter 1999 DoubleClick had employees in twenty-two countries, served 4,300 advertisers and sold advertising space for 14,000 websites worldwide.[31]

Hoping to become "the premier online destination targeted to women," iVillage proposed to make acquisitions that would give it "new vehicles to reach and capture our target audience, provide new solutions for advertisers and add to our ability to grow our overall business."[32] Objectives included: "build strong brand recognition," "aggressively grow membership," "pursue strategic acquisition and alliance," and increase revenues from sponsors, advertising, and e-commerce. To this end iVillage launched a $40 million marketing plan to run from mid-1999 through 2000, much of it on NBC. Its acquisitions in 1999 included Online Psych, Lamaze Publishing, Family Point, and iBaby, Inc. By November 1999 iVillage was attracting 5.5 million visitors to its website a month.[33]

StarMedia also stressed pumping up so as to become "the leading Internet media company targeting Spanish- and Portuguese-speaking markets worldwide." Tactics included: "Aggressively extend the recognition of our brands" so as "to make our brands synonymous with the Internet in our markets"; and make alliances and acquisitions so as to "expand our user base, revenues and competitive position."[34] In fall 1999 StarMedia acquired three companies (PageCell, Webcast Solutions, and Paisas.com). From the spring of of 2000 to the spring of 2001 it used stock to acquire three more: 71,000 shares and $2 million cash for Ola Turista LTDA, 8 million shares of stock and $5 million cash for AdNet, and 1,125,000 shares of stock for Obsidiana.[35] StarMedia increased the "page views" on its network from 471 million in 1998 to some 3.6 billion in 1999—an increase of 675 percent.[36] By 2000 StarMedia had offices in Barcelona, Bogota, Buenos Aires, Caracas, Madrid, Medellin, Mexico City, Miami, Montevideo, Ottawa, Rio de Janerio, San Francisco, San Juan, Santiago, and São Paulo.

Although many of their new employees were located elsewhere, the explosive growth of the national contenders supercharged New York's spectacular (but brief) rise as a New Economy hotspot. Just as important, their lightning-quick expansion—and resulting leaps in revenue—dominated media narratives of Silicon Alley, keeping in motion the train of evidence suggesting that a new kind of firm and economy had emerged—and that New York had a new engine.

PRODUCTION'S OUTWARD MOVEMENT

Silicon Alley's vitality depended on extending its connections with New York's economy and labor market. The special nature of new media production had driven its incorporation (and alteration) of a wide variety of businesses and occupational groups. The new media, like various industries, developed flexible means of supplying specialized "inputs" for unstable markets. In Silicon Alley's case, "What customers want, and what it is possible to produce both technically and creatively, shift again and again."[37] Its firms have adapted organizing models from other Manhattan industries (e.g., consulting and advertising), particularly, projects, teams, and interfirm networks.[38] These organizational forms were key devices through which the new media extended into new domains.

Beyond Firm Boundaries

Silicon Alley firms use projects and networks to bring together various kinds of collaborators (workers from assorted disciplines, business partners, and clients). Monique Girard and David Stark found that web design firms used projects to assemble "business strategists, interactive designers, programmers and other technologists, information architects . . . and merchandising specialists" and sometimes client reps. Moreover, projects were supported by a web of external collaborators:

> technology "partners" (. . . arrangments through which the web developer can offer access and support for new technologies); hardware and network affiliations through which the web developer offers server space, maintenance, and network security; venture capitalists . . . other web development firms (when different parts of a project are distributed among different firms . . .); vendors to the client (whose information systems must be reconciled with the . . . [new] site) . . . and so on."[39]

Heydebrand and Miron report an impulse among Silicon Alley firms to move into "transorganizational domains" while drawing "external units, suppliers, and clients" into their own firm. By combining competition with cooperation, firms extended their networks to a wider range of firms. They cooperated with potential rivals in order to swap jobs, share ideas, and gain feedback on innovation. One executive noted that collaboration let one find out, "what's hot, what's going on, who's doing what"—allowing firms to avoid direct competition. Mixing social and business ties also enabled them to extend their networks: "Relations with family members and friends from school and college . . . fuse effortlessly with more business-oriented and market-oriented ties and strategies."[40]

Into the Labor Market

Networks were the most important means through which Silicon Alley firms extended themselves in the labor market—and workers linked up to new media employers. A study of the Silicon Alley labor market—by a team from Cornell—concluded that new media workers were rooted in "personal networks that help them find jobs, identify and learn new skills, build careers, and secure their futures."[41] The importance of networks reflected the fact that workers changed jobs frequently. One manifestation of this mobility was the large numbers who were freelancers, part-timers, or temporaries (see table 4.1). Furthermore, although most were full time, the Cornell team found evidence that "full time does not necessarily mean long term." In their large sample[42] the average job tenure of workers who were classified full time was only six months. They argue that this mobility reflected the use of projects by firms and the "opportunity, ethos, and career paths" of Silicon Alley workers; the professional identity and standing of workers, as well as advancement to more desirable work, pivoted on acquiring a "marketable portfolio of specialized skills and prestige projects"—not on staying with an employer for an extended period. Thus, worker mobility was a double-edged sword. A Silicon Alley manager they interviewed, observed: "We use no independent contractors, although our new media people behave as though they are. They will quit in a minute and go across the street for five dollars and then return three months later."[43]

Networks help both employers and workers cope with the fact that "the demand for skills is constantly changing and includes not only technical skills but more elusive abilities": the latter include creativity, problem solving as well as being "able to work in a team" and to "manage client relationships." Core workers were, in essence, *hybrids*. Networks were critical for the amassing of experiences and skills by workers. Most workers in the Cornell study gained their skills "on their own, informally, or through colleagues and friends." When asked to name the most important sources of skills 87 percent of the respondents cited "self-teaching," some 73 percent named "informal on-the-job training," and 52 percent cited "peers and colleagues." Only about 15 percent named "college degree" while some 11 percent cited "employer training." The nature of skill acquisition and the lack of standardized credentials made it difficult for employers to recruit and select workers. Consequently, the networks of workers have been the most important means for matching job seekers with jobs. When asked to name the most important sources of jobs some 81 percent of the respondents named "friends and colleagues," 56 percent cited "Internet job postings," while 42 percent named "professional associations" such as NYNMA.

As Silicon Alley workers advanced careers through changing jobs they hope to move eventually from the status of full-time employee to that of independent contractor or entrepreneur. Barriers to moving up include the money required for equipment and software and the time it takes to acquire enough skills—and job contacts—so that one can avoid spells of unemployment. Workers absorbed most of the risks entailed in acquiring skills and jobs. They invest some 20 hours a week (on average) in maintaining or boosting their employability: an average of 6 hours a week in looking for work and 13.5 hours in unpaid learning.[44]

CULTURE'S ROUND-ABOUT MOVEMENT

Researchers stress the pragmatic nature of new media production: It is driven more by immediate exigencies and emergent solutions than by commitments to particular models or institutions. Yet, this general condition itself hints at the existence of a complmentary culture—sets of norms, values, and sensibilities that encourage one to cross boundaries, blend roles, and to engage in continuous reinvention. The culture that supported Silicon Alley in the late 1990s was not a straightforward derivative of the production system but a hybrid—formed through a circuitous mixing of elements of external, as well as local, origins. At the level of the district was the deconstructionist "spirit of Silicon Alley" and the cultural commitment to professional community. At the level of the firm, culture helped hold together organizations lacking strong structures. Thrift argues that New Economy firms induce workers to "do more, be passionate and flexible"—through using company "narratives" and "events" that kept a "current of inspiration going."[45] One can see such cultural controls in Silicon Alley. Take for instance, a start-up in the Financial District. Most of the workers were twenty-somethings; many were children of recent immigrants. A co-owner provided a narrative about their movement toward upward mobility that mixed a local version of the American Dream with extreme capitalism à la New Economy:

> Most people here didn't go to the right school, didn't go to Columbia, but they have this attitude, grew up in middle-class neighborhoods, like I did in Queens. . . . You can teach anybody to be a programmer but you can't teach them to be a warrior entrepreneur. There is an intense atmosphere. Anybody can do anything. People have desire, vision. Everybody is here before 9 am and stays at least until 7 pm, six days a week. We look out the windows down on the Wall Street crowd and say, "look at the ants coming to work, leaving work all at once." We see we aren't like that. There is fulfillment in what we do.[46]

Revels and Revelations

Inspirational currents also flowed in abundance through the Silicon Alley party circuit, which was a source of status for those who could put their centrality on display. Andrew Rasie, founder of the Digital Club Network, advised that the secret to being "cool" in Silicon Alley was "to know what party is hot tonight . . . to be going to the coolest events."[47] Some start-ups linked up with the party circuit hoping that occasional bouts of extreme partying would signal their New Economy soulfulness—their central position in the culture—to investors and corporate customers, as well as to workers. At Pseudo the stigmata of the New Economy—its charismatic blemishes—were on display 24/7. In *Bamboozled at the Revolution* Motavalli recounts a tour of Pseudo given to investors that ran into,

> a "full monty" of drugs, constant and public sex, and an unreal, day-for-night atmosphere . . . the first sight greeting them was a guy "with his forehead pierced riding a skateboard." Later, as the group ventured further into the loft,

they became engulfed in a huge cloud of marijuana smoke. Everyone smiled, as if this . . . was an integral part of the New Economy.

The hapless tour guide—a newly hired CEO who was Pseudo's first professional manager in that spot—noted that the investors, some of whom were executives, "thought it was cutting edge . . . they just said to themselves, 'This is the Internet and we don't know anything about it. This is cool, hip, edgy content. We just have to let these guys do their thing."[48]

Unlike Pseudo, Razorfish combined serious debauchery with serious business. Well known for pushing company culture to the limit, it hosted periodic over-the-top revels along with more formal inspirational events for "fish" (employees). After its IPO Razorfish held a May Day party featuring Brazilian drummers, barely clothed samba dancers, a techno DJ, and a massive inflatable moon walk.[49] Even more over the top (much more) was "Fish Fry"—a $2 million party held in Las Vegas in 1999. An ex-"fish" reports that, the company "brought in everybody who worked for Razorfish around the world." The formal inspirational component—a "pep rally"— was "masterfully done." The employees filed into four bleachers that were set up opposed to each other, facing large video screens. "Out comes our CEO who stands in the middle on a revolving circular platform." As the video screen displayed a game of "pong"—the classic video game—the four groups of employees competed with each other to see who could cheer the loudest—the volume affecting how the game of pong proceeded. The party side consisted of "lots of drugs and sex"—with the head table "blowing" massive amounts of money in conspicuous consumption of drugs. The potlatch character implied that no rival could match Razorfish. The "vibe" the firm gave off was, "We are going to take over the world." Another ex-"fish" recalled, "when they flew in all the employees from around the world to Las Vegas I thought, 'they must be doing something right.' "[50]

Tales and Translations

We have seen hints that the broader New Economy cultural mobilization was a second force that—in conjunction with the outward movements of the production system—contributed to the extension of the new media in New York. The mode of its influence was one of "translation." Silicon Alley actors embroidered New Economy narratives with local sensibilities in ways that made sense of conditions in New York—and promoted their own centrality in district networks.

On the work front, New Econony narratives of "free agents" provided a new spin on insecure employment. The new media, like Manhattan's other cultural sectors, had been able to get underemployed creative types to work at insecure jobs with relatively low pay in a bittersweet trade-off for the opportunity to do creative work.[51] Let's call it the "Rent" syndrome (after the Broadway show). A rosier storyline about the New Economy's "free agents" has appeared due, in large part, to self-promotions offered by firms operating websites that match employers with contingent workers (independent contractors, freelancers, moonlighters, and part-timers). This narrative was brightened by references to new opportunities—for cultivating a lifestyle as well as a career—opened up by the demise of the employment bargain once offered by corporations. The owner of FreeAgent.com, a Manhattan-based firm, states that, "The free agent has a much better lifestyle . . . they can go snowboarding; they can decide when they want to work. . . ." A key element in the narrative is the shift away from centralized firms to "virtual corporations." He uses a rather glamorous analogy—the Hollywood film industry: "In Hollywood, when you produce a movie, it's not about a corporation, it's about all these individuals who have complementary skill sets: they come together, they work on a team, they produce something and they disperse. This is what I envision the future of work being."[52]

Ads for FreeAgent.com featured the slogan, "For a Brave New Work Force," implying, an observer notes, that "today's heroes take risks." The Hollywood analogy and the bravado did not originate with FreeAgent.com (nor from a Silicon Alley workplace) but in the inspirational currents of the New Economy cultural circuit. The free-agent storyline took off after *Fast Company*, a New Economy management publication, featured a "Free-Agent Nation" cover story in its January 1998 issue. The cover announced that, "25 Million Americans Declare Independence. Are You Ready to Join Them?" The spin and "facts" offered about free-agency were then repeated in publications like the *Wall Street Journal* and *Newsweek*.[53]

A more crucial influence of the New Economy cultural circuit on Silicon Alley was the advocacy of stock options as a new currency for workers. Use of teams and projects were established practices in some New York sectors; giving options to ordinary workers was not. Silicon Alley entrepreneurs initially struggled to get their workers to take options in lieu of salary. Fernando Espuelas of StarMedia reported, "We try to get people to really think about the stock being their major compensation."[54] The year before iVillage's IPO its founder, Candice Carpenter, proposed that IPOs would help develop a Silicon Valley–type culture in New York and establish the value of options as a new currency in the eyes of its workers:

> A series of successful IPOs would be good for Silicon Alley . . . no one here has a next-door neighbor who hit it big. . . . New York needs the kind of culture Silicon Valley has . . . that believes that options and upsides and incentives are really worth taking as a big part of your package. . . . Initially, a lot of the people we hire were still very hung up on salary. . . . We're like, "Hello? Excuse me? Your salary is to pay your rent. That's all it is. You should take as little as possi-

ble." . . . Well, I've been glad to see people around here . . . say, "Can we take it all in options?" Which is a really great change, where they're beginning to believe that options are the best form of currency.[55]

Talk about options became a lot more credible after the IPO run began. On the first day of trading, iVillage's new currency was as good as gold—its stock rose to over $113 a share. iVillage employees were hardly alone in their apparent good fortune. In 1999 a benefit plan administrator estimated that, on paper, IPOs had created more than one thousand millionaires among the founders and executives of Silicon Alley firms; another two thousand accumulated between $500,000 and $1 million.[56]

Other firms were forced to offer options or boost salaries in order to retain workers. A special impetus was a problem unique to New York—the difficulty of competing with Wall Street for talent. Local perspectives shaped the meaning given to options. The owner who spoke of "warrior entrepreneurs" wove options into his narrative of how the firm and its workers would move upward together:

> In our firm we develop an atmosphere where you come in on Monday and you can be president in a year. . . . When we raise capital we offer stock options to workers. If there is a cash flow problem, we principles don't get paid. The workers do. We may write them a personal check. . . . We're real people. They see we go to the well for them so they go to the well for us. We tell them, "this is where we think we can go" and ask them to buy in.[57]

More evidence of local sensibilties is provided by an @NY editorial discussing the "Silicon Alley Syndrome"—the "inability of the big companies to attract and keep talent." It evoked a New Economy theme—the undermining of hierarchy: Refugees from corporations had forsaken security, comfort, and vacations but, "they're not kissing the chairman's ass any more. . . ." Yet, the details resembled those in the narrative of Jason Calacanis. The target of the insurgency was the old media:

> Working for old media while looking forward to . . . that big Internet gig is this generation's equivalent to waiting tables. Working for a network is slumming it. Suits and long corridors and brass plates and doormen are a signal of failure. . . . Tina Brown is an icon only for people of . . . a certain age.

The old media titans were being bypassed by history—and a generation that envisioned careers without job ladders and associated rituals of subservience:

> You have to feel for the Gerald Levins and the Sumner Redstones [the heads of Time Warner and Viacom, respectively]. They've got these huge businesses, bringing in gazillions in revenue, and they can't attract the best and the brightest any more. That's because one of the many things the Internet has changed forever, is the way talented young people think about a career. No more production assistant gigs . . . or coffee-fetching jobs. Equity rules.[58]

Betting the Future on Silicon Alley

Aggressive accountants did it with sharp pencils. Lawyers did it over lunch. National contenders asserted that their employees most certainly had done it when they decided to come on board. The grand irony of the New Economy was that while venture capitalists—who were supposed to do it—were not doing it very well, people in all sorts of occupations were assessing the relative risks of investing in new media firms. Our concern here is with New York's business services.

Assuming the Position (New Economy Player)

Some of the most compelling evidence that the new media were becoming New York's new engine was the growing involvement of Manhattan business services. Media stories suggested that an ensemble of specialized services was gearing up to assist Silicon Alley with technical training, consulting, recruiting, software duplication, language translation and the like.[59] The trend accelerated by the end of the decade. Business and professional service firms reportedly had created "tens of thousands of jobs" in a "scramble to serve Silicon Alley," including many that were "once dependent on Wall Street . . . advertising firms, lawyers, accountants, architects, contractors, printers and caterers."[60] Many of these firms provided more than services. Heydebrand and Miron remarked that Silicon Alley's lawyers had played multiple roles in extending new media networks, acting as "consultants and matchmakers, as well as network creators";[61] lawyers even helped create ties between start-ups and venture capitalists.

But how was it that business services came to participate in the new media and what was the nature of their participation? One possibility is that new media firms successfully recruited them: It seems natural that a growing sector would attract services. Yet, new media firms were not just another set of potential clients—as was evident in a *Crain's* story crediting the new media with driving the growth of New York's business services: "[T]he new media sector is helping double or even triple the business—*if not the bottom lines*—of the city's accounting firms, lawyers, architects, contractors and real estate services." Firms were taking risks in "starting new divisions, changing their fee structures and hiring employees who understand the freewheeling ways of the new media world." Many service firms agreed to "flexibility" on compensation since many start-ups were short on cash. A partner at a CPA firm commented:[62] "We had to rethink the way we provide services and how we get paid. . . . We'd always been taught that the longer we worked, the more we get paid. We think now about how to make a company successful, not how to get paid." Like many others, his firm had begun to defer fees, accept flat-rate billing, or take equity in new media clients—many of whom had not gone public yet, but could offer "warrants" that might be used to acquire stock once (if) they did.

Why agree to such terms? A productionist explanation suggests one possibility: In trying to adapt to the needs of the new media, service firms might develop relationships that lead to the development of trust. However, something more than responsiveness to client need was involved—many firms began to seek actively equity arrangements as investment opportunities. And trust (or faith) seemed to occur early on in the development of relations. Take, for instance, the case of Sunny Bates Associates. This executive search firm, which previously asked for a third of the first year's salary received by a placed executive, began to ask for a third of their first year's stock options. It had made twenty such deals by early 2000. Sunny Bates, the firm's owner and an NYNMA board member, stated that these deals "guarantee a different kind of relationship. If you're a stakeholder, you give freely of your introductions and your time, your contacts."[63] In other words, taking a risk produced a special tie, not vice versa.

In fact, the rapid development of faith in, and ties to, the new media was influenced by the broader New Economy cultural mobilization. Services flocked to serve the new media, at least in part, because of New Economy models that touted the leading-edge nature of the new media sector and the injunction to seek a piece of the stock market action. Richard Sennett argues that the advent of a New Economy has been accompanied by a new "risk culture" where risk-taking is "no longer meant to be the province only of venture capitalists."[64] He cites the New Economy injunction that people be entrepreneurial in changing jobs: As corporate job ladders crumble, upward mobility depends on finding positions with strategic leverage—the sort that intermediaries (or "brokers") gain. One should not be immobilized by a fear of failure—the only real failure is a "failure to move," to "make a break," "to act." In this culture, "risk is a test of character"—to take a risk is to choose "self-assertion rather than submission to what is given." The call to take risks is, at the same time, a put-down of the complacent individual who remains "dependent on hierarchy."[65]

The player's mentality was evident in an interview of a Silicon Alley lawyer by Heydebrand and Miron: He focused on forming ties with other people who "are in the middle of deals" such as "consultants" and other "intermediaries who see deal flow."[66] The way in which these brokers interpreted their possibilities was influenced by cultural entrepreneurs within their own ranks and by local media narratives—both of which stressed the desirability of options and the example of Silicon Valley where service firms built portfolios of equity in other firms.

Like Cisco's Lawyer

Lawyers played a prominent role in promoting the "Silicon Valley" model in New York. In 1999 when NYNMA's Venture Capital Forum drew a record seven hundred attendees, it seemed as if there were as many lawyers as there were financiers. Nine law firms spent as much as $10,000 each to sponsor the event in the hope of making themselves known to new media firms. The *New York Law Journal* reported that they dreamed of hitting it big, like Brobeck, Phleger & Harrison had—the Bay Area law firm that landed Cisco Systems as a client back when it was a fifty-employee firm.[67] Brobeck had prospered by representing the firm in acquisitions and investment deals ($3 billion in 1998 alone). If a law firm could hook up with a Cisco it might gain business for all facets of a practice: financing, mergers and acquisitions, intellectual property, licensing, litigation, real estate, and tax work. Brobeck was off to a fast start in New York. Its ad in a November 1999 issue of *Crain's* boasted that it had acted as counsel for thirteen Silicon Alley IPOs.

New York firms originally began Internet-related work to aid corporate clients that were experimenting with the Internet. As start-ups became stock market hits law firms began to create or expand practices in the area of "new media" (or "technology"). They sought entrée to the new media community by attending events such as NYNMA's "special interest group" for law and the Venture Forum. As one lawyer put it, participating helped in "building a brand in the market and building a reputation." Firms such as Greenberg Traurig and Howard Smith not only sponsored the Venture Forum, but also hosted "rehearsal sessions" at their offices so that start-ups could "come in and practice their pitches."[68]

The Authority Business

A host of Manhattan business services joined the local media in creating a local circuit of New Economy cultural authority. Media coverage of the burgeoning Silicon Alley phenomenon featured business professionals who—in the manner of venture capitalists—took risk "positions" in exchange for equity. Efforts to make sense of this novel trend often evoked the "Silicon Valley" or "California" model. For instance, a *Crain's* story about Brown & Wood—a local law firm whose drive to target new media firms had landed it eighty clients—-reported that it was "inspired by West Coast firms that have successfully built their business plans around the new economy."[69] The headline, "Law Firm Scores a Technical Knockout," alluded to the kind of pay-off from high tech start-ups that now even New York lawyers could aspire to and seek. A wireless communications start-up that Brown & Wood had taken on in 1998 had raised $1.3 billion via bonds and an IPO and then been acquired by another firm for $5.3 billion. The headline in a *New York Times* story summed up the larger phenomenon: "The New Economy's Currency Is Stock, Stock, Stock." It gave numerous examples of Manhattan business services that were accepting equity in new media firms as compensation. It reported that this was common practice in San Francisco among law firms, executive search firms, PR firms, consultants, building contractors, and commercial landlords. The story featured a co-owner of a San Francisco PR firm serving tech firms who reported that thirty to fifty firms approached his firm each week, many offering stock. He advised that his firm's expertise in technology meant that it could pick whom they would work with: "You're acting like a venture capitalist when you do this."[70]

The new media's bid for cultural authority not only made for good headlines, but also made for good business for an array of advertising services that were comfortably nestled alongside the media. Much of the advertising was geared to stirring up buzz in New York. The new media became the second leading advertiser on local radio in 1999—spending $64.1 million.[71] Dot-com ads seemed to appear everywhere: in print, radio, phone booths, and on a balloon in Macy's Thanksgiving Day parade. Of course, the use of the Macy's parade—a widely televised event—also points to nationally or globally focused advertising. Dot-com ads were also placed in commercial spaces that were located within Manhattan but whose images were circulated to global audiences. For example, Giftcertificates.com boosted its 1999 Christmas campaign by paying for a 67- by 25-foot billboard in Times Square.[72] The high (or low) point of dot-com campaigns was the blizzard of ads that affixed themselves to the Super Bowl spectacle. Hotjobs.com, an obscure firm, helped set the pattern when it became a national contender after spending $2 million (half of its 1998 revenue) for a thirty-second ad in the 1999 Super Bowl.

Other business services used ads targeting new media clients in an effort to display their command of New Economy sensibilities. For example, a Hale and Dorr ad sporting the banner—"Counsel to Silicon Alley"—paid tribute to the new media's revolutionary aspirations: "You laugh at the conventional wisdom. You leapfrog the industry standard. You rewrite the rules." Of course, the not-so-subtle subtext was, "Hale and Dorr gets it." An ad in *Crains* by Insignia/ESG, a commercial real estate firm, advised new media firms that a real estate provider was another element of the network they needed to support their all-important stories.

> You've got a killer .com business plan and venture capital to make it a reality. *Don't risk your vision* with shortsighted real estate advice. Turn to the best commercial real estate talent in New York—Insignia/ESG, and our specialists in New Media. We'll not only find you the perfect Silicon Alley location with the right technology; we'll also arrange the kind of lease flexibility that can accommodate explosive growth.

The quest for cultural authority helped turn new media firms into important customers for the hospitality industry. An executive at a hotel that raked in $15,000 to $25,000 per new media event, commented, "They really seem to want to spend money right now."[73] New media start-ups vigorously celebrated their passage through an accelerated life cycle: launch, secure financing, go public. Thus, the new media generated 30 percent of the business for Apogee Events, a caterer with its four hundred–capacity facility, Tribeca Rooftop. Apogee could earn $5,000 from a meeting or as much as $200,000 from a full-scale product launch or "media event." The serious business of gaining and displaying status as a New Economy change agent figured heavily in such revels. One notable example came in 1999 when Apogee catered the $100,000 wedding of the president of the Gay Financial Network. The event was attended by two hundred guests and broadcast live to 200,000 over the Internet. Furthermore, new media seminars and conferences—lucrative mainstays for hotels, caterers, and event planners—were also components of the New Economy cultural circuit. Such events, Thrift notes, disseminate "new business knowledge" and provide "motivational fuel."[74] Apogee profited from serving buzz meisters such as *Silicon Alley Reporter* and Jupiter Communications, which hosted meetings, parties, and press events. Tribeca Rooftop was the venue when Jack Hidary warned the old media to take the new media seriously (or face assimilation).

Other services supplied elements of material infrastructure for the new media. Even in the design and construction sector, part of the service was to help the new media signal its pedigree—through artifacts (and artifice)—postindustrial decors and props such as banks of computer screens (or a bus) in the lobby. Dozens of architects, contractors, furniture dealers, and lighting designers became New Economy players as they reorganized, or started up, to renovate offices for new media firms. Some accepted options as compensation: When a construction firm renovated the offices of eFit.com, it accepted 75 percent of its $120,000 fee in equity.[75] One architect termed his firm's reorganization "an investment in a new wave of entrepreneurs." Some became extensions of the financing system. A flooring supplier created a project management firm to handle design, construction, and equipment installation for new media firms; it also offered financing for the work. The founder remarked that his firm exploited the need for speed—essential because new media firms "run through a lot of money fast. The sooner they get set up, the sooner they can raise more money."[76]

MORPHING MANHATTAN

The new media's blitz across Manhattan brought modest physical changes (a bit of rewiring) and a great deal of reimagining of space. Yet, for all the talk of epochal change—and a very real reorganization of space that displaced other kinds of firms—the new media occupation had an ephemeral quality. New media firms etched their mark on interior spaces, but left few traces at street level. To understand how their "moment in time" left New York a different place, we need to turn to their hooking up with the real estate sector. New productive and cultural impulses propelled the new media expansion, but when it came to assembling property a traditional New York power was in the driver's seat—commercial landlords.

Manhattan's commercial real estate market, which followed the financial sector into the tank in the early 1990s, was slower in climbing out. During the 1990s financiers never regained their appetite for bankrolling the construction of speculative buildings (see table 4.2). In the period 1993 through 1998 there was virtually no new construction of commercial buildings in Manhattan. However, the market for existing space began to rebound in the mid-1990s. The vacancy rate for Manhattan commercial real estate dropped from 16.8 percent in 1996 to 9.6 percent in 1998. By decade's end rents were soaring while vacancy rates plummeted. In 2000 the vacancy rate for Manhattan was 4.5 percent while that for the Class A segments in Midtown and Downtown were, respectively, 2.4 and 2.1 percent. From 1997 to 2000 the average Manhattan rent rose from $31.07 to $46.85 a square foot while the averages for the Class A segments in Midtown and Downtown, rose from $40.91 and $32.76, respectively, to $62.36 and $47.35.[77]

The new media was implicated in real estate's robust rebound. A rush of new media start-ups into the market was spearheaded by the IPO stars who were willing and able to pay premium rents for large spaces. For example, iVillage and Jupiter Communications each leased over 100,000 square feet at $40+ a square foot while about.com signed on for 170,000 square feet at $50 a square foot; DoubleClick leased 400,000 square feet.[78] A January 2000 report estimated that one hundred new media firms were looking for offices in the range of 60,000 to 100,000 square feet.[79] During the first half of 2000 the new media and other tech firms leased 5.2 million square feet, displacing the financial sector at 3 million square feet as the number one leaser of new commercial space in the city. In the second quarter the new media and tech firms accounted for nearly 31 percent of the new space rented in the city in comparison to 17 percent for the financial sector.[80]

Narratives of Industrial Succession

For an ensemble that was supposed to be the cutting edge of New York's economy Silicon Alley had a peculiar image problem—it was virtually invisible on the street. New York, as a premier merchant city, was manifest in

Table 4.2 Average Annual Vacancy Rates, Average Annual Rents, and New Construction in Manhattan, 1985–2000

Years	Manhattan Vacancy Rates			Manhattan Rents			New Construction Completed (in millions of square feet)
	All	Class A Midtown	Class A Downtown	All	Class A Midtown	Class A Downtown	
1985	6.3%	7.2%	10.2%	$46.28	$56.28	$51.90	6.606
1986	8.4	7.0	7.9	46.27	55.96	50.20	5.430
1987	8.5	7.1	9.9	45.54	54.34	54.29	7.492
1988	10.1	9.4	8.1	44.14	54.87	49.87	2.700
1989	14.1	10.5	11.1	46.44	53.25	44.95	7.832
1990	16.1	13.3	12.6	42.19	51.28	41.86	4.804
1991	17.6	13.0	13.9	38.66	46.07	38.95	0.170
1992	18.6	12.8	16.4	35.21	41.43	38.11	2.254
1993	18.1	13.2	16.1	32.64	38.65	34.38	0
1994	16.9	10.5	15.5	31.24	38.39	33.26	0
1995	16.6	9.4	14.5	30.94	37.75	33.35	0
1996	16.8	8.1	12.9	30.81	37.85	32.71	0
1997	13.5	6.1	7.5	31.07	40.91	32.76	0
1998	9.6	5.3	4.1	34.67	48.26	39.70	0
1999	8.2	4.0	3.3	40.02	50.47	40.49	1.500
2000	4.5	2.4	2.1	46.85	62.36	47.35	0

Source: Group of 35, 2001.

Fig. 4.1 "DoubleClick Welcomes You to Silicon Alley" sign tucked behind Flatiron Building (Photo by author)

a forest of towering masts and a dense collar of piers; as a center of the garment industry the city revealed itself in fleets of racks that shuttled garments between shops, lively sidewalk deal-making, and showroom windows. But as a new media center, just about the only visible sign was literally a big sign—"DoubleClick Welcomes You to Silicon Alley"—erected near the Flatiron Building. To make the enclave more visible the *AlleyCat News* even sponsored a Silicon Alley Street Fair at Union Square Park. The fair showcased sixty firms, most of whom set up booths demonstrating their websites. Its publisher noted, "People read about Silicon Alley, they hear about it, but they don't come face to face with it."[81]

Media coverage, particularly by the business press, was vital for sustaining Silicon Alley as a sociological entity. In a city burdened by questions about its future, and a swooning real estate market, the business press interpreted the new media's explosive expansion as a historic turnaround for the city. Even though the most cyclical of forces propelled it—a stock boom—the new media was featured in tales of *industrial succession* and *the march of technology.*

A flood of media accounts, such as a 1999 *Crain's* story, cited the new media for having "reclaimed buildings and neighborhoods forsaken by the traditional business community."[82] The implication was that real estate was restructuring as the tech sector drew marginalized (or vacant) industrial areas into the market mainstream. Conversions of large industrial properties were used to symbolize the passing of industrial New York. Take, for example, a *New York Times* story about the Starrett-Lehigh Building on the West Side—a railroad terminus born of a time when railroad cars were ferried across the Hudson River on barges:

> The Starrett-Lehigh Building was constructed in the early 1930's for a world that no longer exists, when the West Side of Manhattan was crowded with rail lines and docks that brought raw materials to the thriving manufacturing sector of the city and then shipped finished products out. . . . The building is attracting a different sort of tenant these days, as are many of the onetime factories and warehouses on the West Side. Office users are flooding [in].[83]

Constructed at a gargantuan scale—its elevators were capable of lifting entire trucks to upper floors—the building contained more rentable space (2.3 million square feet) than the Chrysler Building. Martha Stewart helped tidy up the behemoth's image when her Internet unit (Living Omnimedia) joined Silicon Alley start-ups such as Screaming Media and Concrete Media in leasing space.

The cultural side of the new media advance was stressed in a *Crain's* article about the leasing of space in the Astor Place area—located between Greenwich Village and the East Village—by Jupiter Communications. Jupiter was "the first major new media player to move into the Astor Plaza area, where manufacturing tenants have been replaced over the last decade with advertising and publishing businesses."[84] The move had added symbolic weight as the building being leased was a "landmark" that "began life as the Mercantile Library of New York and served for many years as the headquarters of United Auto Workers' District 65." The previous tenants were avant gardes in their day. The Mercantile Library Association was formed in 1820 by clerks from merchant firms; the library—once the largest circulating library in the United States—hosted evening classes and lectures by the likes of Frederick Douglass and Mark Twain. District 65— founded by communists as a textile workers' union in the 1930s, later pioneered the organizing of white-collar workers. Jupiter—a partisan prophet— was no less ambitious in aspiring to vanguard status.

Real estate interests also put their spin on the transformation. A twelve-page special advertising section in the March 21, 2000, edition of the *New York Times* featured conversions in Queens, Brooklyn, Long Island, New Jersey, and Manhattan. It included the rewiring of a factory in Long Island City (Queens) to serve

> telecommunications, Web-hosting, dot-coms and high-tech back offices. . . .
> The building could stand as a metaphor for the march of technology since its construction in 1911. It was first a manufacturing site for horse-drawn car-

riages; then it was an auto manufacturing building. Its next iterations were in airplane manufacturing, followed by garment manufacturing.[85]

The next stop in technology's march was the New Economy. The building owner said of the high tech tenants he sought, "Their growth is almost boundless because capital is almost boundless." Another real estate tale concerned the solving of the Downtown question. One *Crain's* article bore the headline, "Downtown Re-emerges as Office Mecca." Another, entitled "Downtown Catches Midtown Office Fever," reported that, "The downtown office market is finally catching fire" and, in comparison to the past, its recovery seemed to be "on firmer footing. . . . There is no speculative office construction to fill . . . and the tenant base is becoming far more varied, lessening the area's dependence on financial services firms. Dot-coms are leading the diversity parade. . . ."[86]

The Wired Difference

Various interests mediated the new media's expansion. These included landlords, a new breed of telecoms who scrapped for the right to connect tenants to the Internet, and assorted services that enacted "new rules" in housing new media firms. Their mobilization of new media images provided content for media coverage—making the new media's settlements "visible" to a broader circle of actors.

Recognition of the Silicon Alley name was due, in part, to the pioneering efforts of Rudin Management and the Alliance for Downtown to rewire buildings for Internet firms. Other landlords began to follow suit in the hope of boosting the image of their properties. By 1999 a real estate executive could argue, "If a building isn't wired, it's out of the game."[87] The "game" featured not only landlords and new media firms but also small telecoms. These telecoms, emboldened by forecasts that Internet use would continue to explode, hoped to bypass Verizon (formerly Bell Atlantic) and service tenants in commercial buildings. However, landlords had ties to established telecoms and hesitated to open the doors to new telecoms. The upstarts offered to wire buildings if landlords would grant them access to their tenants. They also offered them a cut of the revenue (e.g., 5 to 10 percent) and in some cases, warrants to buy their stock. Telecoms invited landlords to distinguish their properties through telecom infrastructure. For example, the CEO of Eureka Broadband noted that his firm helped landlords "differentiate their buildings" through measures such as creating a website for building tenants.[88]

Crain's reported that a number of New York landlords began to sign on so that they could market their properties as "temples of cutting edge technology."[89] In fact, rewiring buildings may have represented more of a commitment to new telecommunications technology than to the new media.

Rewiring cost much less at $50 to $100 per square foot than what it would cost to develop a new building—$505 a square foot in Midtown and $438 a square foot in Downtown.[90] A number of landlords also dealt space to telecom hotels—heavily air-conditioned warehouses for computer servers. For example, in 1999 Rudin Management purchased AT&T's former headquarters and embarked on a $60 million effort to turn the 1.2 million square foot complex into a "new economy telecom and dot-com facility."[91] Between 1998 and 2001 5 million square feet in the New York area was leased or purchased for telecom hotels. From New Jersey's Meadowlands to Manhattan's West Side property owners were "looking to cash in on the telco hotel craze."[92]

At any rate, many landlords were cautious when it came to embracing new media tenants—and broker pitches invoking the New Economy's new rules. Like other business services, real estate brokers tried to use New Economy norms to better their position vis-à-vis the "deal-flow." One broker encouraged new media firms to think of landlords as potential investors who must be sold on their potential: "We have to convince them that a visit to the landlord is like a road show selling their concept to investors. We encourage our clients to get ready . . . and to be prepared to tell their story at a moment's notice."[93] Other brokers advised clients to entice landlords with options and to stress the financing they had received. Some landlords did accept equity to seal deals.[94] Pseudo obtained a third floor in its building through offering the owner equity; its president Josh Harris (perhaps surprised) remarked, "They believed in us."[95] Rudin Management lead the way in accepting options.[96] Wary landlords were more apt to adopt another New Economy practice—they asked "to see business plans . . . about a company's backers, the size and shape of the funding, its 'burn rate' and 'exit strategy.' "[97] But, a broker was not likely to get a client in just by flashing its New Economy currency. A leasing agent noted, "Relatively uneducated brokers look at their [venture] backing and think, isn't that great? But that's the price of admission; it doesn't give the tenant credibility."[98] As the market tightened, landlords used their leverage to ensure that they could harvest some of the bounty before the new media tide went out. Normally, commercial tenants paid security deposits equal to two or three months' rent on a five- to ten-year lease. New media firms, lacking credit records and sound finances, often had to pay one, two, or even three years' rent for security—and a rent premium of 10 to 20 percent.[99]

Once a firm gained a space, various services helped inscribe it with new media sensibilities. An observer remarks that during the 1990s, "Virtually all of the creativity in Manhattan building design went into interiors . . . creating the bare-bones dot-com look."[100] A real estate executive noted that new media firms would pay over $40 a square foot for "the aura of space" even if it "lacked . . . elevators, air-conditioning and heat."[101] They favored spaces with "exposed lighting . . . exposed piping," "brick-and-timber warehouse-type space," and "the right kind of industrial steel."[102] Besides putting a postindustrial burnish on industrial surfaces, offices were designed to express new media work culture. DoubleClick installed a basketball court; Razorfish was "dog-friendly."[103] Lancit Media had a "womb room" where workers "brainstorm in overstuffed floral print chairs that look like they've been lifted from a wealthy aunt's East Hampton sunroom." An architect noted that the new media lifestyle featured "expresso bars, working all night, headphones, CD-ROMs, surfer shorts and net surfing . . . they don't play by the same rules." A designer remarked that spaces expressed egalitarianism: "There are no doors, no corner offices and no cubicles. We see workers enveloped in a beautiful web of technology and color." Equal access to natural light was achieved through translucent walls or making do with few walls. Concrete Media, where walls were in short supply, provided movable metal racks to hang diagrams on. The deconstructionist spirit burned even more brightly at Knowledge Strategies where all the furnishings were "mobile." Its CFO commented:

> The new organizational paradigm for new media is a flat organization that has project teams. We have wheels on all our chairs, tables and file cabinets so people can continuously reconfigure their work spaces. People here roll freely into clusters, then break apart and move toward another buzz of energy where a problem needs to be solved.[104]

(Dis)associations of the Seamless City

Many new media firms looking for space found themselves in new territories. One of these was madscience.com, which moved into a twelve-story building in Chinatown to take a space vacated by Destiny Fashions; it later acquired a second space when another garment firm left. The co-founder of madscience noted, "It was a bit of a gamble moving in here. But in a couple of years we think this area is going to be very hot." A *Crain's* reporter noted that as the madscientist spoke, a steady stream of Chinese workers filed into the building, which still hosted numerous garment shops. However, the new media expansion put the industry in peril. Chinatown landlords had converted sixteen buildings from sites of garment production so as to attract tech firms; another twenty were in the process of being converted.[105] The erosion of the industry raised doubts about Chinatown's destiny.

So it was that "the others" began to appear in media accounts of new media forays. Only ghosts of the industrial past were supposed to be left in the dead zones being revived by the new media. But, garment workers, printers, and the like who were expelled during the new media's Great Trek were other-worldly only in the sense that they did not belong to the brave new world of the New Economy.

Vacancy rates for commercial real estate at the center of the original Silicon Alley enclave, the Flatiron and SoHo Districts, fell from 22 percent and 15 percent, respectively, in 1994 to 2.6 percent and 5.6 percent in 1999. In the same period the average rent (per square foot) in the two areas soared: from $24 to $34 in Flatiron and from $14.50 to $34.50 in SoHo. As commercial spaces in the original center of Silicon Alley became rented up, or much more expensive, new media firms pushed into new territories: first, Downtown, and second, the southern edges of Midtown such as Chelsea (west of the Flatiron District) and the Garment District (ten blocks north of Flatiron). In Lower Manhattan, the new media moved into Chinatown, the Printers' District, the Flower District, and Tribeca. Rents spiked while vacancy rates plunged. For example, from 1994 to 1999 the average rent in Chelsea rose from $17.40 a square foot to $36.05.[106]

A notable example of displacement in Chelsea was the Starrett-Lehigh Building where new media firms, paying $30 a square foot in rent, dislodged mattress firms and warehousers who had been paying rents in the single digits.[107] Trinity Real Estate stopped renewing the leases of dozens of printers as their district—west of SoHo—became a prime spot. Printers had paid as little as $7 a square foot in rent; Trinity asked new media firms for rents approaching $40 a square foot.[108]

The new media also made serious encroachments in the Garment District. Much of it was protected by zoning, but the city had stopped its enforcement inspections. Landlords converted vacant space, refused to renew leases, or demanded higher rents. For example, Heung Fook Fashion, the company that manufactured clothing for Kathie Lee Gifford, moved out of a space that it rented for $7.25 a square foot—and was replaced by Resume.com and Netcentives.com, which paid about $30 a square foot.[109] The new media expansion threatened to uravel the nexus of specialized resources that made up the district. The sector, hard hit by competition from Asia, was staggered by a doubling and tripling of rents in the Garment Center and Chinatown from 1999 to 2001. The number of apparel shops in the city fell from 3,591 to 3,260 between 1998 and 2000, while the number of production jobs dropped from 70,100 to 60,700. Aparel and textile-related wholesale jobs fell from 132,900 to 113,800 between 1998 and 2000.[110]

Real estate interests celebrated a "new social reality" emerging in the wake of the new media's advance. Speculators began to invest in newly chic areas in the Meatpacking and Flower Districts now associated with the "new economy" and "new media lifestyles."[111] Warehouses in Tribeca that had rented for $1 a square foot in the 1960s were converted to condos that sold for $500 to $600 a square foot.[112] Some brokers stated that they were changing their maps—old place identities such as the Garment Center were "anachronisms" and new "submarkets" were emerging. The business district was extending to new corners of Manhattan and even to other boroughs, producing a "new frontier" for providers of office space.[113] Some real estate interests chirped about the emergence of a "seamless city"—a prime segment extending from 60th Street through Lower Manhattan.[114]

In fact, real estate interests took the lead in promoting new place identities and boundaries. Trinity Real Estate revived a historic name to rebrand the Printer's District—Hudson Square—that appeared on maps two hundred years ago. A Trinity executive said the idea was "to create an image of an area that had historical significance and cachet."[115] Chinatown landlords who were converting sweatshops to tech shops floated the name "SoHo East."[116] The president of Max Capital, which paid as much as $30 million a building to remodel garment factory sites, asserted, "The garment district is just another office market at this point."[117]

The grand irony of the new media's lead role in making over Manhattan was that it become increasingly difficult for them to set up, or remain, in the new hot spots. In part, the new media became caught up in a wildfire that it had helped ignite—a space race that sent rents into orbit. But, the aggressive use of the new media to change the image of properties—and the later problems of new media firms in securing space—suggests that more was involved in the reorganization of space than comparative purchasing power alone. It is difficult to pin a single motive on landlords—and the thinking of many no doubt changed over time. Several possibilities are likely: They believed in the new media at first—or were willing to give them a chance—and perhaps grew skeptical; they believed in the New Economy in general—especially the prospects for wired infrastructure; or they embraced the new media as a temporary, or even, cynical gambit.

Many landlords suspected that it was new media firms who would not be long for this world. As one real estate observer put it, "How do you finance a building full of these? If the Internet market crashes. . . ."[118] Another said of landlords, "The balance sheets of Net companies in their embryonic state really frighten them. They're concerned that some . . . companies won't be around in a year."[119] The head of the city's second largest real estate provider stressed that new media firms were poor risks because of their lack of credit ratings: "If you are a credit tenant landlords will work to get you in. We had lots of opportunities to lease to dot-coms and decided not to." He ventures that the new media firms that were unsuccessful in bidding on his space, "probably thought it was full."[120]

Even a major success story suggests that the relationship between Manhattan real estate and the new media was a shaky marriage of convenience.

One Friday in March 2000, iVillage called Newmark Realty, saying that it needed 100,000 plus square feet; on Monday it signed a deal for a Newmark property in the Garment District. The space was one of two Newmark properties in the Garment Center that were near Times Square. Newmark wanted to highlight their proximity to Times Square, hoping to raise the rents from $15 to $35 a square foot. Its president recalled, "This was at a time when the garment district was still the garment center. But we realized it was close enough to Times Square to change the perception."[121] iVillage agreed to pay $44 a square foot, and Newmark reported that the deal changed the images of the building and the area. However, despite the happy alignment of agendas, and the fact that iVillage was one of Silicon Alley's most prominent firms, Newmark extracted an eight-figure security deposit.

Some analysts have warned that the digitalization of space would produce segmented territories. Occupants of areas that were connected to advanced telecom networks would be privileged over those residing in areas without access.[122] The New York experience suggests that this image was unduly mechanistic. Elements of the built environment were brought into new media networks through the efforts of diverse interests who created narratives, relationships, and images as well as telecom devices. And areas were given new associations by pulling them away from existing ones—tenants, identities, and boundaries of older industrial districts. Moreover, it was real estate owners, not a technological elect, that possessed formidable devices for assembling physical facilities. They have legal claims to particular properties and wield great influence with public-private partnerships and quasi-public entities that are devices for redevelopment. In contrast, the new media's position in Manhattan's new wired corridors was contingent on their stories remaining compelling—and their reserves of capital holding out.

CHAPTER 5

OVER THE RIVER AND
THROUGH THE 'HOODS

Let's craft policies to keep the boom going, and let's make sure the boom is
inclusive—that it doesn't just reach graduates of the Brown University
Semiotics program, but also graduates of [the] Borough of Manhattan
Community College, that it gives jobs to [not only] people from SoHo but
[also] people from the Bronx, Brooklyn, and the Lower East Side as well.
—President of the New York Software Industry Association, June 1999[1]

. . . we can duplicate the success achieved in Manhattan's Silicon Alley district.
New companies in the Harlem Internet Way 125 district . . . will be large-scale
employers who will provide the critical mass for migration of new media firms to
Upper Manhattan, and drive the creation of business service companies in the area.
—President of the Upper Manhattan Empowerment Zone, April 2000[2]

A ceremony held on April 19, 2000, outside the Adam Clayton Powell Building in Harlem hinted at a bridging of divides: the institutional, geographic,
and racial fractures that criss-cross New York. The Upper Manhattan Empowerment Zone (UMEZ) announced that the city's Economic Development
Corporation had designated a corridor on Harlem's historic 125th Street as a
high tech district in its Digital NYC program. UMEZ used the occasion to
welcome Urban Box Office (a new media firm) as the anchor tenant for "Harlem Internet Way 125" (HIWay125). Relations between the Empowerment
Zone—a Clinton administration initiative—and Guiliani's administration
previously had been frosty. The mobilization for HIWay125 also seemed to
cross institutional and social boundaries. Organizations pledging to "help
identify, recruit and establish" high tech firms in the enclave included the City
College of New York, Columbia University, several utilities, and the New York
City Investment Fund (NYCIF)—an elite group of investors that had begun

to assert itself in new media affairs. UMEZ, which had a fund of $250 million and federal incentives at its disposal, promised to give Urban Box Office (UBO) a loan of $4 million. Digital NYC, modeled on Downtown's Plug 'N' Go program, would provide marketing money for the district and help reduce its energy costs and taxes.

The formal goal of Digital NYC was to address the new media space crisis in Manhattan by helping establish enclaves of low-cost wired space in other parts of the city. Besides Harlem, the program supported districts in the minority communities of the South Bronx, and Red Hook and Sunset Park in Brooklyn—and in other old port or industrial areas such as Long Island City (in Queens), DUMBO (a rapidly gentrifying neighborhood in Brooklyn), and Staten Island. Anticipation ran high that the new media could help jump-start revitalization in these areas (as it had in Lower Manhattan). The Harlem site (an old industrial area called Manhattansville) was pocketed with long-abandoned properties. Yet, UMEZ declared, that with the "strong team of partners" and UBO acting as "the district's flagship," the project might produce, "a 24/7 commercial environment uptown."[3]

Could an innovative ensemble that depended so heavily on personal ties reach across a cityscape fractured by race and class—and a developmental divide that set off Corporate Manhattan from the "other" New York? While Manhattan possessed one of the densest concentrations of Internet connections in the United States—and seemed to be gaining a Starbucks on every other corner—it took the intervention of a nonprofit entity to get the Bronx its first cybercafe (CyberCase) in early 2001 (but no Starbucks).[4] Especially daunting was a racial faultline that ran across the new media itself, which was dominated by white males. The 2000 U.S. Census showed the city population to be 24.5 percent African American and 27 percent Hispanic, but a new media survey released that year reported that only 8 percent of its workers were African American while 6 percent were Hispanic; only 38 percent were female.[5] Observers also noted that the rise of minority entrepreneurs in the new media was stunted by their lack of ties with Silicon Alley venture capitalists.[6]

UBO seemed a promising base for boundary-crossing. It hoped to transcend ethnic niches by appealing to a broader "urban mindset" market with a network of sites dealing with "urban music, arts, sports, and fashion." UBO aimed to exploit the fact that hip hop drew a mixed audience: inner-city teens from diverse backgrounds and white suburban teens. UBO had a well-known co-founder—George Jackson—the producer of the film *New Jack City* and a former CEO of Motown Records. And, thanks to Flatiron Partners, Chase Capital Partners, and NYCIF, UBO had just received $16 million in financing.[7]

A promising nest of institutional ties seemed to be forming around UBO. But were these ties of a sort that would allow new media firms to address their most fundamental challenge—to become less dependent on speculative capital? New media firms needed support that could help them develop sustainable (i.e., profitable) ties with product markets as well as cope with immediate problems of procuring workspaces, skilled workers, and operating capital. For a new sector to create, or connect with, such institutional supports required a new industrial politics—one that could mobilize a broad spectrum of participants and produce a cultural fabric that would cause the general public to embrace (and support) the sector.

The outlines of a new industrial politics did emerge from New York's digital industries by the end of the decade. Among other things, it called for the inclusion of less advantaged segments and territories in technology-related growth. However, the stock boom that propelled new media–related growth exerted a powerful hold over efforts to create institutions. Instead of helping buffer firms from the vicissitudes of the stock market, the new industrial politics tended to organize institutional arrangements around ties to the financial sector. And the prominence of the new media's financial associations (and the sense that few benefited from "instant" dot-com wealth) stunted the new media's public appeal.

A (NOT-SO) SMART REGION

The release of a study by the city Comptroller's Office in April 1999 was a watershed in the emergence of a new tech industry politics. It documented a huge boom in the city's "software/information technology industry" between 1992 and 1997. The number of computer services firms and employees nearly doubled in the city, growing at a more rapid rate than in the United States or in New York's suburbs. The study, in a sense, "deconstructed" the prevailing definition of Silicon Alley that revolved around Manhattan's new media, drawing attention to various features of New York's tech industry that had been overshadowed by the new media's stock market exploits. The area industry possessed a sizeable "pure tech" segment and a regional structure, yet faced myriad institutional challenges. The study—the brainchild of the New York Software Industry Association (NYSIA)—signalled a shift in how tech industry identities, interests, and territories were defined in the New York area. It also highlighted the fact that the new tech industry politics was making itself felt in the realm of electoral politics. The study was the first attempt by a city agency to measure the high tech boom and to address the broad range of institutional issues it raised. In a setting where the tone was set by a Republican mayor and governor, the report of the comptroller (a Democrat) issued a rare call for active government intervention on a broad front: "The City and State need to pay more attention to the industry and take actions to improve the climate for software companies in each of four critical areas: costs (especially of communications and space), education, finance, and regional partnerships and consortia."[8]

One dimension of the report struck a familiar chord—the injunction to follow the Silicon Valley example. In this instance, the Silicon Valley model referred to a regional web of institutions—the appropriate focus if policy moved away from a company-based development strategy to an industry-based one. Silicon Valley was the point of reference throughout in discussions of tech education, venture capital, university-industry partnerships, and regional cooperation. Other institutional actors weighed in to support a regional approach to developing the tech sector, proposing that it was at the level of regions that competition for tech investment occurred. An editorial in *At New York* (formerly *@NY*) stated, "It's time for a regional look at the advantages and challenges facing Silicon Alley"; unless we as a "region are ready to plunge ahead with development policy . . . we'll always be playing catch up to places like Silicon Valley and the northern Virginia/Washington, DC corridor."[9] Similarly, the New York Academy of Sciences—which assisted in the comptroller's study—argued that "for New York to compete with other regions of the country and the world," the region's tech employment numbers and research funding had to be aggregated to draw investors.[10] The academy's president proposed, "We would then be able to put together a case to somebody like Bill Gates who has real money to put on the table"; he also stressed the need to "apply the region's science and technology assets to economic growth"; finally, the academy pushed for the creation of a "regional technology council" to broker ties among universities, corporations, and governments so as to bring more research dollars in and, eventually, to inform policy: "We hope to have mapped out what the most successful regions do in terms of regulatory regimes for knowledge-based industries."[11]

These recommendations resonated with a body of research on the rise of regions as units for economic organization, especially for knowledge-based industries.[12] Such areas are often called "smart regions": They possess institutions that allow participants to assess their strategic situations and to create (and continually evaluate) industry supports. The work on innovative regions follows the lead of Annalee Saxenian, who applied the model of industrial districts (discussed in chapter 1) to explain the "regional advantages" of Silicon Valley. She stresses the role of entities such as civic organizations or trade associations in providing regional institutional frameworks for an industrial politics that crosses governmental and institutional lines.[13]

However, other researchers see the creation of regional economic institutions to be more problematic, especially when the region extends across political boundaries.[14] Moreover, myriad efforts to emulate Silicon Valley have fared poorly, perhaps because of the region's unique incubation as a subsidied Cold War hot spot.[15] It may be especially difficult to institutionalize the regional growth that neoliberal policies promote; an economy that initially grows through exploiting deregulation is unable to respond when problems emerge in the supply of labor, real estate, and capital.[16] And encouragement of free flows of capital often promotes a competition among localities that is the bane of regionalism.

The case of the New York City region largely fits the less rosy vision. To paraphrase Karl Marx, the New York technology ensemble is a region "in itself" but not "for itself." Various industry surveys have presented compelling evidence of the technology industry's substantial regional structure, but there is little regional consciousness or institutional framework to complement it. Particularly striking was a 2000 NYNMA survey[17] that found an estimated 8,431 new media firms to be located in the region (consisting not only of parts of the state of New York but also New Jersey and Connecticut as well); of these 3,831 were located in New York City while considerably more—4,600—were located in the rest of the region (see table 5.1). Moreover, the rate of growth in firms from 1997 to 1999 was higher in the region

Table 5.1 Growth of New Media Firms in the New York Region, 1997 and 1999

Area	Number of New Media Firms		Change	Percent Change
	1997	1999		
Manhattan				
South of 41st St.	1,106	1,675	+569	+51.4%
Midtown (41st to 59th St.)	451	855	+404	+89.6
Uptown (North of 59th St.)	571	592	+21	+3.7
Other New York City	473	688	+215	+45.5
New York City subtotal	2,601	3,831	+1,230	+47.3%
New Jersey	974	2,397	+1,423	+146.1
Connecticut	610	895	+285	+46.7
New York Region total	4,881	8,431	+3,550	+72.7%

Source: PricewaterhouseCoopers, 2000.

Table 5.2 New Media Employment in New York City and New York Area, by Employment Status, 1995, 1997, and 1999

	Employment Status		Change	Percent	
	1995	1997	1999	1997–99	Change
New York City					
Freelance	6,150	12,680	20,773	+8,093	+63.8%
Part Time	2,800	11,280	12,820	+1,540	+13.7
Full Time	18,350	32,013	104,665	+72,652	+226.9
Total	27,300	55,973	138,258	+82,285	+147.0%
New York Area[a]					
Freelance	17,000	24,478	38,659	+14,181	+57.9
Part Time	8,600	22,526	25,363	+2,837	+12.6
Full Time	45,900	58,767	185,617	+126,850	+215.9
Total	71,500	105,771	249,639	+143,868	+136.0%

[a]The PricewaterhouseCoopers study defines the New York Area as including New York City, Long Island, the lower Hudson Valley of New York State, northeastern New Jersey, and southwestern Connecticut.

Source: Pricewaterhouse Coopers (2000, 29).

as a whole (72.7%) than in New York City (47.3%) and much higher in New Jersey (146.1%). With regard to the number of new media employees, the rate of growth was higher in New York City than in the region as a whole. Yet, if we subtract the city subtotal from the region total we see that the number of new media workers in the region outside the city was still impressive, at over 111,000 compared to 138,000 in the city (see table 5.2).[18]

However, New York City's regional economy is a political orphan—possessing neither a constituency nor governmental authority. The most vocal proponent of regional planning and development—the Regional Growth Association—has modest influence at best. The most important regional authority—the New York/New Jersey Port Authority—has a limited mandate: It controls major transportation infrastructures in the vicinity of the city, including ports, buses, trains, and airports. Its only major foray into the realm of economic development was, in fact, a notable one—the construction of the World Trade Center.

The dominant approach to "development" by state and local governments in the region is to raid their neighbors through recruitment—or to defend against such tactics through offering generous subsidies to "retain" existing businesses. The imprint of this competitive mentality can be seen in the limited regionalism espoused in the comptroller's report—it stated that it didn't focus on the "non-NY state parts of the NYC region."[19] In fact, for all practical purposes "regional" initiatives to support the New York–area tech industry have consisted of reaching beyond the borders of Corporate Manhattan into the rest of the city.

A New Industrial Politics

The comptroller's study, in part, stemmed from the desire of NYSIA to establish itself as a political interest and to forge an identity for technology firms that was distinct from that of the new media. Though NYSIA's president noted the overlap between new media and "software/information technology" firms, he contended that the latter were a distinctive segment that gave a city and a region credibility: "For New York to truly be considered one of the hot tech cities, there has to be a strong base of techies. Whether applications . . . are financial, new media, or e-mail servers and development tools, you have to have programmers and software engineers. . . . Artists and writers who know how to use technology are not enough to make a region a high-tech center."[20] After the comptroller's report was issued, NYSIA expressed satisfaction that it had gained "formal recognition of the size and scope of the 'hard-core' tech sector."[21] Despite its challenge to the industry's identity and boundaries, NYSIA embraced the Silicon Alley moniker—and the NYNMA as an important ally.

While NYNMA and NYSIA were very active, their efforts paled in comparison to Silicon Valley where over a hundred trade and professional associations were involved in labor market programs. Moreover, in Silicon Valley assorted local and county governments participated alongside schools, nonprofit organizations, and firms in Joint Venture: Silicon Valley—a regional governance body that identified and addressed collective problems in the industry. In contrast, New York's digital industries and their institutional allies had to labor mightily to get state and city government to respond to the new ensemble's needs.

Initially, NYNMA led the way in lobbying government to support digital industry. In 1995 it began to criticize the city's economic development strategy for consisting mainly of handouts to corporations rather than nurturing the capacities of small firms. The group asked the city to provide small firms with tax relief and to create support mechanisms that would aid in commercializing technology. NYNMA also criticized the location of the New York Information Technology Center, noting that the Wall Street location—which fit the city's agenda of boosting Downtown real estate—was not convenient for Silicon Alley's clients from the publishing and entertainment industries located in Midtown.[22]

In 1997, NYNMA and NYSIA joined several other entities in forming a new coalition—the Emerging Industries Alliance. In 1998 the group took advantage of state elections to call for a tech policy. It criticized Govenor Pataki's consolidation of economic development agencies and the lack of aid for technology firms.[23] Silicon Alley notables joined the critique of policy. In 1998 one of the Flatiron partners complained of government inaction to address industry problems:

> The public sector should be an ombudsman. They should be identifying problems, opportunities. . . . Local industry is being strangled by a lack of labor. All the local universities should get together. Our competitior is a firm like Goldman Sachs. The new media can't pay $150,000 for computer science grads. . . . As firms go public with this problem government could support a conference to get the universities together and then get out of the way. The universities probably could not set it up. . . . You need strategic vision.[24]

Around the same time, a *Silicon Alley Reporter* editor called on City Hall to:

> . . . provide tax incentives, support putting the technology in the schools, internship programs, adult technical education. . . . They should showcase the industry. When I was in LA I saw banners along the streets that said, 'LA is Number 1 in new media jobs.' Why not banners here on 5th Avenue that say, 'Silicon Alley'? . . . There is a battle to become the lead ecosystem for Internet companies. . . . In LA government is . . . doing tangible things for the industry.[25]

Even *Crain's New York Business* (a reliable Republican supporter) supported the critique of Pataki's policies offered by the Emerging Industries Alliance and endorsed its proposals in an editorial ("Pataki Must Help High Growth Firms").[26]

Bringing the State (and City Hall) Back In

The new industrial politics began to send ripples through the domain of electoral politics as politicians (usually Democrats) began to embrace the policy agenda of the digital industry lobby—and its critique of Republican policies. In 1997 the speaker of the City Council, Peter Vallone, endorsed much of the NYSIA agenda as he geared up for the 1998 gubernatorial campaign. He called for the state to grant a five-year tax moratorium for small firms, create an advisory board to assist start-ups in "emerging industries," and authorize a city technology office to help commercialize new technologies.[27] In 1997 the Democratic-dominated City Council passed the "Emerging Industries Job Creation Program"—a $30 million loan fund for small tech firms. As they geared up for the 2001 mayoral campaign (a term-limited Rudy Giuliani could not enter) several Democrats—including the Public Advocate Mark Green and the city comptroller—called for active government support of digital industries. Green's office issued a report calling for an effort to make New York "the Internet City" of the United States. In response to a request by NYSIA, most of the Democrats issued long position statements supporting tech firms. The leading Republican candidate, billionaire Michael Bloomberg, did not respond, but stressed his credentials as an information age entrepreneur.

As the industry gained support from business boosters (e.g., the New York City Partnership) the Pataki administration agreed to give $600,000 to the Emerging Industries Alliance in 1997. The Guiliani administration was slow to respond. It delayed implementing the City Council loan program and resisted requests to meet with new media reps. As Democrats made inroads in Silicon Alley, City Hall finally met with new media reps in early 1999 and created a Mayor's Council on New Media.

Besides the Plug 'N' Go program for Downtown, the main assistance the city provided took the form of traditional recruitment and retention packages. The head of the Economic Development Corp. claimed to have helped recruit twenty-four new media firms to New York between 1996 and 1999.[28] The city extended its retention program to new media firms in December 1998 when it offered a $4.8 million incentive package (e.g., tax breaks) to keep DoubleClick from moving some of its employees to New Jersey. It offered similar deals to theglobe.com, about.com, StarMedia and Jupiter Communications. Critics questioned whether web firms would really leave the cluster of specialized resources. The case of StarMedia certainly added to the suspicion that more than a little posturing was involved: The firm gained $2.76 million in incentives after announcing that it was thinking of moving its headquarters to Connecticut or New Jersey—or maybe Uruguay.[29]

Although they did not turn down these handouts, the tech industry maintained pressure on the city to offer more systematic aid that was tailored to the sector's problems. One of the biggest concerns was the need for affordable wired space. Actors as diverse as the city comptroller, the City Council speaker, NYSIA, and *Crain's* called on the city to extend a program in the Plug 'N' Go mold to other parts of the city. A *Crain's* editorial supporting the proposals of the Council speaker remarked, "The city could begin to develop buildings in every borough similar to 55 Broad St.," but "the Giuliani administration has shown little interest in such programs."[30] Just before the City Council was scheduled to take up the issue, NYSIA's president ratcheted up the political pressure, remarking that the extension of tech boom required a "partnership" with the public sector—and the "inclusion" of less advantaged populations and neighborhoods. He proposed that government help set up "technology districts" outside Manhattan by subsidizing "incubator construction" in league with landlords who agree to "keep rents affordable."[31] NYNMA was less enthusiastic about locating new media firms in the outer boroughs. In early 2000 NYNMA's head commented, "People want to stay in Manhattan because they want to be part of the creative energy here."[32] She proposed that firms might locate in the neighborhood around Columbia University, advising this might create the kind of ties between industry and academia that was evident around elite universities such as MIT and Stanford. In contrast, the executive director of NYSIA called for government to help connect tech firms with the city's public college system, the City University of New York (CUNY)—"the primary point of access for working class people into good jobs in the high tech economy."[33]

PLUGGING IN THE "OTHER" NEW YORK

Two major initiatives with public sector support appeared at the end of the 1990s in response to a perceived new media space crisis. Both used the imagery of the new media in order to extend the zone of territorial transformation. The first was the Giuliani administration's Digital NYC program. Using the Plug 'N' Go program as a template, Digital NYC encouraged local development corporations, universities, building owners, and telecoms to set up wired enclaves outside Lower Manhattan. The city offered to pay up to half the marketing cost (up to $250,000 per district) and promised to set up special arrangements to lower property taxes, provide cheaper energy, and reduce rental rates.

In fact, the program seemed a framework for forming minigrowth coalitions that would change the image and value of industrial properties. In order for property owners to receive funds, they had to partner with nonprofit entities such as development corporations, universities, or NYSIA. Seven districts were established in a mix of industrial areas and low-income minority neighborhoods in Brooklyn, Staten Island, Queens, Harlem, and the Bronx.[34] A May 22, 2000, column in *Crain's* proposed that the Digital NYC program would soon reveal "how much faith landlords have in the digital revolution and in the other boroughs."[35] Renovating an industrial building for tech firms was expensive (and risky). Since landlords in factory districts generally lacked the financial resources a more speculative type of property owner was probably needed. The case of one Long Island City participant in the program shed some light on the kind of landlord who had the capital. David Brause, the owner who was converting a larger factory to take advantage of the "boundless" nature of tech firms and capital, was (like William Rudin) a member of a major real estate family. The Brause portfolio included sixteen Midtown office buildings as well as twenty strip malls in five states.

The gamble was made more attractive in the other boroughs by the promise of becoming sprinkled with a bit of new media pixie dust. A real estate broker in Queens reported that landlords there did not make the onerous demands that they did in Manhattan: "Out here . . . the dot-coms have a lot of sex appeal, so the credit issue is not as critical."[36] In a number of cases the bet was sweetened by packaging telecoms in with the new media firms. For instance, a telecom hotel was the anchor for a site at Brooklyn's massive Bush Terminal, a twelve-building complex possessing 5 million square feet of space. A real estate executive claimed the complex was now positioned to exploit a new wave of demand as most businesses would come to need the kind of wired facilities that dot-coms had.

However, Digital NYC initiatives revealed the dilemma posed when high-value development was directed toward industrial neighborhoods: It threatened to extend the zone of displacement for industrial firms. For example, manufacturers that had settled in Bush Terminal after being pushed out of Manhattan were uprooted again as the rent was raised from $5 a square foot to $20. The situation was especially worrisome in Long Island City, New York City's largest remaining concentration of manufacturing. At the opening of a Digital NYC project there, the EDC's president announced that "Silicon Alley's boundaries are now extending beyond Manhattan,"[37] oblivious to the implications for a cluster of 2,400 industrial firms employing some 43,000 workers.[38]

The second major initiative followed the release of a report in January 2000. It estimated that only 25 percent of the one hundred new media firms that were currently looking for large blocs of office space would find it in Manhattan. Armed with the report New York Senator Charles Schumer called the space crunch, "a troubling storm cloud on the horizon that could cause New York City to stagnate or even decline. . . . If we don't address [the office space shortage] and mitigate it, another city—possibly a city even outside the United States—will surely replace us as the world capital of the ideas economy."[39] As a response Schumer assembled the "Group of 35," an extraordinary coalition co-chaired by then–Treasury Secretary Robert Rubin—and by the president of the New York City Investment Fund. Besides the usual growth coalition actors—utilities, universities, unions, a state development agency, and real estate interests (including William Rudin)— the group featured blue chip representatives of more cosmopolitan entities (e.g., Time Warner, Goldman Sachs, CitiCorp, Chase Manhattan, and the Federal Reserve Bank of New York) and CEOs from several of Silicon Alley's national contenders (Agency.com, DoubleClick, StarMedia). NYNMA and NYSIA served on committees providing technical assistance. Senator Schumer outlined the following strategy for a public-private partnership:

> . . . the city puts together a large parcel of land . . . provides the transportation infrastructure with help from Washington, zones the space . . . and then reclaims all or part of the expense by selling parcels of land to private developers who will build there with or even without signed up tenants.[40]

Thus, a network linking various levels of capital and government would mobilize to spur (and subsidize) redevelopment—even if it was speculative in nature (i.e., "without signed up tenants"). The Group of 35 reported that it was considering three neighborhoods as high tech zones: Long Island City, Downtown Brooklyn, and Manhattan's West Side.[41] While the first two sites were also featured in the Digital NYC program, mention of the West Side raised eyebrows. That turf was especially difficult, having been successfully defended by community groups against the development plans of none other than Donald Trump.

The plot had thickened since the time that The Donald was dumped. The Jets had expressed interest in having a stadium constructed in the area as did a group that was preparing a bid for the 2012 Olympics. It seemed that the new media was a pretext for latching onto a space coveted by powerful interests.[42]

INTELLECTUAL CAPITAL, CAPITAL'S INTELLECTUALS

The outlines of a new industrial politics was most evident in efforts to build intellectual infrastructure (training, research centers). But, the creation of collaborative partnerships among public entities, private actors, and universities did little to buffer the ensemble from dependence on Wall Street; on the contrary, such efforts focused on increasing the linkages of support systems to the financial sector.

City and state government began to offer more assistance to the tech industry, but they showed little inclination to provide sources of financing that would lessen the enclave's dependence on Wall Street. A public-private investment fund that the city set up—the Discovery Fund—had begun to invest in new media firms since 1995. Originally targeted to generate "thousands" of jobs, the fund was reoriented to fill Silicon Alley's venture capital gap. Though only five hundred jobs were created the city amassed a rich portfolio because of several big IPOs.[43] A second fund—the loan program for tech firms set up by the City Council in 1997—only made one loan before the money was diverted to another use in late 2001.

In 1999 the state's Jobs 2000 program included several items that NYSIA and its allies (including the New York City Investment Fund) had been lobbying for. It set up a new state agency to oversee the expansion of government- and university-based technology initiatives, and it allocated $120 million to support university research centers—the bulk going to the "five whose research projects show the most promise for economic development."[44]

The state program, along with the rapid expansion of Silicon Alley, spurred efforts by New York City universities and colleges to seek new ties with the tech industry. It also helped the New York City Partnership and its affiliate—NYCIF—become a nexus for institution-building on behalf of the tech industry. The partnership was founded by David Rockefeller in 1979 "to formalize the public-private partnership that was created during the city's fiscal crisis"; it was made up of some two hundred top executives of corporations and other institutions. Having merged with the chamber of commerce, the partnership was "the city's most prestigious business group."[45] Yet, up to this point, it was debatable whether it had exerted much influence in economic development. However, as Silicon Alley appeared on the scene the partnership's investment arm, NYCIF, had become a prominent participant in efforts to support the new media. The private fund was set up in 1996 to spur job growth by Henry R. Kravis (whose exploits as a corporate raider helped define the 1980s). The fund, which had raised $100 million by April 2000, used volunteers from the financial sector to identify industries with growth potential and to work with entrepreneurs. Manufacturing was originally a fund target, but most of the firms in its portfolio by 2001 were technology firms.[46] In fact, the fund announced in April 2000 that it was ending its efforts on behalf of manufacturing firms to focus instead on high tech industries. NYCIF argued that it made sense to redirect its money, given the city's strength in media and finance—and the fact that blue-collar jobs were being created in sectors such as telecommunications.[47]

In fact, from early on NYCIF developed institutional ties to give itself a central position within Silicon Alley. It worked with venture capitalists, including Flatiron Partners, to fund Silicon Alley start-ups such as StarMedia and theStreet.com. In 1997 it provided a loan of $750,000 to Ericsson to help support its Cyberlab project. As was the case with venture capital, it was the ties that came with the money that were of great interest—in this case, Cyberlab could gain relationships with the likes of Citigroup, Bear Stearns, and J. P. Morgan. Representatives of elite fund members took seats on Cyberlab's board of directors, and NYCIF proposed that it would utilize its "network of corporate leaders, venture capitalists, and media and technology experts to identify and sponsor projects for development through Ericsson Cyberlab."[48]

NYCIF's most notable efforts came in conjunction with the efforts of local schools to develop programmatic ties with tech entrepreneurs. City colleges and universities were facing increasing pressure to upgrade their efforts at applied tech research and to develop ties to business. NYSIA and policy institutes such as the Center for an Urban Future had especially focused on the untapped potential of the massive CUNY system. The system operated twenty-three campuses—ranging from community colleges to the Graduate Center—and employed 6,000 full-time faculty to teach 200,000 students. The CUNY Graduate Center, known for its liberal arts, law, and business curriculums, began to invest in technology teaching and research facilities. In a joint venture with NYSIA, the Grad Center created the CUNY Institute for Software Development and Design. A vice-chancellor remarked, "We're looking to quickly become a major center for software design and development."[49] Other schools also became more active. For example, Polytechnic University (an engineering school in Brooklyn) made a $25 million investment in computer science and engineering in order to "redefine the role of a technological university in a global city," in the words of its president.[50]

Science and education were hardly the only considerations. The director of the Media Research Lab at New York University reported that the Internet stock boom had altered the mindset of his students: "Young people in this field think they should be millionaires."[51] This was especially true after Yahoo paid $12 million (in stock) for "Webcal"—a web calender that one of his students created in the lab. Stock market glory was also on the minds of university officials. In January 2000 a distance learning venture at New York University (NYUonline Inc) was thinking ahead to an IPO less than a year after it opened. An analyst at Credit Suisse First Boston advised that brand names in education (e.g., Columbia University, NYU) could be translated into sizeable online businesses.[52] Even community colleges aspired to be New Economy players. In 1999 the Borough of Manhattan Community College (BMCC) (a CUNY campus) joined with two venture capital units (Bear Stearns Constellation Ventures and the Psilos Group) and the NYCIF to create the New York Telemedia Accelerator (an incubator for start-ups in digital television and other digital media). The facility (in the shadow of the World Trade Center) supplied seed funding, office space, and services to "accelerate the growth of early stage companies focused on broadband content, enabling technologies and e-commerce applications" such as "video-on-demand."[53] In return, BMCC was to receive a 5 percent share in the project. This lead BMCC's president to embrace a new dream: "Let's say one of the companies becomes successful like Microsoft and we make a lot of money. We could be the only community college in the country not to have to charge tuition."[54]

NYCIF had an intimate role in lining up the Telemedia Accelerator deal and the facility became a linchpin in the fund's attempt to position itself as a broker in a new institutional ensemble linking universities, government, tech firms, and the financial sector. Using the accelerator as a template, NYCIF worked with four other CUNY colleges to devise similar partnerships and incubators fitting their respective strengths. Henry R. Kravis characterized the accelerator as a model for how to fill infrastructual gaps: "The Telemedia Accelerator is a model of the kind of infrastructure New York City needs to support her high tech entrepreneurs and to connect . . . educational institutions to businesses that are generating jobs in the new economy."[55]

For its part, CUNY proposed to use a share of the state's big new tech fund in order to "clone" the accelerator at its other campuses. CUNY's new chancellor— who had spearheaded tech-related reforms—noted, "We are breaking the boundaries between what separates people on a campus from the business community"; the head of NYCIF agreed that the accelerator "directly responds to the issue of CUNY having been . . . out of touch with the growth sectors of the city's economy."[56] NYCIF added that the facility would create opportunities for minority and poor students. A letter to the *New York Times* by the president of BMCC also echoed these sentiments (and those we heard earlier from NYSIA's president):

> CUNY has the potential to be the engine driving the economic development of the metropolitan region by applying its intellectual capital to stimulate growth in technology and by offering educational opportunities tailor-made to accommodate the needs of potential workers and the existing work force in the new economy. Universities can no longer afford to be quasi-monastic entities that exist at arm's length from the experience of working Americans.[57]

The punchline was that CUNY needed "engagement with the community" in the form of partnerships with business. In part, the rhetoric concerned CUNY's internal politics. Many faculty criticized the tech initiatives because they privileged applied over basic research. They also feared that academic integrity would be compromised by a mission to serve business and gain access to equity. Ironically, they also thought that the CUNY system was developing a stronger central authority as it reorganized for the New Economy—supposedly a hierarchy-adverse domain.[58]

VENTURE CAPITAL RULES

The objections of the CUNY faculty to being commercialized raises a fundamental question about the New Economy's (not-so) long march across the institutions: Given the New Economy's new rules, what sort of rules were now supposed to govern noneconomic spheres such as government and education? Or to use the lingo of sociologists, What rules, norms, and sensibilities were to guide social behavior? The evidence we have seen thus far suggests that "venture capital rules" were fast becoming a new "master logic" for institutions. A broad range of actors tried to emulate venture capitalists as they invested careers, business futures, public budgets, and intellectual assets on behalf of the new media. In essence, the venture capitalist role model suggested that an investor could become a rational actor through developing inside ties (and privileged access to information) that allowed them to manage their risks. The carriers of the model were the media, various business professionals, and venture capitalists themselves. It seemed difficult for any other logic to stand up against the venture capital rules.

This was illustrated vividly in the effort of Flatiron Partners to institute a new approach to philanthropy that it termed "social entrepreneurship in the new economy."[59] On April 3, 2000, the firm announced that it had set aside $5 million to start up the Flatiron Fund and the Flatiron Foundation. The fund was a venture fund for for-profit enterprises that have "socially redeeming goals." Examples might include businesses that have a "social mission" such as

> helping children become prepared for life in a digital society; educating and encouraging entrepreneurship among minorities, women, and others with less traditional access to capital; and finding ways to encourage new and experienced entrepreneurs to turn their attention to social problems.[60]

The Flatiron Foundation would use "the disciplines of a venture capitalist" in funding nonprofits; Jerry Colonna noted, "We normally need to see a five-or-ten times return in order to invest. This fund can invest in things that only have a potential for a 2-X return if they are good for society."[61]

As was often the case with New Economy players, Flatiron set forth its program as a model. Fred Wilson commented, "a lot of people copied us" when Flatiron set up its original fund and "now we're saying that social entrepreneurship will be big, and we hope even more people will follow suit."[62] Flatiron offered to help entrepreneurs start their own foundations. More basically, it proposed to help nonprofits become more self-sustaining through placing entrepreneurs and venture capitalists on their boards and using tactics of the venture capital world, such as "syndicate" funding (organizing a group of investors). Colonna implied social entrepreneurship would redistribute New Economy wealth; it was a way to "harness this new economy to give back."[63] Since the program was also a means to address social problems, it seemed to grasp for core roles played by the public domain.

Flatiron had proved beyond a doubt that it could profit tremendously from entrepreneurship. As of April 3, 2000, when Flatiron announced its philanthropic initiative, the fund had cleared a profit of $3 billion, which meant that the partners had made somewhere around $600 million if they received the usual 20 percent cut.[64] However, before two weeks had passed, serious doubts had been raised about whether New Economy entrepreneurship had been of much benefit to the new media industry—or even to many entrepreneurs who *had been* rich on paper.

THE ETHIC THING

Ever since Max Weber wrote *The Protestant Ethic and the Spirit of Capitalism*,[65] sociologists have found it difficult to refrain from trying to identify the ethos that supported the rise of some new epoch (they also have trouble resisting the impulse to identify the emergence of new epochs). Although most observers now are more skeptical that the New Economy circa 1999 represented the onset of epochal change, it is useful to ponder the core cultural impulses that drove the New Economy as we knew it at its zenith. Indeed, the reception of the public to this ethical foundation may provide a hint about the New Economy's long-term staying power (or lack thereof) as a general institutional foundation. Moreover, this provides an opportunity to assess claims made about the progressive nature of the Silicon Alley version (recall the narrative of Jason Calacanis).

In his epic, three-volume, account of the rise of an "Informational Society"[66] Manuel Castells cites "creative destruction" as its ethical foundation, a notion that sounds like the way academics talk rather than New Economy activists and participants. Closer to the action, Andrew Rasie (founder of the Digital Club Network) commented on the Silicon Alley ethos: Money was "secondary to how much of a change agent [you can] be," which was related to the sense "that you're smarter than the rest of society, that the rest of the society doesn't get it."[67] But though that weathered notion still may have mattered for staking claims to status within the enclave's social circles, the domain for change agents had shifted to the financial sector by 1999. The New Economy crowned its heroes in the stock market. And, at the high tide, much was imagined of how the wealth they won might filter down, as the extension of the industry transformed the boroughs and various institutional spheres in ways that would benefit the rest of us. But stripped of technotrappings, the base ideology had a familiar ring.

For Whom the (Closing) Bell Tolls

Rituals often provide a glimpse of core norms and beliefs, especially when they involve moments when people genuinely seem to lose themselves, such as the ecstasies of spiritual possession in a religious ceremony or the equally exotic ritual that we witnessed over and over on the evening news in the late 1990s—the moment when a group of visiting notables rang the closing bell for the NYSE and the group—along with the ever-present Richard Grassio (president of the stock exchange)—broke into rabid applause and wild grins. What had possessed these worldly Americans?

What sticks out is the fundamentalist quality of New Economy culture—more specifically, three strands of fundamentalism: the market fundamentalism that surges in Anglo-American capitalism from time to time; a renewed faith in technology (with hints of millenarian fervor); and a resurgent nationalism—a mythic America *uber alles*—that Ronald Reagan helped bring front and center.[68] In the eyes of many, the wonderous dot-com stock market signalled that it was morning in America again. Michael Deaver, Ronald Reagan's former deputy chief of staff, remarked that the Gipper's "optimistic message of individuality, distrust of government and reliance on markets undoubtedly would make him a dot-commer."[69] (Deaver did not indicate whether Reagan might have worked for Pseudo or perhaps been a "fish" at Razorfish.)

The 1990s—which were supposed to be an era of technological "convergence"—saw a convergence of a more ideological nature. Neoliberalism morphed. The stock market was supposedly "democratized." American capitalism with its emphasis on free markets, entrepreneurism, and risk was deemed "real" capitalism—not only by free market extremists but also by the Clinton administration as it tried to force neoliberalism on other countries. In a 2000 interview by the New Economy magazine *Red Herring* (appropriately entitled "Charles Darwin, meet Adam Smith)," Treasury Secretary Summers not only wove together Darwinism and free markets, but also added American culture and the stock market exploits of tech entrepreneurs:

> Evolution is an "invisible hand" process . . . it inclines one toward a set of policies that support . . . a lot of different people trying to do a lot of different things rather than . . . laying out a blueprint for the future. We're the only country in the world where you can raise your first $100 million before you buy your first suit. That's a cultural strength of our country and a reflection of our courts and laws.[70]

It no longer seemed so odd that Alan Greenspan, a former acolyte of free market fundamentalist Ayn Rand, had become the New Economy's head oracle. Indeed, many Silicon Alley philosophes had graduated from Foucault to Ayn Rand. When the *New York Times* asked a panel of Silicon Alley stars who their "model" was, iVillage's Candice Carpenter cited Rand as a "champion of capitalism" while DoubleClick's Kevin O'Connor revealed that Rand's "philosophy of capitalism and the individual is just how we pretty much run the company."[71] Henry R. Kravis—notorious corporate raider of the 1980s, respected civic father in the 1990s—was the hero for Razorfish's Jeff Dachis, who liked to describe himself as a "brutal capitalist." Another ethical touchstone was the question of why one had become one of the elect. Dachis, as befits a brutal capitalist and dance major, nimbly sidestepped the issue of whether he was worth a couple of hundred million dollars:

> I don't want to be lumped in with the hucksters of the world, because we have the real deal. I feel completely and utterly entitled to whatever success comes our way. Not everybody's good, not everybody has the winning idea, not every idea deserves to be funded or to be public. I'm sorry, but there are sheep and there are shepherds, and I fancy myself to be the latter.[72]

Other members were mostly mystified by their inclusion in the elect, although they seemed to think they were in alignment with larger forces. Candice Carpenter remarked, "For some reason, some number of people have been tapped on the shoulder, like 'you're going to be part of this thing that is going to be born. There is nothing that's going to stop this . . . trans-formation." Though it might have sounded as if she had been touched by an angel, Carpenter clarified that the higher power she walked with was American culture: "The risk of walking away from what's known and guar-anteed and starting over in one room that you're sharing with eight people, in retrospect, looks like no big deal. But when you do it, you're taking a big risk. Our culture happens to reward that behavior, which is one reason it's a great country." It was the magic of perfect market alignment for Fer-nando Espuelas—"we win when the stockholder wins and not otherwise, which is a perfect alignment of value." Kevin O'Connor did not know why he was worth a billion but, in the face of irrepressible forces, he managed to face the fact with serenity and acceptance: "Am I working a million times more than or smarter than someone else? No. Am I overpaid? No. It is what it is."[73]

Of course, Silicon Alley also retained a "liberal wing"—which takes us back to the Flatiron Partners, proponents of government support for tech businesses—and social entrepreneurship to take care of the disadvantaged. Colonna and Wilson and many prominent Silicon Alley figures were big supporters of the Democratic Party. For instance, a Silicon Alley fund-raiser for Hillary Clinton's senatorial race raised $750,000, with the tab ranging from $1,000 to $25,000 a head. Colonna and Wilson hosted the event along with Kevin Ryan of DoubleClick and Jeff Dachis of Razor-fish.[74] Which raises the question, How much distance separated New Econ-omy liberals and conservatives during the 1990s?[75]

What does stand out is the disjuncture between the lofty intentions to spread the wealth and the reality of financial sector domination (with its dog-eat-dog approach to life) and the reigning free market ideology (neo-liberalism). Many New Yorkers certainly seemed to "get it"—the yawning gap between the geeked up ideology and the reality—and they did not much care for it. Though the media never seemed to tire of the New Econ-omy story, there was a lot about its tenor that repelled a great many New Yorkers—the superficiality, the self-satisfaction, the excess—especially when it was embodied in the persons of digerati who acted as if they really thought that they were smarter, more creative, and more worthy—instead of merely being the benefactors of insider ties during a speculative stock market. Not to mention the fact that most residents were left out of the ex-plosion of wealth. The Internal Revenue Service reported that 75 percent of the capital gains earned during the boom accrued to just the richest 2 percent of New York taxpayers. The rest of us, a *New York Magazine* writer commented, have often felt "like hired help at a dot-com launch party."[76] At any rate, the ascension of the dot-com elect did not go over well with many in New York—as evidenced by the three hundred plus responses that came in when, at the end of January 2000, a *New York Times* column posed the question, "What do you call a dot-com lout?" The responses included: "technotrash, dot-compost, e-coli, cyberscum, barbarians at the portal, World Wide Weasels, netjerks." The winning entry was unprintable. Two runner-ups—"I.P.Oaf" and "Cyboor" were defined thusly:

> *I.P.Oaf*: A foolish or graceless person who has been suddenly enriched by the initial public offering . . . a member of the Internet nouveau riche, a parvenu faulted for conspicuous consumption, poor taste or overbearing manners.

> *Cyboor*: A rude, stupid or arrogant person seeking to profit from commerce on the Internet, esp. one regarded as undeserving of wealth or esteem.[77]

One dot-commer offered a spirited retort to the contest: "I bet the Neanderthal on seeing the approach of Homo sapiens thought they were pretty damned rude. Tough." However, it was his kind whose moment in time was just about up.

CHAPTER 6

SILICON ALLEY UNPLUGGED

The growth we've see in the industry is going to keep up at the same pace.
That's what our deal flow is telling us.
—President of New York City Economic Development Corp., March 2000[1]

If there really were a dot-com crash, it should have slowed the New York economy. . . .
The sector's prospects remain reasonably bright, as do those for the city.
—*Crain's*, July 2000[2]

With the pending merger of entertainment giant Time Warner and the
8,000-pound Internet gorilla that is AOL, Silicon Alley took the first significant
step toward fulfilling its potential as the center of the new New Economy.
—*Silicon Alley Reporter*, January 2001[3]

In January 2000 the new and old media worlds were rocked by the news that AOL and Time Warner would merge into one company. The deal was the climax of the new media's rise and the ultimate use of New Economy currency. An Internet upstart would use its stock to buy out the world's preeminent old media power. For some observers the deal clarified Silicon Alley's destiny and the likely exit for its firms—to hook up with some new sort of hybrid corporation.

Many commentators saw the merger as giving AOL a huge advantage—Time Warner's vast supply of "content" properties. In various ways, the new situation would benefit Silicon Alley. Both New Economy firms (e.g., Yahoo) and Old Economy firms (News Corp., Sony, AT&T) would have to add rich content components (or augment their offerings) to remain in contention. Silicon Alley's content producers could take advantage if they hooked up with a "real world" firm to gain a major distribution outlet. Corporations would acquire smaller Silicon Alley firms. And AOL Time Warner could use its cable system to expand broadband access, spurring demand for rich new media programming created by Silicon Alley firms such as Push Media Group, ACTV, Pseudo Progams, BigStar Entertainment and thoughtbubble.[4]

Broader opinion on the merger was mixed. *The Industry Standard* called the deal a "bombshell" that signalled "the end of the Internet as an alternative realm outside the bounds of traditional media."[5] The positive view was that this was "a brilliant innovation—the best of both worlds, now working in tandem." The merger would "allow for previously unimaginable combinations of video and interactivity."[6] To critics, the concentration of control that would result suggested an old media conglomerate. AOL Time Warner would own six of the top fifteen most-trafficked news and information sites on the Internet. Besides antitrust concerns, there were questions about the new firm's strategic course and the balance of power between the two groups of executives. AOL stockholders were shocked (but not awed). The merger with an old media firm threatened AOL's New Economy pedigree and the prospects for "rocketlike" growth. They were skeptical that a "corporate ship with 80,000 deckhands and decades of corporate baggage" would be able to "sail on Internet time."[7] The deal also would dilute their stock value. Even though AOL's market cap was 20 percent higher, Time Warner shareholders would get 1.5 shares in the new firm for every 1 share of Time Warner; the ratio for AOL stockholders was 1 to 1.

Thus, the New Economy's biggest deal bore a big contradiction: One of its champions was taking over an old media power; yet, its leaders had agreed that its currency was worth 50 percent less than that of the old media conglomerate. Was AOL conquering new domains or cashing in while it still could?

One is tempted to find in the AOL deal (or some other news in early 2000) the lethal blow that did in the bull market—that punctured investor enthusiasm and the stock bubble. Such news may have contributed, but it was unlikely (by itself) to cause a decisive turn. The boom had withstood negative evidence before. I propose that New Economy narratives still dominated until the New Economy investment gambit was undone by its signature success—producing Internet IPOs while allowing insiders to cash in. When the supply of new IPOs swelled in early 2000 at the same time that insiders were cashing in en masse on previous IPOs, it destabilized the market. Wild rises and drops in stock values—and a rash of media exposés that followed—eroded the hold of New Economy narratives on investors; the ensuing market crash set in motion a slow erosion of Silicon Alley rather than an immediate unraveling.

The severing of the lifeline to financial capital created a crisis—especially for the national contenders. Yet, Silicon Alley proved rather resilient. The momentum produced by the New Economy lasted well after the market crash. And new media entrepreneurs hoped they would be asked to take the revolution into hybrid giants such as AOL Time Warner—the heir apparents of the new media.

To Believe and Believe Not

Economics offers little help in understanding why investors and others embraced the New Economy in the face of conflicting evidence—and then apparently "lost faith" in early 2000. Economists can only advise us to have faith in markets, which they claim are driven by calculations of individuals who weigh information on the relative merits of various courses of action and then choose one that will maximize their benefits. This heroic portrait of individual rationality rests on a dubious assumption: masses of individuals have access to adequate information.

On the surface, many of the new media people seemed to have the right stuff to live up to the expectations of economists. They appeared responsive to market developments as evidenced by their flexibility and aptitude for reinvention. They also dutifully positioned themselves to get strategic access to information. For their part, ordinary investors could closely monitor the new financial news—or Internet chat rooms—gaining unprecedented access to information. However, the value of responsiveness and positioning to assorted participants was derived from certain expectations and beliefs that they held (in whole or in part): New rules and new kinds of firms were supplanting old versions, some new firms would be able to create and dominate profitable new markets, and other new firms had a good chance of being bought out by the winners. What needs explaining, is why these expectations and beliefs held up in the face of very ambiguous evidence.

Sociologists show that one's attention can be directed to certain aspects of a situation (rather than others) and that preexisting categories determine what is learned (and not learned). Individual perceptions do not reflect exposure to information in some direct fashion (as economists would have it). They are mediated through systems of classification, representation, or interpretation that organizations (or sets of organizations) provide members.[8] Recall the promotion of business models by intermediaries who aspired to be New Economy players in Silicon Alley—a process that resembled a social mobilization. Sociologist Paul DiMaggio proposes that collective mobilizations are factors in the rise of "optimistic expectations" that drive stock speculation. When investors lack information they may still invest if a collective mobilization provides them with a narrative that leads them to believe that the market is likely to rise—and that *people like them* can reap the rewards.[9] We have seen that New Economy narratives did precisely this.

Why did New Economy narratives prove to be so resilient even in the face of contradictory evidence? Michael Piore proposes that a group that is organized around some narrative—be it at the level of a district or a national movement—acts in ways that can be interpreted along the lines of that story. A narrative provides them with both a means to interpret past events and acts (including their own) and "a template for future action"; the "constant repetition on all sides" of such storylines "gives them their power."[10] Ambiguous developments that arise in the normal course of events can be dealt with, without causing a breakdown in the narrative— or even bringing conscious reflection. If ambiguities become intense enough, a breakdown may occur that leads them to reconsider the framework that guides them. Otherwise, people have a stake in narratives that link them to others. A narrative helps the group to make sense of itself and assures individuals of the coherence of the actions that they have taken.

Interactions among New Economy participants may well have bolstered the hold of these narratives—and their optimism. Sociologist Randall Collins argues that if people engage in "ritual" interactions that reaffirm their shared identity and their standing as "equals," it tends to create energy and optimism.[11] This is an intriguing lead. New Economy doctrine announced the end of hierarchy in general and the "democratization" of the workplace and the stock market. And ritual interactions based on New Economy norms and identities were common (events, parties). Investors could have somewhat analogous experiences. IPO "road shows" that played to institutional investors (and the allocations underwriters set aside for them) signalled that they too were insiders. Allocations stoked their enthusiasm through providing material benefit and by suggesting that reciprocity existed between them and bankers. And though ordinary investors were in disadvantaged positions, unbeknownst to them, they too could also join in rituals that helped them feel like "equals" and "insiders." These interactions were of a more virtual nature—chat room encounters with fans of particular firms and "tipsters" as well as access to inside "tips" by analysts appearing in the financial media.

NOTHING BUT NET (LOSSES)

A burgeoning stream of New Economy buzz built up to support waves of investment in Internet IPOs and stocks through the end of the 1990s. Skeptical or negative assessments—and even exposés—surfaced in the media alongside the New Economy buzz, but punctured neither the spirit of participants nor the stock bubble.

In part, the ebb and flow reflected the weaving and bobbing of analysts and other "experts" who worked market peaks and troughs to channel whatever momentum could be summoned up. On the basis of a *Crain's* article in September 1997 one might have thought that the heyday of Internet IPOs was over. It reported that investment banks were backing only the most promising candidates for IPOs. An analyst proclaimed, "These companies cannot go public anymore based on just expectations. Investors want a clear idea of where profits will come from."[12]

More damaging potentially were exposés. A flurry of exposés appeared in 1998 as stock values plummeted and several dozen firms that had filed for IPOs stood paralyzed on the sidelines. An editorial in @NY complained,

> For too long, investors have bought the vision of a mythical digital Oz, a friction-free market place where even the slightest hint of a viable business plan will bring riches in the form of stock gains, not corporate profits. Egged on by venture capitalists, institutional investors, and day-traders alike all looking for maximum return in the shortest possible time, companies have made their single-minded goal raising money and going public.[13]

When EarthWeb and theglobe.com—two obscure firms—broke the drought, it fueled further critical commentary. *Crain's* November 16, 1998, report ("Up in Smoke") accused Silicon Alley firms and Wall Street of running "Ponzi" (pyramid) schemes. The subheadings were telling: "Gold Rush Attracts New Age Opportunists," "Wall Street Earns Its Bucks Promoting CyberSchlock," "It's Always Possible to Find Another Sucker." Regarding the start-ups it stated, "No one had a clue as to whether the ideas were viable" but "those in the know are happy to live off of investors' Microsoft fantasies."[14] Long a cheerleader, *Crain's* now raised doubts about stars such as DoubleClick, StarMedia, RareMedium, and iVillage: "With unproven technologies and half-baked business models, a generation of technophiles has received vast sums of money because venture capitalists, who would have required exacting credentials of any fledgling manufacturer or retailer, have applied few of the standard tests when it comes to new media."[15] Yet, after this special report, *Crain's* returned to its previous posture, using the New Economy storyline to frame the new media as New York's new engine.

Negative evidence and analysis that occasionally surfaced in the media hardly slowed up the New Economy bandwagon. Indeed, the unending New Economy buzz prevailed. Moreover, apologists could give plausible explanations for the uneasiness of skeptics—they still clung to Old Economy rules. Note, for example, the letter that NYNMA's head sent to *Crain's* after the "Up in Smoke" story.

> What's described in the article is . . . what happens when new technology-based industries are built. Market share is valued over profitability. . . . The

> stock market, recognizing the huge potential, reacts by placing bets. Failures occur . . . but . . . wealth is created for the regions that give rise to these firms. Think, for example, the PC [personal computer] industry and its impact on Silicon Valley. That industry was founded by twenty-somethings . . . Michael Dell, Bill Gates, Steve Jobs and Steve Wozniak, and produced—along with risk . . . and failure—the largest legal creation of wealth in the history of [the United States].[16]

The president of the Alliance for Downtown also responded. His letter blended New Economy values with fundamental values of *American-style* financial capitalism.

> Wall Street's—indeed New York's—role as the nation's financial center was due . . . to financiers and investors with big dreams who were willing to take chances on new ideas. . . . I doubt that J. P. Morgan is rolling over in his grave. . . . He and others whose vision and daring established this country as the most powerful economic power in the world are enthusiastically applauding the fact that the firms they established are now financing the new information age.[17]

Celebrity owners and CEOs used New Economy sensibilities to deflect skeptics and neutralize bad news—especially as losses soared (see appendix C). Kevin O'Connor claimed the market had given DoubleClick a mandate to spend its way to the top:

> It's clear what the market's telling us. They want to give us a lot of money, so we take it and invest . . . what was the biggest mistake that we made? We should have invested even more money. We should have lost more money . . . this is the biggest thing that's ever hit. Market share is everything.[18]

(DON'T) DRINK YOUR KOOL-AIDE

Just as the common view is that irrational beliefs set up investors for a fall, one might think that the new media—transfixed by New Economy beliefs—walked in lockstep toward the precipice. However, Silicon Alley was not sociologically vulnerable to the failure of a single set of beliefs. Workers, for example, did not walk away en masse when investors did. The fatal flaw of most national contenders was their failure to develop a means to create commercial applications of the Internet that could pay for themselves. Certain New Economy norms played a role in weakening their focus on applications, but only as they were reinforced by material arrangements—namely, the intertwined circuits of capital and buzz. Regardless of whether firm owners believed in these norms (they often did not), they were under great pressure to conform to them in order to gain credibility.

The cultural tapesty that held together Silicon Alley drew on a variety of sources. The respective subcultures of different groups (managers, creatives, techs) drew on some elements of New Economy doctrine, and not others. Andrew Ross reports that even in firms with strong cultures, workers keep their own cultural space and a critical distance: According to a Razorfish worker he interviewed, "We practice cynicism to the point of rejecting whatever we have been spoon-fed, whatever we have been programmed to believe about how workplaces are supposed to be, including our own management's version."[19]

In fact, developing a tentative understanding among different occupational groups was the defining problem in making new media applications. Monique Girard and David Stark note that the creation of a website design, for example, required ongoing negotiation and compromise to resolve (for a time) differences among the disciplines involved (e.g., software engineers, web designers, marketing specialists).[20] Work groups did resolve such tensions to some degree (websites did get built). Yet, this tension reflected a serious faultline: Silicon Alley firms strained to reconcile the innovative impulse with the need to make commercial applications. An executive commented that the firms do "a really good job at . . . coming up with an idea that seems novel" and at "creating a whole buzz"[21] but are not as good at applying ideas. One manager blamed the ethos of Silicon Alley workers. They "are interested in what's hot—trends, skills, content—not in the people they work with or the impact of the project. . . . They care so little about the business that they don't even see the need to justify 'neat' projects in terms of a business rationale, or to provide a reason for the costs expended."[22]

However, many executives were slow to take on the problem of reconciling creative and business concerns. An ex-Razorfish worker recalled a meeting where the firm's founders once asked, "What should we change?" Some workers said, "We have so many clients. We aren't really selective. We need fun clients. Cool Clients."[23] Another ex-"fish" commented that the firm sometimes "fired" clients. "You would have 22-year-olds walking out of meetings because clients didn't 'get it.' " The firm did not exercise much control over costs. The first worker recalled, "One time our manager comes out and says, 'we just got the budget. We got three times what we need. What kind of stuff do you want to get?' " This was an invitation to put in orders for expensive toys. The second saw evidence of haphazard staffing: "I wondered about the different roles that people had. What do they do? Do they really have to be on the team? I'm not sure some of them were working. They were playing Quake a lot."[24]

Part of the problem was that rapid growth at firms like Razorfish disrupted the culture and teams they depended on. For example, a former worker noted that after Razorfish acquired i-Cube, its straightlaced workers were stunned by an over-the-top Razorfish party in Las Vegas: "The i-Cube people were scared shitless. They wondered if they sold the company to lunatics."[25] The situation was worse at some firms that jumped into the new media business without having experienced people. Take, for example, the case of 360hiphop.com. A Silicon Alley vet who was recruited to serve as an editor at the firm, was dismayed by what he found: "Everybody who was there was from print or the financial sector. Few people there knew what a website was about." Money was blindly thrown into the venture. The result could not have been further from the vision of the lean, nimble start-up. 360hiphop "employed 80 people to do one content site . . . the site never worked properly. It was the biggest piece of shit. It was the Titanic." Discouraged from hitching their future to one firm, workers had little reason to care much. He noted, "I was so excited by the money" but could see it would end: "There was no accountability, no structure. . . . I got paid for doing nothing for 8 months. I would show up at noon. Have lunch. Check my e-mail at 1:00. Surf the web, hang out in the lounge. Work a little. Go to the bar."[26] One of the former Razorfish employees also remarked, "I saw things that were wrong but ignored it. . . . My attitude was, it didn't matter if they were making money if I was making money."[27] An ex-"fish" also complained about a lack of recognition:

> During the high point, when there was a focus on all the money, the people you were reading about were all in management. It wasn't the people that made code. The real Silicon Alley is a bunch of sweatshops with underpaid people doing HTML. Anybody who does code doesn't get any glory, status, money. All the managers that were running around, they didn't even use the Internet.[28]

Razorfish, he said, tried "to build a cult around the idea of global domination through the Internet. They wanted you to drink the Kool-Aide. My friends and I used to always say, 'Don't drink the Kool-Aide.'"[29]

BOUNCING A VIRTUAL MARKET

At the start of 2000 some analysts were reportedly "cracking down" on Internet start-ups. Henry Blodget had chided Amazon.com and its peers, stating that they should commit to a "path to profitability"—a course of action that ended at a date when they would report profits.[30] And firms could no longer count on cheap capital courtesy of the Fed; Alan Greenspan had proclaimed that he intended to slow the economy so as to ward off the threat of inflation. By February 24, 2000, the Fed had raised interest rates four times in eight months. Yet, the flow of positive buzz (and money) was still going as strong as ever. DoubleClick hosted a Willy Wonka party at the Roxy in January 2000: Purple-skinned go-go girls held the stage while orange-skinned OOmpa-Loompa bartenders served two thousand guests amidst towers of candy and creme-filled boulders. UBO announced its "arrival" with a $100,000 bash on Ellis Island for three thousand people. As of mid-March 2000 the year's IPOs were averaging 100 percent gains in the first day of trading compared to 60 percent gains in 1999.[31] A total of eighty-four IPOs had filed to go public by April. Most dramatically, the NASDAQ Index went above 5,000 on March 9, little more than four months after it first pushed past 3,000. A March 10 story in the *New York Times* noted that while other stocks were falling (in the aftermath of a Fed hike) "the enthusiasm for the 'new economy,' dominated by the Internet, has only increased."[32] Under pressure from investors, mutual funds were shifting more funds to tech stocks. An investment strategist commented, "Given the fact that I don't see the end in sight, I don't think they are being foolish."[33]

What then, rocked (and ultimately sunk) the boat? The factor that contributed most was escalating stock volatility rooted in the structure of the market itself. The wild swings in stock values, *Red Herring* reported, were due to a "virtual market" structure: There was, and had always been, a basic imbalance between the number of Internet stock sellers and buyers. At the start of the boom many people were eager to buy Internet stock but few Internet start-ups existed to sell it. And firms that did go public often issued a small supply of stock, so as to engineer a spectacular rise in its stock value on the opening day of their IPO. Insiders (e.g., venture capitalists and firm executives) held on to most of the stock.[34] In early 2000 at least some industry insiders feared that a big increase in the supply of Internet stock— there were somewhere between two hundred and three hundred Internet IPOs depending on how you define the category—was probably going to cause a big drop in share prices. For example, a hedge fund manager commented in January 2000: "A year ago we were actually talking about a shortage of Internet stocks. Well, the investment bankers have taken care of that, and now there are too many. There is going to be a shakeout in the whole sector."[35] A huge secondary effect of the 1999 IPO wave loomed: The six-month "lock up" period would end for insiders, allowing them to sell their stock. On March 19, 2000, the *New York Times* reported that 2.4 billion shares of stock from IPOs held in 1999 would be free to enter the market over April, May, and June 2000. This amount was more than twice the number of stocks trading in those firms.[36]

Big increases in the supply of Internet stock roiled the stock market even as the NASDAQ hit its all-time high (5132) on March 19, 2000. From 1988 to 2000 there was a total of ten days when the NASDAQ index closed with a gain or loss of at least 3 percent; by March 10 2000, there had already been twelve such days (six big gains, six big losses) during the year.[37] A growing series of dizzying drops and rises in market valuations inspired several exposés that had a new bite. Paul Krugman, in his March 12 *New York Times* column, said the market for tech stocks was like an "accidental Ponzi scheme."[38] Critics soon went further, striving (like Toto) to pull back the curtain and reveal the machinery behind the wizardry. A cover story in the March 20 issue of *Fortune* skewered entrepreneurs, venture capitalists, and investment banks, accusing them of consciously creating Ponzi schemes.[39] *BusinessWeek* released its cover story on the "Wall Street Hype Machine" on April 3.[40] That same day the NASDAQ lost 7.64 percent of its value. On April 4 ("Seesaw Tuesay") the NASDAQ, at one point, was down 575 points (13 percent of its total value); it then bounced up 500 points.[41] On April 7 it went up 4.19 percent. *Barron's* dropped a bomb at the start of a week that ended with the New Economy's version of Black Friday (April 14): It listed Internet firms with their rate of expenditure, their remaining cash reserves, and the estimated date when they would go bankrupt if no further money was forthcoming. The NASDAQ lost 7.06 percent of its value on April 12 and another 9.67 percent on April 14 (the worst loss since 1987). Overall, the NASDAQ had lost 34 percent of its value since its March 10 high. The market rallied 6.57 percent on April 17, but this proved to be the last hurrah.[42] The seesaw ride left investors with a queasy feeling: People would now surely worry that market momentum could give out at any time—and if suddenly no one was willing to buy, you would helplessly watch your holdings melt away.

UNPLUGGED

A new storyline emerged in Silicon Alley after the crash: Firms were now exposed to "the market," but the resulting purging would be healthy for individual firms and the district. The reality proved to be much more harsh. The NASDAQ's value fell from $6.7 trillion on March 10, 2000, to $3.2 trillion a year later—a loss of $3.5 trillion (52.3 percent).[43] Silicon Alley stocks took an even steeper dive. However, for much of the rest of the year the district was buffered by continued venture capital spending and New York's still-healthy economy. Silicon Alley's circuits seemed to be intact.

Exposed

Before the dust had settled from the crash, assorted experts issued their take on the new reality. An April 17 *New York Times* story quoted venture capitalists, executives, and economists as saying a healthy culling of the Internet herd was underway. A venture capitalist remarked, "It will mean we have two or three Web sites selling pet supplies instead of seven. That's hardly a loss."[44] *At New York* was almost giddy. It noted, "So much of what we call Silicon Alley had more to do with the buying and selling of money than with innovation"; the crash had killed off a market that "seemed like an infected vestigial organ" that had "leaked weakened companies and corrupted the body." Firms now would have time to develop ideas and venture capitalists would be able to act like "smart money."

Now think of the scores of real innovators hard at work in Silicon Alley and around the world, busily planning the next stage in the digital transformation of the planet, an era that has at least a generation yet to run. They went to work today with a jump in their step, jazzed by the innovation itself . . .[45]

The healthy shake-out storyline continued through the summer even as lay-offs began. A *New York Times* story on June 22 quoted an economist as stating, "The industry is doing well by any economic measure. This is a company phenomenon, not an industry-wide or economy-wide phenomenon."[46]

While many of the star firms were shielded (for a time) by big cash reserves, big reputations, or big partners, market exposure proved to be more corrosive for some of Silicon Alley's more problematic champions. As of July 10 eight firms, including theglobe.com, were in danger of being "delisted" from the NASDAQ: Their share prices had sunk below or near $1 a share. GSV (Cybershop) was the first to receive a warning: It would be delisted if, by September 10, its stock did not trade at least at $1 for ten consecutive trading days.[47]

However, the district's circuits of capital and buzz seemed to be adjusting. Venture capitalists were still investing money at a near-record pace. Nationally, $26.8 billion in venture capital was invested in the first quarter of 2000; despite the crash, the amount invested in the second quarter increased to $27.8 billion, and reached $26 billion in the third quarter.[48] In New York, the amount invested in the second quarter—$1.1 billion—was just below the first quarter total of $1.4 billion—but still above the fourth quarter in 1999 ($984 million). Wit SoundView Ventures raised $270 million for its Dawntreader II Fund in April; VenRock Associates raised $800 million in July.[49] Venture capitalists did subject their portfolio firms and new prospects to a new critical scrutiny. A venture capitalist advised, "The mantra today is 'path to profitability.' "[50] Firms were pressured to identify how they could at least break even by the end of 2001. Venture capitalists also began to perform "triage" on portfolios, cutting off from further assistance firms that seemed destined to be "losers."

The New York New Media Association—trying to change (or salvage) the image of the new media—published the finding of a minisurvey in January 2001 showing that 56 percent of its members had been profitable in 2000 while 18 percent broke even; firms expressed optimism about the future and 75 percent expected a profit in 2001.[51] In line with NYNMA's back to basics theme, *Crain's* added that "The bulk of Alley companies are small, self-funded Web content developers and design firms that essentially need to make money to survive."[52] While this was true, the standing of content firms was severely damaged by the deepening dot-com debacle. Venture capitalists moved away from e-commerce and content firms to firms that were doing something requiring more technological expertise such as software or infrastructure.

The buzz apparatus quickly shifted the spotlight. A partner at Price-waterhouseCoopers technology practice remarked, "Silicon Alley started out as the content capital of the world, but now New York is getting on the map in other technology areas."[53] A *Crain's* story also announced the sea change: "As dot-com fever has broken, and many of the more delirious business plans have succumbed to reality, a new and healthier layer of the Internet economy has been revealed in Silicon Alley: companies that develop software which performs useful functions."[54] For a time, firms and rainmakers tried to organize around "wireless" firms—thought to be the next new thing. In June 2000 Flatiron announced it would invest $100 million to $150 million in wireless firms over the year. The *New York Times* touted New York as "the nation's center for wireless Internet applications, financing and advertising," noting that "much of Silicon Alley is recasting itself in a wireless role." It added, "The New York wireless scene is buzzing so much that an online magazine has been created to cover it all" (*Unstrung*); Nokia's venture investment arm announced plans to set up an office in New York, with one of its principals stating, "New York is getting hot very quickly." A discussion on the wireless Internet hosted by NYNMA in July drew 1,100 (with hundreds turned away at the door). The director of Ericsson's Cyberlab stressed New York's new centrality in the area, because of its strength in services. Among the budding stars was Vindigo, a wireless firm (Flatiron's stable) that provided maps and information from restaurant guides and the like for use on portable devices (e.g., Palm handhelds). Silicon Alley firms such as Razorfish and Agency.com expanded their wireless operations in New York. The head of Agency's mobile business for Europe remarked, "we're ready to promote a knowledge bleed from London to New York because this is where the action is."[55]

Bodies in Motion

The sunny tone carried over to the subject of new media layoffs. Many new media firms continued hiring through the summer. The lack of alarm was on display in a *New York Times* story on June 22. It featured a large photo of a windswept young blonde sitting on a pier, with San Francisco Bay providing a glorious blue backdrop. She was, the caption said, a laid-off employee of Third Age Media who viewed her layoff an "an extended vacation." In the text she remarked, "I would imagine that if I want a job at the end of the next week, I'd have one."[56] A *Crain's* story at the time stressed the ease with which laid-off Silicon Alley workers were being recycled. One worker, who lost a job when Brandwise.com folded in May, was hired as a manager at Clickthebutton.com after only one month of looking for a job. She exclaimed, "If you have experience in the Internet space, people just start calling you."[57] The "people" in question—recruiters—were just as much a feature in the story as the job seekers. The recruiters advised new media workers to think about a new job before the pink slips started; one now needed to subject prospective employers to more scrutiny—a chore that strategically positioned recruiters could help with.

One recruiter hit upon a novel means for connecting with laid-off new media workers—hosting a "pink slip" party at a Silicon Alley watering hole. About thirty people came to the first party organized in June by Hired Guns (a "New Economy Outsourcing Company"). In true Silicon Alley fashion, Hired Guns linked its gathering to the party circuit and fanned perceptions that it was a hot spot—sending out e-mails to one thousand people warning that those carrying pink slips would get first priority to enter. It later instituted color-coding for everybody: glowing pink armbands for the unemployed, green for recruiters, and blue for everyone else. At a pink slip bash held in December 2000, forty-five recruiters showed up—along with five camera crews representing ABC, CNN, and stations from Germany, Italy, and Japan.[58]

Even in early 2001, when the crisis of the new media industry had hit with full force, the city's robust economy seemed capable of absorbing unemployed new media workers. Observers noted that the supply of workers let go by the new media was a boon for other sectors who once had been priced out. Now nonprofits, the public sector, and a wide range of businesses could hire skilled technology workers at discount prices.

THE URGE TO PURGE

On September 18, 2000, Pseudo closed, leaving 175 workers without jobs and stunning Silicon Alley. Several other content producers closed shortly thereafter: iCast (219 jobs lost) and APBnews.com (140 jobs lost). UBO, the anchor firm for the Digital NYC enclave in Harlem, closed (300 jobs lost) just as it was to move in.

The shutdowns, especially of Pseudo, ratcheted up the sense of crisis. They also intensified the "purging" impulse, drawing out—from all quarters it seemed—proposals for what needed to be excised. Some Silicon Alley veterans eulogized Pseudo as an avant-garde enterprise. One noted, "They imagined a world where programming wasn't just spoon fed to the viewing public but instead involved the viewer's active participation."[59] The *Silicon Alley Daily* was sympathetic, but added, Pseudo "has always been more about buzz than product."[60] Most observers called for a break with the past. Another story in the *Silicon Alley Daily* asserted "Silicon Alley . . . is a whole new industry. Fiscal responsibility and corporate pragmatism are now more important than trailblazing, and a cool idea no longer passes for a business plan. In the new business landscape, there's no room for a Pseudo."[61] The consensus of "Alley experts," *At New York* reported, was that a "glut" of content producers called for "the cool efficiency of dot-com Darwinism."[62] Some assailed Pseudo as embodying all that was excessive about Silicon Alley. The *New York Times* depicted Pseudo as a refuge where children of the middle class went to escape and smoke marijuana "for lunch"—and snort coke "for supper": "you didn't really have to work. You surfed the Net. In the office, there was an electric water pipe that five people could smoke at once. It was the way out of their fathers' 9-to-5 work world. Then there were those options that would be worth millions when some witless investor took the bait." The reporter tracked down two dazed refugees. One (now playing music in the subway) said, "We were making art"; a second, a former art director (found in a bar trying to forget about his worthless stock options) recalled, "It was wild and the Wall Street suits would come to the parties and get high and write us a check in the morning. We ate from the trough of the venture capitalist pigs. . . . It's over. Now I'm crawling back to the corporate dog bowl."[63]

The creative rank-and-file vented their own views about who or what needed to be purged: mercenary managers, vapid New Economy visions, and middle-age bourgeois opportunists. The rhetoric heated up on the Netslaves website (Disobey.com) as layoffs hit in July 2000. On July 2 one of the founders of the site posted a fierce criticism of "clueless, abusive bosses" and "horrid working conditions": "Between the quick buck artists and the business plan from hell folks, a lot of people have been screwed. They're tired of the false friendly and the forced conviviality. After work parties and dogs in the office do not make up for 18 hour days and crazy bosses."[64] An August 3, 2000, posting on the site (by "Disgusted") presented something of a "Creatives" manifesto that savaged both managers and "the techs":

> Most of the . . . creatives are smart enough not to buy into stock option, get rich quick nonsense . . . it's just that they can make a . . . living designing web pages as opposed to working as print designers or freelance artists. . . . Project managers are . . . shitheads. They treat the "creatives" like children and have disdain for them. . . . These are the people who buy into the dot-com, yuppie, beamer [as in BMW] new economy bullshit. . . . The techs are in [a] world of their own . . . many of them are arrogant little fuckers who think they're better than the creatives.[65]

After the defunct Pseudo had been ridiculed in some press accounts, the *Silicon Alley Daily* published a "rant" by Mike Rinzel, a writer/musician who had worked for Pseudo from the early days. It was a classic Silicon Alley narrative, drawing on the sensibilities of "Generation X" creative types. He blasted the baby boom ("Boomer") generation as the perpetrators of the

New Economy and encouraged his "Xer" peers to resist the Slacker persona, even as it seemed a lot like 1992: "You may start seeing the word 'slacker' banded about the media again. But don't buy into it. It's just a code word to cover up another Boomer spectacle: dot-com fallout." He contrasted the shallow concerns of the Boomer bourgeoise and the creative impulse of firms who "were the cultural story of New York in the '90s":

> In the end, all of the creative Xer Power we harnessed was crushed by the pomp and circumstance of Boomers, urging us to spend big, burn fast, roar like lions. Build something huge! . . . But they did a 180, all bailing out when their 401(k)s took a hit in April. Boomer VCs snapped shut their wallets. . . . Wall Street Boomers were no longer sweet on the newly IPOed. Boomer managers showed their true colors all over the Alley—hacking staffs and dismantling many companies in arbitrary attempts to make their flawed business models work. . . . The ones out on their asses? Xers . . .[66]

THE PATH TO PROFITABILITY (DEATH MARCH)

The continuing slide in the stock market hit Silicon Alley's firms especially hard. The combined value of stocks in the "Alley Fund"—a composite of forty-six Silicon Alley firms that were publicly traded—fell from $1,519 in January 2000 to only $276 by the end of October 2000—a drop of over 80 percent.[67] The carnage at some leading firms was remarkable. On its IPO day in March 1999 iVillage had boasted a peak price of $113 a share; by October of 2000 the value had plummeted to $2.09 a share. Other firms had similar drops: DoubleClick fell from $249 to $14.50; About.com from $90 to $26; Razorfish from $96 to $4.44; RareMedium from $80 to $5.03.[68] Earning statements for 2000 did nothing to improve investor opinions. Losses soared as advertising in general was slipping into a depression, and firms lost the business of other troubled dot-coms. Whereas thirty-seven public firms in Silicon Alley lost a combined $433.4 million in 1999, their combined net loss in 2000 was almost $3 billion; nine of the firms lost over $100 million (see appendix C).

Silicon Alley's national contenders faced increasing pressure to establish that they were "good corporate citizens" who could cut costs and find a "path to profitability." Many entered into a "call and response" relationship with Wall Street analysts who offered "advice" as well as ratings. Wall Street demanded cuts, and this—in combination with the worsening situation—caused Silicon Alley's thirty-seven national contenders to lay off over fifteen thousand during 2000.[69] The travails of iVillage, StarMedia, DoubleClick, and Razorfish offer a feel for the fiery reentry firms experienced after the crash. All four kept their eyes on the prize—becoming the leader in their market. They raced to hit "the black" before rivals did—or before their capital gave out. As the four firms (like battered wagon trains) pushed across an increasingly desolate landscape, they jettisoned all sorts of "excess" baggage: workers, business models, and celebrity founders.

Of the four firms, iVillage began the quest in the most problematic position. Racked by high losses (over $116 million in 1999) and turmoil in the executive ranks, it hired a new president in 2000—a cable veteran who had helped launch the Lifetime network. He proposed to pitch iVillage to advertisers as a lower cost alternative to cable TV, which was becoming pricey.[70] In July 2000 he became CEO, replacing Candice Carpenter, who became one of the first founders to hop overboard so that their firm could signal that it had broken with the "old" days. Though iVillage's stock price sunk to $2.00 a share, it managed to outlast its rival—Women.com from San Francisco—whose stock had fallen to 70 cents a share and was facing delisting. In a February 2001 merger iVillage absorbed its rival. Hearst Corporation, owner of 46 percent of women.com, agreed to commit $40 million to a new combined company while iVillage paid $27 million (in stock) to women.com investors.[71] Serious cost-cutting soon followed. iVillage had a work force of 450 in July 2000; in June 2001 it announced plans to reduce the combined work forces of the two firms to just under 200, hoping to reduce expenses by $25 million to $35 million by the end of 2001.[72]

As the new media crisis worsened in September 2000 StarMedia became one of the first major Silicon Alley firms to use staff cuts to signal its "responsiveness" to Wall Street. It cut 125 workers in "nonessential positions"—as designated by a consulting firm brought in for the occasion. Though its share price had sunk to $10 and it faced a bevy of serious rivals (AOL Latin America and major firms from Brazil, Argentina, Mexico, and Spain), analysts responded to the cuts with strong ratings.[73] However, as time passed Wall Street became concerned about the firm's intension to remain independent. Analysts were afraid that StarMedia would miss out on an opportunity to sell out to a big firm, and they doubted that the firm had enough cash to last until it could become profitable. StarMedia claimed that a booming online ad market in Latin America would help it break even by the end of 2001. A simpatico analyst who gave the firm an "outperform" rating advised, that regardless, the firm had lots of room left to cut costs.[74] StarMedia took the hint, but disaster ensued. In May it laid off 25 percent of its staff in an effort to break even by the end of 2001; service cuts caused it to lose millions of users. On August 8, 2001, with the share price down to 60 cents, Fernando Espuelas (a co-founder) stepped down as CEO.[75]

Of all of Silicon Alley's national contenders DoubleClick had the most muscle to make good on the pretensions. Besides being the leader in the advertising network category and possessing a fair amount of technologi-cal expertise, it also was blessed with massive cash reserves: $900 million (as of December 2000). And DoubleClick still could use its stock to make acquisitions. In buying @plan (a market research firm) in September 2000, it used its stock to pay for 80 percent of the $120 million price tag.[76] Dou-bleClick was also willing to make bold moves to keep its image as robust as its bank account: One of its co-founders was eased out in the summer of 2000. In December 2000 DoubleClick was again keen to make a gesture to Wall Street: Dot-coms accounted for half of the revenue in its main business, and its share price had sunk to $12.19. It decided to lay off some-where between 150 to 170 of its 2,100 workers.[77] When online ad revenue continued to free fall through mid-2001, DoubleClick made decisive moves to shift away from its media business toward more technological pursuits. It became a major force in e-mail marketing, delivering 2 billion e-mails a day for 250 publishers. As of July 11, 2001, its share price was $10.87 (and it had $814 million in cash).[78]

After the crash Razorfish's over-the-top image loomed as a handicap; so did the bulk it put on just before the crash as it expanded in anticipation of a big rise in business. For some, Razorfish was only marginally less outra-geous than Pseudo. Razorfish became the poster child for New York new media firms that possessed more attitude than expertise. In December 2000 *The Economist* remarked, "The flashing web designs that were the hallmark of 'nose-ring' New York firms such as Razorfish are now seen as slow and confusing. Yahoo's credo of fast, functional and boring has won the day."[79]

The corporate world presented a two-edged challenge to web service start-ups like Razorfish: on the one hand, their corporate customers were sharply cutting back on technology expenditures; on the other hand, the big consulting firms and giants such as IBM were now competing for their business. Razorfish was one of the few national contenders to have made a profit. But, in December 2000 it noted that it would suffer a big loss due to a large drop-off in revenue. Its share price ($1.84) stood in stark contrast to its work force—one thousand nine hundred employees at fifteen offices around the world. Final totals for 2000 would show that the firm had lost $148 million. However, the firm founders—having begrudgingly laid off two hundred workers in October 2000—fended off Wall Street's demands that they cut more. Andrew Ross provides a rich account of what followed. Analysts attacked, questioning the firm's future. CEO Jeff Dachis assem-bled the New York employees and reaffirmed the firm's vision. "We're a company, not a stock, and we're playing to win the revolution, not the stock market. This . . . is a company of true believers."[80] But in February 2001 they gave in, laying off four hundred to start a reorganization and "rebranding" effort. When "fish" complained that the culture was being eroded, "they were told that the old culture was out of synch with what clients wanted ... features of the ... past profile—'cooler-than-thou,' 'Bleeding edge,' 'downtown New York'—were regarded as exclusionary and intimidating. . . ."[81] Yet, its stock continued to slide. With the share price at $1.22 on May 4, 2001, co-founders Jeff Dachis and Craig Kanarick left. The ritual sacrifice did not suffice. By July 25, 2001, Razorfish faced delisting with a share price of only 49 cents. It cut down to only 670 workers by August 15, 2001. The end of the trail loomed. At the close of the second quarter—a period in which it had burned through $15 million—Razorfish had only $15.1 million in cash left.[82]

Embracing the E-Vile Empire

As their situations worsened, new media firms felt increasing pressure to find some means to connect with corporations. The locus for new media enterprise—and for the deconstructionist impulse—shifted evermore toward the corporate world.

Plan B (Back into the Matrix)

As stock market ties gave way so too did the idea that new media start-ups could dominate some market niche as "first-movers" who were free of Old Economy ties. A new notion dominated the "buzz" in the Silicon Alley circuit: To make headway a start-up had to position itself to fit into the market webs of corporate giants. A July 2000 issue of *Crain's* advised, "To even have a shot at succeeding, web content initiatives require the involvement of established media players as well as a cross-media strategy."[83] Thus, at the same time that APBnews.com was shuting down, Court TV launched a "crime news and entertainment" site—Crime.com—which it could promote on its cable network while making use of the Court TV video library; it also hired the producer from the TV show *Cops*. Many speakers at the "Silicon Alley Uptown" conference held at Columbia University in November 2000 stated that corporations would be at the center of new media industry. At a panel discussion ("The Path to Profitability") a partner at a consulting firm claimed that the "Internet-only" model made sense in only a few situations. More likely was a "hybrid online-offline" model dominated by large firms: "Old Economy firms," he advised, "will adapt to change, absorb Internet firms, or put them out of business." He added, "Plenty of New Economy firms . . . will survive but they will be marginal. . . . They will have enough profits to keep only 12 or 14 employees."[84]

At the "Alley Talks" conference at New York University in March 2001 the managing director of the Dawntreader Fund noted, "venture capital as we all knew it is dead," but there was a possibility that "venture capitalists may start to act as R&D for corporations." Corporations "are no longer dinosaurs. They can turn on a dime. You can't target them and say they are slow-moving."[85] The big firms were also in mind when NYNMA convened its "State of the New York New Media" panel in January 2001. A Ziff Davis executive proposed that, "A lot of people came into the business for the wrong reason—to try to escape corporations for the 'safety' of entrepreneurialism." Buoyed by AOL Time Warner's announcement that it would locate its headquarters in Manhattan, she commented, "they will take charge" and local firms will feed in their wake.[86] The founder of About.com said the merger showed that new media entrepreneurs could take the revolution inside big firms: "How AOL operates their company is fast, crisp, decisive. . . . Many people with entrepreneurial zest will bring that to traditional corporations. They will be intrapreneurs. Time Warner works at half the pace of AOL. They will have to catch up. We can use Internet energy in New York corporations."[87] Jerry Colonna added that the type of skills that were now important for the new media were those of "people who know how to run a business lean, mean, fast."[88]

Now the best evidence of one's credibility was that corporations wanted to connect with you. IBM set up a Silicon Alley center for its e-consulting unit: Wanting to cultivate start-ups that might turn into major customers, the center's director proclaimed, "It's up to me and my team to get into the fabric of Silicon Alley."[89] High-profile acquistions by corporations raised hopes that a few of the tarnished national contenders could take a second path to New Economy riches. A watershed was Primedia's October 2000 announcement that it planned to swap stock worth $690 million to acquire About.com. Primedia owned over 220 magazines and had revenue of $1.7 billion in 1999.[90] Primedia's main investor (the leverage-buy-out firm run by Henry R. Kravis) had directed it to take a digital leap. Though About.com's revenue was only $27 million, it was one of Silicon Alley's top prospects: It was the seventh most-visited website and had $133 million in cash (and no debt). *Crain's* noted that Silicon Alley firms with "the best chance of surviving as stand-alone businesses" might end up "trading their independence for the comforting embrace and deep pockets of large corporations."[91]

The rising fortunes of SonicNet founder Nicholas Butterworth also spoke of the rewards of becoming part of a corporate empire. MTV bought SonicNet in May 1999, but his playing field extended much further as MTV's parent was corporate giant Viacom. He became head of MTVi—an entity that integrated Viacom's online sites (MTV.com, VH1.com, Sonic-Net)—and SonicNet became a linchpin in Viacom's larger plans to develop "convergent content" across its online and offline units. Viacom's president claimed that it would become "the first 21st century media company" on the basis of its "brands . . . world-class content . . . and the best distribution system in the business in both the established and the new media."[92] By March 2001 Butterworth was integrating cable channels with Internet sites: The hope was that viewers of a cable program such as MTV's *Total Request Live* would use MTV.com to contact each other through "instant messaging" or to download music.[93]

The news in January 2001 that AOL Time Warner would locate its headquarters in Rockefeller Center had special importance. At a time when fifteen Silicon Alley firms were in danger of delisting, enclave boosters proclaimed that it had gained a new heavyweight champion and renewed credibility. *Silicon Alley Reporter* exclaimed that AOL was a new media company about which "analysts and [mutual] fund managers remain bullish . . . the 8,000 pound Internet gorilla."[94] Silicon Alley now had King Kong on its side.

Imagine You Watching Me Watching You

What exactly was being absorbed into the corporate body? Was the new media still alive in some sense or was it toddling along Zombielike in the corporate ranks? These questions raise a further question: Just what is (was) the essence of the new media? We might revisit one of the pioneers, Josh Harris, who in Pseudo's early days seemed to have a feel for the "soul" of the new media in all its messiness, unpredictability, and willingness to let people try things. After Pseudo's demise Josh Harris outfitted his SoHo loft with thirty-two motion-sensitive webcams and thirty microphones and broadcast 24/7 on a website—Weliveinpublic.com—that was available to paid subscribers. Harris asked America, "Is it better to live in public, or is it better to live in private?" A question he raised about the project itself seemed directed to new media observers: "Is it art? Or is it a business?"[95] The high/low point came when Senator Charles Schumer hosted a virtual town meeting in the loft in February 2001. While the unsuspecting senator spoke about the virtues of technology in the New York economy, a bathroom "toilet cam" turned on to reveal someone urinating. Soon thereafter, Harris shut down the operation and announced plans to relocate upstate to grow (and barcode) apples.

Perhaps Weliveinpublic was Harris's farewell gift to Silicon Alley or maybe like many of his creations it was a self-indulgent parody. But perhaps one reason that Pseudo was so gleefully maligned in the press was that it embodied the new media's challenge to mainstream media: *As the technological potential for interactivity increases, how does the self-consciousness of the media user become part of the experience?* A few media firms such as MTVi have begun some very tentative and limited experiments, but for the most part, the media's answer has been to *simulate interactivity* as a sort of branding exercise. When Pseudo held its first SoHo event in 1994, NBC Today opened the first TV studio exposed to the street; but while Pseudo was probing the intersections of media space and real space, NBC Today turned the sidewalks at Rockefeller Center into a pedestrian photo op (in both senses of the word).

At the end of the 1990s, media giants began to cluster in Times Square to set up studios open to the street. The area now hosts, among others, Reuters' new U.S. headquarters, ABC's Times Square Studios, NASDAQ's MarketSite Tower, and MTV's studios. Silicon Alley has representatives on the edge of the ensemble: About.com is next to CondeNet (Conde Nast's digital unit), as is the studio of eYada.com (an online talk radio network). The main agenda is to tap the "branding potential" of having a live audience. During MTV's *Total Request Live*, the camera turns to crowds of kids who mass below the studio window so they can see some celebrity guest wave to them. MarketSite, NASDAQ's chairman avows, embodies the exchange's "ideals to be digital, global, and investor-focused."[96] Its tower gives a "public face" to NASDAQ, which actually has no trading floor. Residing inside the facility are the studios of CNNfn and CNBC. An eight-story-tall video screen on the outside provides passersby with financial news (and allows the networks to broadcast images of people checking out a digital ticker).

Times Square promoters tout it as a "hot" spot where the confluence of people produces the unexpected. But its new digital features add little substance to the interaction. Times Square mostly simulates an interactive space by combining new digital signage with big media sensibilities (photo ops, branding). Silicon Alley did lend some imagery to this landscape. For starters, the interiors of new offices in the area often bear Silicon Alley's mark. Max Capital (landlord for About.com and CondeNet) has used a design sensibility labeled "vintage Silicon Alley" or "Post-Alley Modern" to remodel its properties; an architect reports that CondeNet likes the idea that its space could "make it look like an Internet company, to be less corporate and more casual . . . un-Dilbert-like."[97] Its "showpiece" office essentially simulates a Silicon Alley loft: It features "oddly angled walls, burnished steel columns, exposed ceilings" with "hidden blue lights placed around the ceiling's perimeter" to "highlight the pipes and wires running along it." Max Capital's president remarks that the financial firms he wants to attract are also interested in dot-com style—"casual dress, open layouts, and sleek spaces." And he contends that Silicon Alley actually inspired the "new Times Square style—a hip mix of financial, entertainment, and publishing businesses . . . a melting pot of New York industries." The *Silicon Alley Daily* interpreted this to mean that, "New York is no longer made up of individual neighborhoods dedicated to specific industries."[98]

While Times Square may have incorporated the enclave's deconstructionist spirit (at least superficially), it was clear that the power of Silicon Alley's images—like that of its entrepreneurs—increasingly hinged on their usefulness to the master deconstructionists of American society: the corporate giants.

A year after Silicon Alley had been unplugged from the IPO machine (the Great Wheel of the New Economy) one could still claim it was a site for making history. Until the quest for profitability turned into a death march for many of its champions, it was still possible to think that New York's new media heroes were reaching for the golden ring—but now from a seat provided by some corporate King Kong. As corporate ensembles absorbed elements of Silicon Alley, the January 2001 *Silicon Alley Reporter* hinted at the district's reincarnation. While its cover dramatized the fall of the old Silicon Alley with the classic photo of the Hindenburg's fiery demise, the issue also announced a phoenix arising from the ashes of the New Economy: with AOL Time Warner's headquarters in New York, "Silicon Alley's upper border is now Rockefeller Center."[99] Woven into the fabric of corporate Manhattan, the digital district reached from Rockefeller's trophy complex in Midtown's northern end, to the monument, to the family's postindustrial vision that anchored Lower Manhattan—the World Trade Center.

CHAPTER 7
CREATIVITY UNBOUND
(AND REFRAMED?)

*Places like Silicon Alley captured and fermented the energies, resources, aspirations of the
moment, but they were not built for the ages.*
—Andrew Ross, 2003[1]

*The real opportunity . . . is to help Lower Manhattan become the protypical hub of the
21st Century by accelerating its natural evolution from a center of global financial innovation to a place that feeds creative growth across the region.*
—Richard Florida, July 2002[2]

*As industries with hipster cred—music, fashion, publishing—winnow their ranks,
young, creative New Yorkers are wondering if the jobs they
moved to the city for have disappeared forever.*
—Ethan Brown, March 2003[3]

I caught a glimpse of New Economy ruins on a March 2001 visit to a darkened SoHo office vacated by Razorfish. It was as if I had entered one of
those tombs built for Chinese emperors and that were filled with rows of
terra-cotta soldiers. In this case, the "soldiers" were long gone, but their
presence was commemorated by rows of $3,000 office chairs and $1,000
tables. A polyethylene sheet marked with some sort of conceptual art was
stretched between pillars—an undecipherable relic of a vanished people.
The careers of pricey office spaces as tombs for imperial illusions were
brief—most were soon pulled back into the light by New York's pulsating
market for commercial real estate. Much the same was true in the residential market where not-so-edgy professionals replaced new media casual-
ties. *New York Magazine* offered a vivid account of one apartment-hunter's
encounter with a "pallid" dot-com refugee in February 2001 in an East Village dwelling: "he was sitting in his home office in the dark, his shades

pulled down. He was wearing a dot-com t-shirt and surrounded by derelict computers. He was drinking wine in the dark at like two in the afternoon."[4]

The real estate boom had begun sweeping creative types out of parts of Manhattan before the crash. Between 1996 and 2001 real estate prices and rents exploded in the traditional bohemian havens: In the East Village, lofts that had sold for between $500,000 to $600,000 now sold for $900,000 to $1.1 million; studios/one-bedroom apartments in SoHo that had rented for $2,500 to $3,500 per month now were $4,000 to $5,000; and in Chelsea lofts that could be rented for $3,500 to $4,500 in 1996 ranged from $6,500 to $11,000.[5] *New York Magazine* observed that the "values" of upscale Manhattan had begun to "permeate every neighborhood and make them all somehow the same."[6] After an influx of couples and young professionals into Greenwich Village, the only "true artsy people" left were NYU students with rich parents; the gentrification of Chelsea's gay enclave (one realtor's motto was "A Castle for Every Queen")—left it "not-so-gay"; Lower East Side "punk-bohos" were replaced by "people who don't want to be called yuppies but are yuppies"; and middle-age professionals who once would have settled in the Upper East Side flocked to Tribeca's textile warehouses (with high ceilings!).[7]

The New Economy tsunami also rolled on across commercial real estate in New York. Even as the fall of Pseudo and other firms rocked Silicon Alley in late 2000, large firms were fiercely competing for spaces to use as "urban campuses." In particular, financial giants—which had been farming their back-office functions to Connecticut, New Jersey, and even Texas—were now anxious to create "corporate corridors" in the city. When a firm vacated a fifty-one–story building in Midtown the suitors for the space included Chase Manhattan (which had just acquired J. P. Morgan), UBS A.G. (a Swiss financial giant that had just acquired the PaineWebber Group), the Canadian Imperial Bank of Commerce, and Deutsche Bank; also interested were technology firms such as Bloomberg and Cisco. In fact, corporations were turning prime spots into campuses all over Manhattan: Morgan Stanley had one on the edge of Times Square (three skyscrapers) while Goldman Sachs used a half-dozen buildings Downtown; Credit Suisse First Bank was starting a campus near the Flatiron Building. Telecommunications had made it easier than ever to conduct business at a distance, but the *New York Times* noted, firms "are suddenly putting a premium on old-fashioned, face-to-face meetings, boardroom brainstorming and water cooler chitchat." A real estate executive advised, "Campuses are the . . . solution if you believe there is a value to bringing together all your intellectual capital within walking distance."[8]

As global city theorist Saskia Sassen has observed, "Strategic, creative activities—whether economic, cultural or political—thrive on density."[9]

No plot of land in the world hosted more density than the World Trade Center. In 1999 it housed 1,170 establishments (807 in the financial or insurance sectors) employing 34,000.[10] Now a hot item, the World Trade Center was leased in July 2001 to an investment group in a ninety-nine–year deal worth $3.2 billion. The facility, having once been overshadowed by Silicon Alley hype, was back on top of the world. Though few knew it, the center had even become a site for New Economy boundary-crossing: The strategic analysis of finance was being fused with that of national security.

Windows on the World

Even as Wall Street went into a downturn, there was little doubt that it still allowed New York to command the heights of the global economy. Moreover, the position of the United States as the world's only superpower (and its aggressive promotion of neoliberalism) extended the reach of New York and its financial ensemble.[11]

A new application opened up for Silicon Alley when Wall Street and the U.S. Navy began a joint effort to rethink the nature of security risks in a New Economy. In the late 1990s, Cantor Fitzgerald (the world's largest broker of U.S. government bonds, Eurobonds, and sovereign debt) joined the Naval War College to run a "New Role Sets" project—a set of workshops for members of "the global, financial and national security communities."[12] By 2000 Cantor Fitzgerald had passed the lead role to eSpeed—its electronic trading spin-off and Silicon Alley's only public firm in the Trade Center. Some workshops were held at the Naval War College in Rhode Island; others were hosted in the Windows on the World restauraunt perched on top of the Trade Center's Tower One. Among the goals were: "Explore how globalization and the rise of the New Economy" are influencing "how nation-states and national economic interests interact" and determine how these relations altered the context for international security. It was thought that international crises increasingly would involve overlapping problems of "geo-strategic" and "geo-economic" instability.[13] Wall Street's importance for strategic assessments of the global economy was reflected in the project emblem—a mercantor-style projection of the world backed by the looming silhouette of the Twin Towers.

A May 2001 project document proposed that one of the "biggest security trends of the globalization era" was occurring below the level of the nation-state: The threats posed by violence and arms purchases had "shifted downward."[14] One threat was internal to the West, as evidenced by Seattle's antiglobalization protests; another originated outside the West in the form of an "anti-Western rejection of the . . . homogenization fueled by globalization." The report noted, "In many societies, globalization is looked upon as forced Americanization."[15] The document specifically cited the "Asian values" position of several East Asian leaders who had criticized U.S. promotion of neoliberalism. A 1997 workshop posed a scenario that included "cyberterrorism" against Wall Street in combination with a disruption of communications with Southeast Asia.

The project was prescient. However, two books that appeared in 2000 and 2001—*Blowback* and *Networks and Netwars*—proved to be more so: They predicted that the United States would soon be engaged in warfare with international networks of terrorists from Islamic groups such as al-Qaeda.[16] Until September 2001 the threat remained academic. Despite a worsening economy Silicon Alley firms like eSpeed, who served the financial sector, could believe that the future would be good. Revenue at eSpeed tripled during 2000—from $38.2 million to $118.9 million; in February 2001 its share value stood at $31; the firm projected that when the third quarter ended (September 2001) it would report a profit.[17]

Though they did not quite discern its nature beforehand, it is possible that some eSpeed employees literally saw it coming—that they were sitting down to breakfast at Windows on the World, or at their desks on the 103rd floor of Tower One when the threat they had apprehended intellectually, materialized in terrible clarity—a jetliner barreling down the Hudson River straight at them.

THE TWO TOWERS

Silicon Alley partisans had wanted evidence confirming the mantra, "Everything has changed." But as an older saying goes, "Be careful what you wish for. You may get it." Maybe it was the first thought that popped into the minds of "listeners" who slept in after a late night and "tuned in" Silicon Alley Station (a web radio station) for news when the morning calm was shattered on September 11, 2001. The station's manager, who had been on business near the World Trade Center and was now covered in soot and nearly breathless, labored through a shocking live report:

> This is Silicon Alley Station. We are live on the scene at what is now turning out to be perhaps one of the worst disasters in American history. We just witnessed the collapse of the World Trade Center. The Trade Center was bombed by terrorist attack approximately 40 minutes ago . . . in a stunning and shocking . . . way the entire upper portion of the building collapsed. . . . People are in shock. Downtown Manhattan is in chaos. . . . [18]

The collapse of the towers killed nearly three thousand people, sending Lower Manhattan into a state of paralysis for months, and putting the economic future of New York City into doubt. The horror of the destruction dealt a staggering blow to the psyche. Part of the trauma was the terrible intimacy of impending doom as many trapped workers in the upper floors of the towers had time to call loved ones on their cell phones—at first reporting that they were safe, but later saying good-bye. Technology became a vehicle for a new sense of impotence. The day after, the *Silicon Alley Daily* gave a vivid illustration: the increasingly desperate reports of a trapped Cantor Fitzgerald worker to its LA office. "Cantor Fitzgerald staff in Los Angeles listened in horror as the tragic events unfolded at the New York office. 'I think a plane just hit us. . . . Somebody's got to help us. . . . We can't get out. . . . The place is filling with smoke.'" The call cut off shortly afterward.[19] The company, based on floors 101 to 105, lost over 600 employees; its eSpeed unit lost 180 in staff. The trauma of having borne the unbearable was still evident in 2003 when Agency.com's CEO Chan Suh noted that New York still felt like a target. "New Yorkers have taken a huge beating to our self-confidence and entrepreneurship. People are more reluctant to make decisions, launch something, get something started. We know New York is a focal point. . . . We know New York is a symbol."[20]

The attack destroyed or damaged over 29 million square feet of office space and cost some 138,000 jobs. The losses in the city economy were estimated to be $83 billon.[21] By March 2003 the combined job toll from the attack and a deepening recession was 223,000; the city's unemployment rate hit 9.3 percent in May 2003.[22] Brokerage firms were hard hit, laying off 23,000 by 2003,[23] but a study by the Center for the Urban Future reported damage across many other sectors: "The economic pain is being felt by a broad cross-section of the city's most important industries from New-Economy web designers and software developers to Old-Economy printers and apparel manufacturers."[24] The Downtown real estate market was devastated. Even with the loss of the Trade Center's 11 million square feet, its vacancy rate hit 16.8 percent by March 2003; if "shadow space" was included (unused space firms could not sublet) the vacancy rate would be 24 percent.[25] An Agency.com executive noted, "We're stuck with 150,000 sq ft. We probably need one-sixth of that."[26] Some 62,000 workers had left Downtown by January 2002; 27,000 of them had relocated to Midtown.[27]

The impact on Silicon Alley was heavy. NYSIA reported that 50 computer-related firms were displaced by the attacks. The Telemedia Accelerator's offices were destroyed when 7 World Trade Center collapsed on it. Many Silicon Alley firms were among the 3,200 firms (most of them small) that were crippled by being located in a "frozen zone" into which entry was restricted. They were also hit hard by the fact that corporate customers had been disrupted or moved. NYSIA mobilized dozens of public and private organizations to hold a "Relief, Rebuilding, and Recovery Community Meeting" for Silicon Alley on October 3, 2001. NYSIA's president declared, "The Silicon Alley community is an important part of the rebuilding process."[28]

But, the disaster delivered a lethal blow to hopes that anything resembling the old Silicon Alley would survive the end of the New Economy boom.

SILICON ALLEY UNRAVELED

The fall of our society's greatest towers, coming after the collapse of its grandest illusions, had the epic quality of myth. Having been hammered by serial disasters, many of Silicon Alley's maimed champions staggered to ends that were noteworthy for their pathos. Even corporate titans left the arena in disarray. In the wake of the rout, the district's unraveling began in earnest. The institutional ties and narratives that had keep everything lashed together began to quickly melt away, leaving the creatives exposed.

The Contenders Hit the Exits

Seven or eight Silicon Alley national contenders were on their way out before the Trade Center attack; in the year and a half following it, a dozen or so more of the firms exited (see appendix D). At last report theglobe.com, which closed its online community site in August 2001, was seeking a buyer for its online games—and was considering going into the real estate business. Agency.com did not exit the Internet business realm but it did exit the public market; it "went private" in October 2001 as a result of being acquired by Seneca Investments, which paid $147 million ($3.35 a share). Sometimes a big wad of New Economy currency stretched out a firm's demise. Media Metrix, which acquired Jupiter Communications for $414 million *in stock*, closed its own Media Metrix unit in June 2002 after selling its assets. In the spring of 2002 its Jupiter unit sold its online operations for $2 million and its patents for computer tracking for $15 million; it sold Jupiter Research and Jupiter Events for $250,000 and ceased being an independent firm on July 31, 2002. Sometimes the exit was fittingly absurd. InterWorld, once deemed Silicon Alley's best bet, was foreclosed in May 2002 by J Net Enterprises (its majority stakeholder), a Nevada holding company formerly known as Jackpot Enterprises—in its previous life servicing slot machines. It shopped InterWorld around in a last effort to find a new player (before cutting its losses).

Two of the four "stars" that were profiled in this book exited after the Trade Center attack—Razorfish and StarMedia. In July 2002, StarMedia sold its online assets for $8 million to Eres Mas Interactive (Spain); it changed its business model to "mobile solutions" (wireless), its name to Cyclelogic, and its address to Miami. In November 2002, Razorfish—the ultrahip icon whose stock had once been worth nearly $100 a share—was sold to a Utah firm for $8.2 million ($1.70 a share). Of a work force that once approached two thousand only two hundred remained. iVillage and DoubleClick did become the leaders in their categories. Even then, analysts still expected iVillage to be acquired (and were not sure about DoubleClick).

The possibility that Silicon Alley firms could prosper in the role of supplier to some large corporation dimmed (for the immediate future) as most of the giants stumbled in their Internet ventures. The end of voracious dot-com spending for online ads added to the woes of corporate Internet units. In 2001 CNN cut 130 of 750 jobs in its interactive division, NBCi axed 320 in a work force of 700, and News Corp. closed it digital unit—headquartered in Chelsea—throwing several hundred out of work.[29] Some giants, such as News Corp. and Microsoft, experienced setbacks in their Internet ventures but did not see their general competitive situation suffer.[30] With the exception of Viacom, most of the media giants who dreamed of "digital convergence" had a rude awakening. Primedia, which hoped its acquisition of about.com would help its share price approach that of dot-coms, saw its wishes come true—as dot-com values crashed. Its stock, which had hit a high of $34 a share before the acquisition, wallowed in the $2 range in 2002. The firm's late sprint to become digital, brought it to the brink of a break-up.[31] Bertelsmann fired its CEO (an Internet enthusiast) and sharply reduced its online units. Disney and Universal Vivendi's efforts to become New Economy content providers left them stalled (and Vivendi's "American-style" CEO sacked).

The New Economy's biggest deal—AOL's acquisition of Time Warner—turned out to be one of the era's signature scandals. It seems that somebody had been monkeying around with King Kong's books at the time that the merger was pending. As the advertising revenue for the new firm's AOL unit sagged, it wrote down its value by nearly $100 billion—conceding that the merger had grossly overvalued AOL. The top executives who had come from AOL (Steve Case and Robert Pittman) tendered resignations as the board began to question whether it made sense to have AOL as part of the company. The firm is now besieged with legal trouble.[32]

The Buzz Stops Here

Silicon Alley suffered another sort of unplugging as its media circuit flew apart. One by one, the purveyors of optimistic buzz fell out of the air like a fleet of lead balloons. The first to go was the district's flagship venture capitalist. Like a humbled child returning to live at home, Flatiron Partners left its Flatiron office in May 2001 to move in with its chief backer, J. P. Morgan Chase & Co. whose offices were located in Midtown. Flatiron reported that it had made the move to save millions of dollars in rent but it appeared that the bank had been behind the move; the *cumulative return* for the Flatiron Fund since its inception in 1996 had fallen from 400 percent in 2000 to 279 percent as of May 2001.[33] A return of 279 percent is a high rate—if you invested in 1996. The problems was that Flatiron's big backer (Chase) had doled out $500 million to the fund in 2000—meaning that it suffered huge losses as the stock market collapsed. Flatiron cut most of its staff and a year later *Fortune Small Business* called it a "trivial subset of Chase Capital Partners."[34] For its part, Chase Manhattan's efforts to become a New Economy player left it a "three-time loser." One analyst said, "I wouldn't let them run a hotdog stand."[35] Other players fared little better. Brobeck Phleger & Harrison—"Cisco's lawyer" and counsel for over a dozen of Silicon Alley's IPOs—declared bankruptcy in 2003.

Just as stunning was the demise of Silicon Alley's media. *At New York* sold out before the Trade Center attack, while *AlleyCat News* and *Silicon Alley Reporter* (*SAR*) folded just afterward. The closures were the result of a massive drop-off in technology advertising that savaged the major magazine publishers (and the national buzz circuit).[36] At *SAR*, for example, the number of advertisers fell from sixty-six in its December 1999 issue to thirteen in September 2001. In characteristic fashion Jason Calacanis (*SAR* founder and editor) declared victory, proposing that Silicon Alley had helped make Internet usage routine. He noted that the Internet industry was consolidating: "90 percent of the innovation in the Internet space is going to come from [the] top three or four companies (AOL, Yahoo, Microsoft)."[37] However, he conceded that the firms he had covered had been devastated: "The story's over. You can't have a magazine about unemployed people . . . about people who are taking time off."[38] He tried to soldier on with a new magazine that followed venture capital deals across the United States. However, the parent company for his publishing and event businesses was harmed by a steep drop in demand for pricey conferences and seminars. By 2003 it was $2 million in debt and up for sale.[39]

Adieu, Milieu

The framework linking creativity to new media enterprise continued to shrivel up as a range of Silicon Alley institutions collapsed or retrenched. To start with, the fledgling venture capital system in New York proved to be less resilient than those located elsewhere. In the first quarter of 2001, New York firms received nearly $1.5 billion in venture capital, which represented 11.5 percent of the U.S. total. After the Trade Center attack venture funding in the New York area fell from $752 million in the fourth quarter of 2001 to $413 million in the first quarter of 2002 (a drop of 43 percent); the $413 million represented only 6.6 percent of the total U.S. venture capital funding.[40] The nosedive in venture financing meant that otherwise healthy new media firms had difficulty adding employees to exploit demand for their services. For example, the founder of Vanguard Media (a web development firm) estimated that it was losing out on $500,000 in potential revenue because he could not procure the financing to hire four more programmers; a lack of money also caused Eric Goldberg (a long-time Silicon Alley participant and a NYNMA board member) to sell his wireless game company (Unplugged Games) to California interests. Despite his blue chip ties, and deals with five major wireless telephone carriers, New York venture capitalists would not support him. He complained that they didn't "get it" (the nature of tech cycles).[41]

Modest public funds set aside for the new media also evaporated. The city disbanded the $25 million Emerging Industry Fund—the final reincarnation of the idea first proposed in 1997—in late 2001 after having made only one loan. The funds were diverted to companies harmed by the Trade Center attack. The president of NYSIA lobbied (in vain) that the fund be revived, warning that "without this money, the companies won't grow" and the city "risks losing an industry and thousands of . . . high-paying jobs that lend diversity to the city's economy."[42] In fact, the turmoil from the Trade Center attack may have disrupted Silicon Alley's political ties, creating an opening for Michael Bloomberg to upset Mark Green—the heavy favorite to replace Mayor Giuliani and a major Silicon Alley ally.[43]

Public support slid on other fronts, including aid for university research facilities. In 2001 the state legislature denied CUNY's request for funding to develop four new incubators based on Telemedia Accelerator. It did later grant the request, but by then Telemedia Accelerator (still homeless) was on its last legs. The CEO of Telemedia Accelerator stated, "There's not a whole lot of interest on the part of the city in promoting (New York) as a place where entrepreneurs are welcome."[44] After struggling with insurers to recoup losses suffered when its space was destroyed, the Accelerator closed. City Hall's commitment to Digital NYC also seriously weakened—the president of the Economic Development Corporation expressed doubts at a City Council meeting that the program was an effective use of the city's limited funds.[45]

One of the most alarming trends was the downsizing of Silicon Alley's industry associations. The membership of NYNMA—which had soared to 8,500 in 2000—fell to less than 6,000 by early 2002. In April 2002 NYNMA was "acquired" by the Software and Information Industry Association (an international trade association based in Washington, DC). NYNMA did retain its own membership, board, name—and New York focus. NYSIA's standing rose somewhat as that of NYNMA dropped. However, its member firms were hard hit by a loss of business because of a growing crisis among their Wall Street customers. In response to these problems and the move of corporations (e.g., IBM, Accenture, and EDS) to compete for their customers, the smaller computer services made increasing use of outsourcing, sending some kinds of software development to overseas firms. Even NYSIA's president (the CEO of Information Builders Inc.) noted he was outsourcing because, "a guy in India is going to charge $25 an hour, compared with $125 an hour in the US."[46]

CREATIVITY UNBOUND

Brian Horey, the venture capitalist who helped found NYNMA, sounded an optimistic note in a November 2001 *Crain's* story. He proposed that New York now had "a core of people" who understood the methodology through which venture capitalists shepherded start-ups to rich payoffs. He said, "they will stick around to start the new wave of companies. Most of the human capital has stayed in New York, so that is a resource that's waiting in the wings for the next wave of start-ups."[47] However, it became increasingly problematic as to whether entrepreneurs or the rank-and-file would stay put: The frameworks that supported employment and entrepreneurship by creative types in New York had begun to disintegrate.

Will Work for Sushi

As New York's recession deepened, many creative and professional workers who had exploited a new fusion between major sectors found themselves disconnected from the labor market: The industries which had, during the boom, guzzled creatives like a hard drinker on a binge, were now "on the wagon." The dry spell provided a harsh reality check for the flexible work force minted during the New Economy.

Like workers discharged from corporations in the 1980s, New Economy workers found that what had counted previously as "skill" or desirable traits was not necessarily going to be valued. A former Razorfish manager commented, "A lot of the people weren't doing technology. A lot of the people in fields like marketing wasted their time. . . . A lot of people had no real skills."[48] He added that some people did gain "networks" that had value. Managing one's networks—a new imperative during the New Economy for the employed—remained one for the jobless. However, there was a limit to the degree to which good ties and, for that matter—flexibility—could make up for a bad economy.

As New York's economy worsened, especially on Wall Street, the outlook became dismal even for software programmers with experience in premium programs. In early 2003 NYSIA's president reported that ten thousand jobs at smaller tech firms had been lost as were at least another ten thousand IT jobs at large firms.[49] An online job matching service noted that in February 2002 it had only 4,600 openings listed in the New York area compared to 10,000 positions in February 2001; the pink slip parties were cut back to bimonthly affairs as headhunters found fewer jobs to recycle to new media folks.[50] And the reports from the struggles of professional-managerial types to find work were beginning to sound a lot like the experiences of blue-collar workers laid off in the early 1980s. A *New York Times* article in December 2002 profiled an executive (a 41-year-old woman) laid off from Razorfish in the wake of the Trade Center attack who was jobless a year later—despite spending fifty hours a week looking; she reported that half of her friends were unemployed. The Bureau of Labor Statistics showed that 49 percent of the people who had been unemployed for six months or more (as of October 2002) were white-collar workers—the highest proportion since it began to track groups in 1982.[51]

Much as extended spells of joblessness had eaten away at the work norms of workers displaced from corporations in the 1980s,[52] prolonged unemployment is now calling into question New Economy sensibilities about the virtues of flexibility and entrepreneurialism. An April 2003 issue of the *New York Times Sunday Magazine* entitled "Commute to Nowhere" gave a vivid protrait of the problems experienced by middle-age workers displaced from New Economy firms. It remarked, "out-of-work executives are being forced to rethink their professional identities, their personal relationships—and their most fundamental sense of who they are."[53] One of the men profiled ("Lou") expressed a hope to end up "in Denver or San Francisco—near good skiing and cycling—as the chief technology officer of a large company at an annual salary of $1 million."[54] Though this sounded like the footloose lover of amenities envisioned in creative city manifestos, Lou had been unemployed for two years when he offered this vision—and the setting was a gethired.com seminar run by a former "interactive marketing director" (who had been laid off by AOL). Thousands of other unemployed professionals belong to networking groups such as Financial Executives Networking Group (FENG), which offers social support, advice, and—it is hoped—ties that might lead to a job opening somewhere. There is a MENG for marketing types, TENG for tech types, and SENG for strategic executives. Members practice "elevator speeches" with each other (a brief pitch to a prospective employer) and bring three fresh job "leads" to the group a month. In the absence of real prospects, the air is ritualistic, as if FENGs, MENGs, and TENGs were networking cults. In fact, Vicki Smith's study of a job club for unemployed middle-class workers concluded, "Surrounding oneself with others who share an understanding of the public nature of one's personal problems creates a buffer between the unemployed individual and employed friends and family."[55] In contrast, a band of new media workers who faithfully attend events on the NYNMA circuit, trying to keep hope—and ties with working colleagues—alive, seem to be discouraged. A flustered middle-aged woman I encountered after a NYNMA event in mid-2001 noted that she had been unemployed for eleven months. This was the fifth job she had lost in ten years and added, "I know ten people like me." She feared she was "not marketable" because her "experience is so fragmented."

As was the case in the 1980s when some displaced workers futilely keep trying to get back into a big factory, some New Economy entrepreneurs are staying the course even as it eats away at everything they possess. Take, for example, the case of a 50-year-old Internet pioneer who had been laid off from his executive position in May 2001; six months later he had to file bankruptcy because he had amassed $100,000 in personal debt trying to get his own online business off the ground. A year later his wife told him to get a job or get out, and he took a job selling pants at a Gap Store. He recalled, "I had hit rock bottom. It was like I was addicted . . . I had to make a decision to start over."[56] Yet, he is now working on a proposal to show the Gap how it can use the Internet to create and maintain relationships with customers. The plan includes a pitch that he be put in charge:

> False modesty aside, my 18-plus years of senior digital marketing experience will likely surpass the aggregate digital experience of the top three individuals in any given interactive marketing agency or consultancy. Translation: substantially more bang for your interactive buck.[57]

Is this really the Brave New World of middle-age work? Or does this suggest that the new armies mustered by digital industries in the future will be composed of young people with fewer obligations? Actually, employment conditions for young New Yorkers more and more resemble those that spawned Generation X in the early 1990s. A *New York Magazine* article in March 2003 ("Generation Hexed") remarked, "It is the industries on life support—music, publishing, the Internet . . . that cloud much of the optimism for the young and unemployed in New York. These are the jobs that shape our sense of possibility, our sense that what we're doing can be done here and only here. And they're fast disappearing."[58] In March 2003 a 28-year-old online producer, who had lost his job in June 2002, reported, "I interviewed with one Website, and they said, 'We can get a college grad to do this for $20,000 a year' "; many of his friends "are treading water right now . . . we've realized that it's okay to postpone happiness for a while."[59] An ex-Razorfish manager (age 27) who has gone back to earn an MBA observed, "A couple of years ago we all expected to be getting 6-figure salaries. Now I would probably move to Boise for $70,000. I don't have any control over my job. I assume things will go downhill."[60] Another new media veteran lamented, "In light of September 11 there isn't the same feeling here. Emotionally and culturally its different. It feels different, grim. I would leave in a second if I could."[61]

End of (One) Story

As the crisis worsened there was growing uncertainty at gatherings about what the new media—and Silicon Alley—were really about. As more and more firms and signature institutions fell by the wayside, the discussion shifted to whether Silicon Alley was "dead" or not. The debate ended up being a matter of semantics, as there was a general consensus that many elements of Silicon Alley were no longer bound together in the ensemble that had been assembled during the 1990s, but were being incorporated into a broad spectrum of activities and industries.

A NYNMA "Town Hall Meeting" on the crisis in July 2001 revealed a fraying of the new media narrative. Participants debated whether "content" or technology was most important and whether a new media industry existed. Several said creativity had been undermined by money, implying that there was an opening for redemption. Kyle Shannon (Agency.com co-founder) recalled that in 1995 people participated "because of the excitement of what they could do. Then the money came in and changed the priorities. The Internet become 98 percent crap. . . ." Marisa Bowe (former *Word* editor) noted that New York was "the content capital of the US," but argued that money and big firms had undercut the new media spirit. "There is no longer interest in experiencing the medium. And big firms kept putting people in charge who did not love it. Now we're talking about content like it is a dead person on a table."[62] A journalist suggested that new media creativity now crossed the boundaries of different industries: Its not an industry. "It's a community that fuses all the other industries that are in New York—fashion, finance, advertising."[63] Some asked whether the larger role of corporations would hold back creativity. The president for AOL TV called for new conceptions of creativity: "We are going to enhance the experience of watching TV. . . . We have to learn how to monetarize it. It's a different kind of creativity."[64] An audience member asked, "Are we all going to be working for big companies? . . . If we went back to our passions . . ."

A month after the Trade Center attack, *At New York* addressed "Rumors of the Death of Silicon Alley." It proposed that Silicon Alley was becoming "woven into every sector that drives this city's economy." It also discussed the prospects for "biotechnology and nanotechnology research in the area."[65] At about the same time, *Crain's* asked, "What is Silicon Alley today, if anything?"[66] Having just closed *SAR* Jason Calacanis remarked, "Silicon Alley describes a moment in time from 1994 to 2001 when Internet companies were built, absorbed or went out of business." *Crain's* was more optimistic (it was still in business): The technology industry was changing dramatically but that "for now, the name seems to be sticking."[67] However, the currency of the Silicon Alley moniker rapidly declined thereafter. For example, IBM's service center dropped Silicon Alley from their name and in March 2002 DoubleClick took down its "DoubleClick Welcomes You to Silicon Alley" billboard. The *New York Times* ran a story entitled, "Silicon Alley: A Once-Evocative Name Falls Victim to the Bursting of the High-Tech Bubble." It declared, "It's now official. Silicon Alley, the district that presided over a thousand dot-com pies in the sky, is dead."[68]

In truth, the Silicon Alley that had minted New Economy stories (and heroes) was dead (or near dead); the buzz circuit that had promoted the name was defunct and the mainstream media found the name less and less meaningful. This was starkly apparent in the steep decline in media references to "Silicon Alley."[69]

But die-hard defenders argued that Silicon Alley was alive in the sense that elements of the new media ensemble were being incorporated and linked up with a wide range of firms and research facilities. Furthermore, several Silicon Alley interest groups—and some of its most powerful participants—still believed that the tech sector could attain a central position in New York's economy. This was evident in 2002 at NYNMA's State of the New York New Media gathering and NYSIA's annual Software Summit, both of which stressed a new theme: The destruction of the World Trade Center had created an opportunity for New York to be remade as the "first true 21st Century City."[70] At the NYNMA event the idea was introduced by Kathryn Wylde (president of the New York City Partnership and its investment fund) and Alan Patricof (chairman of a major venture capital firm and a participant in NYNMA's Angel Investors program). Wylde proposed that the mobilization to rebuild Lower Manhattan would probably be the main opportunity for tech firms to receive new public aid. Patricof added, "Lower Manhattan is being thought of in a new way—the new city of the 21st Century that will blow your mind." The implication was that the narrative of New York as a futuristic city would allow the technology industry to place itself at the center of a new hot spot.

RETHINKING THE TWENTY-FIRST—CENTURY CITY

The New Economy's fall and the terrorist attack leave us again pondering the nature of cities in an age that is digital and global. A wide variety of groups are considering the question as they debate how to rebuild Lower Manhattan. Despite their diverse backgrounds, they have been drawn to cultural development strategies. This has brought a distinct set of tensions to the rebuilding effort. As Sharon Zukin has shown, spaces of cultural production are marked by frictions between the social control impulse of public and business elites who try to monopolize cultural images and spaces and the efforts of cultural producers to free themselves from such controls.[71] This includes the friction between bohemian "creatives" and corporate distributors of their products as well as conflicts that arise when real estate interests use the presence of creatives to change the image—and value—of the spaces they inhabit (often resulting in displacement of the creatives). A novel twist is the new impulse to make secure space from terrorists, which may constrain how creatives—indeed, all of us—use city spaces. How now should we frame the work of creative enclaves? And what kind of relationship should these districts have to a world gone strange?

Bubble City, Creative City

Immediately after the Trade Center attacks *BusinessWeek* asked, "Are the benefits of concentrating people in a narrow space worth the risks . . . now when the Internet and other technologies are providing new ways to work?"[72] Increasing numbers of firms undoubtedly will use digital systems to experiment with decentralized offices. At the same time, digital technology is also being used to secure city spaces. For example, eighteen Manhattan buildings are using computerized tracking of visitors. A bar-coded pass allows you to visit only certain places for particular periods of time; if you stay too long you become trapped in a digital mousetrap of turnstyles and elevators that will not work.[73] No doubt such systems could be used to secure all sorts of spaces—even entire districts. One anticipates that if new towers are erected, some rational fantasy will be used to fortify them (call it the "bubble over the city" syndrome).[74] Fears about the target value of new towers are widespread and have lead most participants in the rebuilding process to oppose them. Yet, the developer with the site lease and the Port Authority favor new skyscrapers. Thus, the winning entry in the design competition featured a 1,776-foot spire. Still, the politics are so complex that it is unclear which actors will prevail and what will actually be built.[75]

Although there was a sharp difference of opinion about new towers, a report by the Center for an Urban Future ("The Creative Engine") noted that, "Vitually everyone . . . is talking about bringing culture downtown."[76] However, there is little that unites different interests besides a vague sentiment that Lower Manhattan should be a center of creativity and a "24/7" community (an area with housing and amenities). The version promoted by tech industry powers has echoes of Silicon Alley. Wylde claims that the new view of Downtown "is due to seeds planted by IT companies that went down there in the 1990s." Moreover, "The real opportunity," she says, "is to make a technology center that will be broadly focused—biotech to software to new media." The use of technology's imagery to make a hot spot also brings Silicon Alley to mind. The new Downtown, Patricof, exclaims, will be "the place to be."[77] However, there is little about technology in the mayor's vision to use culture to attract international firms. His $10.6 billion plan is to construct an "urban hamlet" featuring amenities ranging from housing, schools and libraries to tree-lined promenades. New York could then be marketed as a "live-and-work-and-visit community for the world."[78]

The widespread interest in culture may, in large part, be due to its perceived power to wipe away bad memories. For example, the Alliance for

Downtown has used a five-month–long festival featuring outdoor concerts to "generate a sense of healing in the area, revive tourist activity, and [issue] a reminder that there is more to Lower Manhattan than the World Trade Center site."[79] But what that "something more" is (or could be) has yet to be determined. So far, the debate has left unanswered basic questions: What kind of "creative engine" can New York host and what kinds of spaces and institutional supports are needed?

From Flatiron to Fargo and Back (Men in Black)

Many visions of Lower Manhattan as a cultural district have featured amenities that attract "creative" people—a key tenet of the creative city thesis developed by Richard Florida and Joel Kotkin.[80] In fact, the two black-clad emissaries of the creative city have not only been active in New York's rebuilding debate, but also are creating their own buzz circuit as they take their message to just about every corner of the United States. This came home to me—literally—when I vacationed in my hometown of Fargo, North Dakota, in December 2002 and found the two men in black offering advice in a Fargo *Forum* series on "Saving North Dakota." The role of the two boho boomers was startling since North Dakota is something like old Greenland (the Norse settled it and then the world forgot it existed). Yet, somehow the advice was similar to that Kotkin had offered for "Saving Silicon Alley."[81] The *Forum*'s front-page article ("Creative Climate Might Be Cure") had a photo of a Fargo webshop whose effort to use a creative workplace to attract workers was said to be in line with Florida's "model for creative communities."[82] Florida himself commented that the cases of Madison (WI), Chapel Hill (NC), and Austin (TX) showed that the key to attracting skilled people was to develop lifestyle amenities—such as a vibrant nightlife and active music scene (not to mention world-class universities). He advised Fargo to "figure out some way to inject some excitement into outdoor activity."[83] He added that amenities might compensate for lower wages. But Fargo is well endowed with amenities; what it does not have is an economy that pays high wages (the reason well-educated youth leave). Kotkin lamented that the New Economy had bypassed the rural heartland, but stated that venture capital programs and "homesteader" tax incentives could attract IT entrepreneurs and, in turn, jumpstart innovation and help a risk culture form.[84]

Of course, culture and creativity are virtues, as are amenities—if they are the kind *your circle* likes. But, as Bob Dylan once put it (perhaps as a result of his brief stint as a keyboardist in a Fargo band), "you got to serve somebody." Who that somebody is, remains the big question for those who would make a living out of creativity—whether they are in Fargo or in Lower Manhattan. In fact, much of the interest in cultural development seems to be more about aspirations to draw in, and then house, clothe, feed, and entertain yuppies through rather conventional means. What then about developing creative districts?

The key mechanism in the creative city thesis is an intensifying place market that is said to confront Fargo and New York with the same problem: "Like all places in the Digital Age New York can have a great future only if enough ambitious, talented and committed people choose to come there."[85] The idea of a place market is not new: The novel contribution of the men in black is to expand the scope and intensity of the putative competition between places. As Kotkin puts it, "Every city is in a natural state of war with each other."[86] The effect is to present all manner of cities with the same anxiety: To draw creatives (astute place consumers), they must attend to an endless range of traits—their amenities.

REFRAMING CREATIVITY

Silicon Alley showed that the viability of ideas depends on support networks that entrepreneurs assemble out of diverse elements. It also reveals problems that emerged under neoliberalism in the late 1990s, underscoring the need to develop new frameworks for harnessing novel technologies and practices. Keeping these insights in mind, I now turn to consider two influential proposals for New York's creative districts and the general problem of reframing the emerging digital economy. This sets the scene for thinking how creative resources—including those produced by Silicon Alley—might be incorporated into new frameworks.

Creativity for What?

With New York's dire situation there is a pressing need to specify just what kinds of goals a creative district should serve. The debate on creative districts for Lower Manhattan tends to divide around three questions: (1) Should some particular industrial cluster(s) be targeted for support? (2) Should government intervene to reserve space for creative firms (and less affluent populations)? (3) Should the state or federal government offer new aid for development? In this section I outline two influential positions: Florida's advocacy of a "free market" approach and the call of Mike Wallace for a "new New Deal" for New York.

Florida's 2002 opinion piece in the *New York Times* touted Lower Manhattan's endowments as a "creative hub"—its diverse neighborhoods, creative culture, and position as a regional crossroads. He detected a virtuous path of development that would continue. Add to this "the financial expertise and capital," and there is "a natural setting for the growth of new ventures." The task then was to "help Lower Manhattan become what it is becoming anyway." He suggested that the city (1) create university branches that draw a variety of jobs and talents, (2) add green space, walkways, bike paths, and waterfront access, and (3) upgrade mass transit. He remarked that Lower Manhattan (like San Francisco, Seattle, and Boston) is one of those centers that "attract talent, are good venues for any business that is creativity-intensive and serve as places for people from many fields to exchange ideas." The difference in the case of Lower Manhattan—the erosion of its economic base—did not concern him. It was "natural" that the financial cluster was starting to dissipate. His only note of alarm was against government becoming too involved: It should not use "public land and subsidies" to "prop up existing industries or to pick winners from among the new ones."[87]

This celebration of the *image* of Lower Manhattan as a creative hub ignores forces that threaten to erode some of its most precious elements. One is the decline of the financial sector, which is a major customer for creative firms and represents 25 percent of New York's total income and 30 percent of its tax base. A second is that redevelopment may reignite the kind of yuppification and corporatization of Manhattan real estate that was pushing out creative firms and workers before the Trade Center attacks. In fact, I propose that real estate developers, along with commercial interests that fuel yuppie consumption, would be the main beneficiaries of this sort of creative city.

In contrast, Wallace (a historian of New York) argues that in the wake of the Twin Towers a "passive reliance on the 'free market' would be . . . inadequate."[88] Given that past strategies focused on granting tax breaks to large firms, he saw a need to develop a "new overall development strategy." He advocated the creation of "industrial district" strategies to assist sectors that involve clusters of small firms such as manufacturing and high tech industries (e.g., biotechnology). This should begin with a "citywide analysis of opportunities and then move to targeted sector interventions" that provide "clusters with R&D support, workforce training, market promotion, export assistance, and the building of support groups" (e.g., industry consortia).[89] He also called for zoning to protect these clusters and the construction of affordable housing. Finally, he argued that the state or federal government should provide financial aid since the city was beset with a massive budget gap. He also favored measures that (as the New Deal had done) provide relief, stimulate demand, and rehabilitate public infrastructure.

In sum, his goals include: creating an alternative economic base, maintaining diversity in the population and in businesses, raising the standard of living for the less affluent, and strengthening economic ties with the rest of the city and region. The Silicon Alley experience reaffirms the need to address these issues.

Reframing the Digital Economy

Let us consider now the kind of frameworks that might allow us to harness the digital economy in ways that serve the goals outlined above. The underlying flaw in the creative city thesis is an unwavering inclination to denigrate government and laud markets. For example, there is little recognition of a need to confront the dominance of real estate interests in cities like New York. More generally, this position echoes the naturalism of Jane Jacobs and even Fredrick Hayek, the neoliberal guru who claims that a free market supports a "spontaneous social order."[90] The point that master plans are ill-equipped to coordinate innovative activities or industries is well taken. But, their stilted conception of how innovation is organized slips into naturalistic imagery that obscures social and institutional mechanisms. Moreover, the men in black ignore serious flaws in the frameworks that neoliberalism provided for innovation. They blame New Economy excesses on irrational behavior—not policies that promoted further deregulation and financialization. We now know that these conditions fueled the spread of a vast seamy side that engulfed many New Economy firms (from dot-coms to AOL).[91]

The new New Deal vision stresses the inadequacy of neoliberal policies to address social problems caused by economic and technological change, especially as they surface in mature cities. However, in evoking the era that preceded neoliberalism, it leaves us wondering how to cope with the distinctive historical conditions marked by the rise of digital technology and increasing globalization. A historical perspective does help us recognize that the United States has encountered and mastered analogous challenges before. Kevin Phillips reminds us that past waves of technological and business change brought financial speculation and scandal—which then spurred the creation of institutions to harness new powers for the broader society while controlling excesses.[92] That last step is our current task.

The Silicon Alley case suggests a need for institutional frameworks that can support rather ill-defined industry clusters that host shape-shifting creative types who regularly cross industry boundaries. The trick then is to mix some kind of structure with a great deal of openness. Neoliberal frameworks selectively give up state control as they open up markets for those entrepreneurial interests that wield the most power. What alternative framework might be developed?

Silicon Alley's Continuing Legacy

A first step in reframing New York's digital economy is to identify institutional entrepreneurs and creative resources that can be brought together. The city's cultural sector does not have much of an institutional framework running across it, but the reservoir of resources is immense: some

150,000 artists, 3,000 arts organizations, and some 2,000 commerical arts firms or professionals.[93] Though the currency of its name has faded, Silicon Alley has left behind some institutional frameworks as well as substantial pools of resources. Over three thousand computer-related firms remain in the city, mostly serving the financial, media, and information service sectors.[94] Some key institutional entrepreneurs remain active, although their relative importance has changed. NYSIA, for example, seems to have bypassed NYNMA in its ability to build institutional partnerships and supports. NYSIA has helped create a labor market consortium as well as various university-business relationships organized around research facilities.[95] The revolving credit fund it advocates would be an important alternative for the vast majority of firms that do not receive venture capital. The New York City Partnership has organized a consortium in an effort to mobilize support for development of a biotech cluster around a Downtown hub facility.[96] The Digital NYC program seems to be on its way out, but several of its districts (e.g., DUMBO in Brooklyn, Long Island City in Queens) are full of tenants. Nonprofits are working with developers to set up WiFi (Wireless Fidelity) hot spots Downtown and elsewhere in New York that provide free broadband access to anyone with a WiFi accessory on their laptop. A last area where new kinds of entrepreneurs and institutions are being formed is a resurgent alternative media that is forming out of partnerships with various cultural organizations. For example, Thundergulch (a nonprofit) was founded to "foster interchange between the world of Silicon Alley and the worlds of art and culture."[97] Joint efforts with New York's lively independent film community have spawned a new generation of new media artists and digital filmmakers.[98] Entities such as the TriBeCa Film Center and Web Lab are helping link the two sectors. Web Lab and its partners are working to develop web environments that lack true authority figures and facilitate the creation of stories by multiple authors. One filmmaker thinks such experiments will produce something resembling "reality" programs on TV, but without the "forced circumstances and settings" and screening of participants.[99]

Open City

A public sociology should discuss solutions as well as problems. Thus, I will conclude with a vision of how a creative district might be woven into Lower Manhattan's redevelopment. I propose that a district be created to support explorations of how interactive media can be built into lifestyle products and services, as well as flexible living and work spaces. There are several inspirations for my "open city." First, is the postwar school of photography that used the metaphor of an open city as a place of "spontaneity and innovation" that was "constantly forming new patterns."[100] Second, are new signs of creative life that are springing up in Lower Manhattan as evidenced by two efforts by creative types to organize their own spaces: the colonization of Wall Street's darkened spaces by young bohemians and TKNY—a "store" that calls itself a "testing space" and "showcase for urban lifestyle technology."[101] A third is the historic mobilization of diverse groups to discuss New York's rebuilding.

Wall Street after Dark

Young bohemians who were pushed out of (or voluntarily left) their traditional haunts, have been colonizing the most unlikely of areas—Wall Street. As Downtown residential rents plummet and Wall Street–related traffic continues to drop, a new arts and music scene is emerging in new galleries—and bars that have lost many of their customers. Edgy twenty-somethings are flocking to "underground clubs" that are organized for weekends in Wall Street bars. For instance, on Friday nights a "Drunk Love" night at the John Street Bar and Grill draws fashion designers, actors, photographers, architects, t-shirt designers, alternative bands, and a Brazilian fashion model now and then. The music is retro or garage. The DJ (a 24-year-old reporter for MTV News) savors a return to spontaneity. "During the economic boom it was really hard to foster any sort of creative community. Anyone who came up with a fresh idea tried to figure out a way to profit from it. It seemed like every art party was sponsored by Skyy vodka."[102] Many who frequent this new party circuit work for big corporations, but the scene is organized around an identity that is vehemently antiyuppie. One of the hosts (an artist) remarks, "Anybody dressed obnoxiously, in a yuppie way" would not be admitted.[103] Not far from the bar is the New York City Urban Experience Museum. A 36-year-old artist who has directed videos for yesterday's rebels (David Bowie) and today's (Marilyn Mansion) says of the gallery, "The energy here feels raw. It's kind of how I imagine SoHo or Chelsea [was] when it first started."[104]

As was the case with Razorfish, these creatives crave spaces that allow them to maintain a critical distance from their employers. The mingling of bohemians and bourgeoisie during the New Economy did not bring a permanent fusion after all. The reason the survival of bohemians matters is provided in Peter Hall's epic book, *Cities in Civilization*. In Hall's studies of great periods of creativity in modern cities (e.g., London, Vienna, Paris, Berlin), he finds that creatives who are near, but not "of" the center are the key actors who occasionally make cities become "crucibles" of creativity. This position allows them to develop an astute critique of the status quo and some new aesthetic; the catch is that their rise to prominence usually depends on support by some faction of a divided elite. Enlightened leaders might draw a lesson here: The presence of critical creatives testifies to the health of a city's culture (not to mention a democracy).[105]

Tokyo–New York (TKNY)

As we saw in the early days of Silicon Alley, the creative workplace a small firm provides may be an important part of the creative scene. TKNY (a Lower Manhattan store and lounge) "acts as a clubhouse for a circle of young expatriates, most from Tokyo, working in design and computer technology." They blend disciplines in exploring a new style ("compact/impact") for "small, efficient furnishings and design with a whimsical edge"; they draw on the Japanese sense of "technology as fashion"—the notion that technological gadgets can have a "fashion moment."[106] One of the owners is a Japanese technology consultant whose wife is a design critic; the other is a Swedish architect. TKNY started up in 2000 as a website where "early adopters" in Tokyo and New York could trade ideas about hot "trends and tools in technology and design." It sometimes exhibits products selected by a "rotating panel of graphic designers, computer programmers and Web masters" who the owners draw from their networks in New York and Tokyo.[107] The store displays product information on thin screen monitors along with Japanese animation; they also use the space to test their own designs, such as NetMeetStreet—a thin sheet of fiber-optic plastic that transforms their storefront window into a continually changing electronic billboard; TKNY sometimes acts as "a talent clearinghouse" for ad firms that are searching for "animators, illustrators, graphic designers and filmmakers."[108] The owners have also used their design sensibilities in organizing their living quarters; the Swedish partner has mobile possessions and furnishings in his Chinatown loft (e.g., furniture on wheels) because, he says, in New York City "nobody has any idea of how long they're staying."[109]

It is not a stretch to see this kind of product development as one main focus for a creative district. Tokyo is filled with clusters of small creative firms that prototype products for diverse industries.[110] What is also striking here is the vitality of creative applications of technology that involve manufactured products (a realm that Japan values much more than the United States). Finally, we see evidence that taking a more open posture toward other societies (instead of a world manager stance) provides special opportunities for creative fusion.

One Last Napkin Scribble

Observers remarked that Silicon Alley was "a moment in time" and "not built to last." It might seem, then, that spaces of cultural production are subject to market forces and can, like an Etch-a-sketch, be wiped clean. However, this seems to me one more rational fantasy. Let me conclude by offering a napkin scribble—a free-flowing vision of how we might build a framework that supports a mutable, interactive space of creative invention—an open city.

To start with, the broad mobilization of civic, professional, and business actors poses a special opportunity. Some three hundred design and architectural firms worked on designs for the Trade Center site while many local groups participated in the debate (one coalition—the Civic Alliance—consisted of some seventy civic and professional groups). We could draw on this critical mass in putting together groups to devise and govern a special creative district—the mandate being an ongoing exploration of the kinds of spaces that cities could provide. The public sector could reserve a sizeable area (the way that Chicago protects manufacturing districts)[111]—and perhaps sign it over to a nonprofit consortium for the rest of the twenty-first century (a strong symbolic commitment). The challenge would be to use a mix of public authority and resources to frame the space for the desired range of activities (e.g., reserve areas for small firms and low-income residents, regulate the corporate presence) and then give up as much control as possible.

Suppose that New York hosted a yearly Open City festival—something like the Sundance film festival—an exhibition and competition for designs of interactive spaces and related products and services. The event could aim to draw designers from across the world and could have numerous categories. Some, for example, could involve unmet needs in developing countries—as well as in places such as the Bronx and Harlem. The special hook is that winning designs would be used to construct temporary demonstration projects for living or work spaces using interactive media. Residents, workers, or students would experiment with these spaces and products, which could be documented. And the complex would serve a variety of visitors (designers, students, and tourists).

My vision is that city space would itself become an economic base. I grant that the idea is rather fanciful, but an interesting aspect is that just about every element within my scheme actually appeared at some time during Silicon Alley's heyday (or more recently). Various kinds of wired and wireless infrastructures could be created (as was done Downtown with Plug 'N' Go, Digital NYC, and WiFi); labs could be leased to corporations or universities at the site (similar to Ericsson's Cyberlab); interactive products and services could be prototyped (by firms like TKNY) and exported around the world; some of the documentation could be used as advertising or a new breed of reality programming (developed by indie film/new media collaborations of firms like Web Lab or perhaps Weliveinpublic.com [Josh Harris–style toilet cams are negotiable]); tourists could pay for admission to some sections: the fashion industry could prototype "wearable" devices;

building product firms could prototype materials for interactive office or living spaces (a chance to expand the demand for the kind of craft workers who make Broadway sets); local government could set up rotating credit associations among small creative firms or specialized manufacturers so they could participate (as NYSIA has lobbied for); and based on the expertise they gain architects, real estate developers, and the like could sell their services to cities across the world that want to make similar spaces (as William Rudin did with the wired building concept). Finally, the district could serve as a September 11 memorial; a living tribute to creative life and peaceful relations with other peoples. The virtues of an open, urban culture would go a long way in giving meaning to lives cut short by intolerance.

The "State" of Silicon Alley

What distinguishes my Open City fantasy from Silicon Alley is the respective frameworks for assembling the elements—a matter that implicates the state. New York and its new media district made a tentative embrace in the late 1990s and found themselves trapped in a financial bubble—despite the fact that many business leaders saw a need to wean the city from Wall Street, many new media pundits and participants recognized that speculation was driving Silicon Alley, and many social critics decried the polarizing effects of finance-based growth and the displacement caused by an unrestrained real estate market. What they all were trapped in, ultimately, was a state framework for development that opened up the economy (and subordinated most everyone else) to entrepreneurs from the financial and real estate sectors.[112] They ended up becoming the main change agents in the new media after the mid-1990s—not just through dominating their own domains, but also through helping hook up the media circuit that figured so much in the construction of Silicon Alley as a social reality. The need now is to institute frameworks for making applications of technology that result in development that is more sustainable, less volatile, and more equitable. The Silicon Alley experience suggests that this will only happen if the state takes a more direct involvement while putting in place a framework ensuring openness.

One goal should be to ensure a more open industrial politics.[113] Government should explictly support innovative places—not just sectors. Instead of having an industry politics that is largely carried out in Washington, DC, by corporate lobbyists there would be a much more accessible political arena at the level of the city. The state should also create a framework at the district level that ensures that industry politics is open to a wide range of stakeholders. In Europe and Japan, where industrial politics is more open, a wide variety of interests collectively develop support systems that help clusters of small firms access labor, capital, and real estate. In contrast to recent practice, the state needs to open itself up to a wider range of interests—such as is done in the Netherlands where firms and other stakeholders are urged to develop collectively agendas for the state to attend to. Another practice from the Netherlands—having government monitor clusters of innovative firms—would help frame a district while tempering the excesses of the buzz circuit seen in Silicon Alley.

APPENDICES

APPENDIX A Changes in Firm Employment Totals after Stock Listed for Thirty-seven Public Companies in Silicon Alley

		Firm Employment Totals			
Firm	**Date Stock Listed**	**Before/At Listing**	**After Listing**	**Change**	**Percent Change**
Globix	Jan. 1996	81 (1996)	850 (2000)	+769	+949.4%
K2 Design	July 1996	27 (1996)	52 (2000)	+25	+92.6
Bluefly	May 1997	10 (1998)	77 (2001)	+67	+670.0
N2K/CDnow	Feb. 1998	173 (1997)	502 (2000)	+329	+190.2
DoubleClick	Feb. 1998	185 (1997)	1,929 (2000)	+1,744	+942.7
CyberShop	Mar. 1998	21 (1998)	42 (1999)	+21	+100.0
RareMedium	Apr. 1998	120 (1998)	929 (2000)	+929	+774.2
24/7 Media	Aug. 1998	117 (1998)	1,327 (2000)	+1,210	+1,034.2
EarthWeb	Nov. 1998	63 (1998)	240 (2000)	+177	+281.0
theglobe.com	Nov. 1998	80 (1998)	197 (2000)	+117	+146.3
Multex.com	Mar. 1999	149 (1998)	561 (2000)	+412	+276.5
iVillage	Mar. 1999	200 (1998)	414 (2000)	+214	+107.0
about.com	Mar. 1999	35 (1998)	61 (2000)	+61	+174.3
iTurf	Apr. 1999	40 (1998)	153 (2000)	+113	+282.5
Razorfish	Apr. 1999	414 (1999)	1,994 (2000)	+1,580	+381.6
Applied Theory	Apr. 1999	190 (1999)	642 (2000)	+452	+237.9
Mapquest.com	May 1999	222 (1999)	335 (2000)	+113	+50.9
Media Metrix	May 1999	88 (1998)	176 (2000)	+88	+100.0
theStreet.com	May 1999	138 (1999)	188 (2000)	+50	+36.2

APPENDIX A Continued

		Firm Employment Totals			
Firm	Date Stock Listed	Before/At Listing	After Listing	Change	Percent Change
Alloy Online	May 1999	25 (1999)	585 (2000)	+560	+2,240.0
Barnes&Noble.com	May 1999	701 (1999)	1,752 (2001)	+1,051	+149.9
Juno Online	May 1999	147 (1998)	332 (2000)	+185	+125.9
StarMedia	May 1999	270 (1999)	779 (2000)	+509	+188.5
InterWorld	June 1999	274 (1999)	280 (2000)	+6	+0.2
Wit Capital Group	June 1999	138 (1999)	450 (2000)	+312	+226.1
Netcreations	July 1999	19 (1999)	40 (2000)	+21	+110.5
Big Star Ent.	Aug. 1999	55 (1999)	78 (2000)	+23	+41.8
Jupiter Com.	Oct. 1999	194 (1999)	706 (2000)	+512	+263.9
Predictive Sys.	Oct. 1999	138 (1999)	691 (2001)	+553	+400.7
Deltathree.com	Nov. 1999	74 (1999)	162 (2000)	+88	+118.9
The Knot Inc.	Dec. 1999	117 (1999)	280 (2000)	+163	+139.3
Agency.com	Dec. 1999	748 (1999)	1,700 (2000)	+952	+127.3
eSpeed	Dec. 1999	370 (1999)	493 (2000)	+123	+33.2
Streamedia Com.	Dec. 1999	7 (1999)	32 (2000)	+25	+357.1
Register.com	Mar. 2000	122 (1999)	240 (2000)	+118	+96.7
LivePerson Inc.	Apr. 2000	73 (1999)	200 (2000)	+127	+174.0
Opus 360	Apr. 2000	155 (1999)	249 (2000)	+94	+60.6
Totals		5,980	19,718	+13,738	+229.7%

Sources: Registrations for Company Stock Offerings and Annual Reports.

APPENDIX B Changes in Firm Revenue Totals after Stock Listed for Thirty-seven Public Companies in Silicon Alley

Firm	Date Stock Listed	Firm Revenue Totals (In Millions) Before/At Listing	After Listing	Change	Percent Change
Globix	Jan. 1996	$14.1 (1996)	$81.3 (2000)	+$67.2	+476.6%
K2 Design	July 1996	1.2 (1995)	5.2 (2000)	+4.0	+333.3
Bluefly	May 1997	0 (1997)	17.5 (2000)	+17.5	na
N2K/CDnow	Feb. 1998	11.2 (1997)	147.2 (1999)	+136.0	+1,214.3
DoubleClick	Feb. 1998	20.0 (1997)	505.6 (2000)	+485.6	+2,428.0
CyberShop	Mar. 1998	1.5 (1997)	7.0 (1999)	+5.5	+366.7
RareMedium	Apr. 1998	4.7 (1998)	110.1 (2000)	+105.4	+2,242.6
24/7 Media	Aug. 1998	5.4 (1997)	146.1 (2000)	+140.7	+2,605.6
EarthWeb	Nov. 1998	3.3 (1998)	73.8 (2000)	+70.5	+2,136.4
theglobe.com	Nov. 1998	0.8 (1997)	29.9 (2000)	+29.1	+3,637.5
Multex.com	Mar. 1999	22.0 (1998)	85.9 (2000)	+63.9	+290.5
iVillage	Mar. 1999	12.5 (1998)	76.4 (2000)	+63.9	+511.2
about.com	Mar. 1999	3.7 (1998)	27.0 (1999)	+23.3	+629.7
iTurf	Apr. 1999	4.0 (1998)	138.7 (2000)	+134.7	+3,367.5
Razorfish	Apr. 1999	83.9 (1998)	267.9 (2000)	+184.0	+219.3
Applied Theory	Apr. 1999	22.6 (1998)	76.3 (2000)	+53.7	+237.6
Mapquest.com	May 1999	24.7 (1998)	34.5 (1999)	+9.8	+39.7
Media Metrix	May 1999	6.3 (1998)	20.5 (1999)	+14.2	+225.4
theStreet.com	May 1999	4.0 (1998)	13.1 (2000)	+9.1	+227.5
Alloy Online	May 1999	2.0 (1998)	33.9 (2000)	+31.9	+1,595.0
Barnes&Noble.com	May 1999	61.8 (1998)	320.1 (2000)	+258.3	+418.0
Juno Online	May 1999	21.7 (1998)	114.0 (2000)	+92.3	+425.3
StarMedia	May 1999	5.8 (1998)	52.3 (2000)	+46.5	+801.7
InterWorld	June 1999	14.6 (1998)	52.3 (2000)	+37.7	+258.2
Wit Capital Group	June 1999	48.6 (1999)	375.5 (2000)	+326.9	+672.6
Netcreations	July 1999	3.4 (1998)	44.8 (2000)	+41.4	+1,217.7
Big Star Ent.	Aug. 1999	0.8 (1998)	9.6 (2000)	+8.8	+1,100.0
Jupiter Com.	Oct. 1999	14.8 (1998)	38.1 (1999)	+23.3	+157.4
Predictive Sys.	Oct. 1999	52.7 (1999)	88.3 (2000)	+35.6	+67.6
Deltathree.com	Nov. 1999	5.6 (1998)	30.4 (2000)	+24.8	+442.9
The Knot Inc.	Dec. 1999	1.0 (1998)	24.2 (2000)	+23.2	+2,320.0
Agency.com	Dec. 1999	26.4 (1998)	202.1 (2000)	+175.7	+665.5
eSpeed	Dec. 1999	34.7 (1999)	91.0 (2000)	+56.3	+162.2
Streamedia Com.	Dec. 1999	0.2 (1999)	0.5 (2000)	+0.3	+150.0
Register.com	Mar. 2000	9.6 (1999)	86.1 (2000)	+76.5	+796.9
LivePerson Inc.	Apr. 2000	0.6 (1999)	6.3 (2000)	+5.7	+950.0
Opus 360	Apr. 2000	0.4 (1999)	11.3 (2000)	+10.9	+2,725.0
Totals		$550.6	$3,444.8	+$2,894.2	+525.6%

Sources: Registrations for Company Stock Offerings and Annual Reports.

APPENDIX C Changes in Firm Net Income Totals after Stock Listed for Thirty-seven Public Companies in Silicon Alley

Firm	Date Stock Listed	Firm Net Income Totals (In Millions) Before/At Listing	After Listing	Change
Globix	Jan. 1996	−$2.6 (1996)	−$132.2 (2000)	−$129.6
K2 Design	July 1996	+0.1 (1995)	−1.9 (2000)	−2.0
Bluefly	May 1997	−0.4 (1997)	−21.1 (2000)	−20.7
N2K/CDnow	Feb. 1998	−28.7 (1997)	−119.2 (1999)	−90.5
DoubleClick	Feb. 1998	−4.6 (1997)	−156.0 (2000)	−151.4
CyberShop	Mar. 1998	−1.8 (1997)	−10.3 (1999)	−8.5
RareMedium	Apr. 1998	−0.6 (1998)	−124.7 (2000)	−124.1
24/7 Media	Aug. 1998	−17.4 (1997)	−799.9 (2000)	−782.5
EarthWeb	Nov. 1998	−0.9 (1998)	−80.4 (2000)	−79.5
theglobe.com	Nov. 1998	−3.6 (1997)	−103.9 (2000)	−100.3
Multex.com	Mar. 1999	−9.7 (1998)	−1.2 (2000)	+8.5
iVillage	Mar. 1999	−43.7 (1998)	−191.4 (2000)	−147.7
about.com	Mar. 1999	−15.6 (1998)	−55.1 (1999)	−39.5
iTurf	Apr. 1999	+0.4 (1998)	−61.9 (2000)	−62.3
Razorfish	Apr. 1999	+4.1 (1998)	−148.0 (2000)	−152.1
Applied Theory	Apr. 1999	−6.9 (1998)	−52.6 (2000)	−45.7
Mapquest.com	May 1999	−3.2 (1998)	−18.5 (1999)	−15.3
Media Metrix	May 1999	−7.2 (1998)	−21.9 (1999)	−14.7
theStreet.com	May 1999	−16.4 (1998)	−62.0 (2000)	−45.6
Alloy Online	May 1999	−1.9 (1998)	−14.9 (2000)	−13.0
Barnes&Noble.com	May 1999	−83.1 (1998)	−65.4 (2000)	+17.7
Juno Online	May 1999	−31.6 (1998)	−131.4 (2000)	−99.8
StarMedia	May 1999	−46.0 (1998)	−210.8 (2000)	−164.8
InterWorld	June 1999	−22.1 (1998)	−55.3 (2000)	−33.2
Wit Capital Group	June 1999	−8.8 (1998)	−22.0 (2000)	−13.2
Netcreations	July 1999	+0.6 (1998)	+4.5 (2000)	+3.9
Big Star Ent.	Aug. 1999	−3.2 (1998)	−18.7 (2000)	−15.5
Jupiter Com.	Oct. 1999	−2.1 (1998)	−0.6 (1999)	+0.6
Predictive Sys.	Oct. 1999	−1.0 (1999)	−3.9 (2000)	−2.9
Deltathree.com	Nov. 1999	−7.1 (1998)	−48.3 (2000)	−41.2
The Knot Inc.	Dec. 1999	−1.5 (1998)	−15.8 (2000)	−14.3
Agency.com	Dec. 1999	−2.5 (1998)	−14.7 (2000)	−12.2
eSpeed	Dec. 1999	−12.6 (1999)	−59.1 (2000)	−46.5
Streamedia Com.	Dec. 1999	−3.8 (1999)	−7.4 (2000)	−3.6
Register.com	Mar. 2000	−8.8 (1999)	+0.3 (2000)	+9.1
LivePerson Inc.	Apr. 2000	−9.8 (1999)	−43.3 (2000)	−33.5
Opus 360	Apr. 2000	−29.4 (1999)	−75.9 (2000)	−46.5
Totals		−$433.4	−$2,944.9	−$2,511.5

Sources: Registrations for Company Stock Offerings and Annual Reports.

APPENDIX D Fates of Thirty-seven Public Companies in Silicon Alley

Firm	Fate of Company
Globix	Filed for Chapter 11 bankruptcy in January 2002 so as to reduce outstanding indebtedness by $480 million.
K2 Design	Acquired by Integrated Information Systems of Arizona for $444,000 on August 30, 2001.
Bluefly	Was taken over by George Soros hedge fund on October 13, 2000.
N2K/CDnow	Merged with CDnow on March 17, 1999. CDnow was acquired for $117 million (@ $3 a share) by Bertelsmann in July 2000. Bertelsmann sold CDnow's online assets to Amazon.com in November 2002.
DoubleClick	Made seven acquisitions since the end of 2000. Diversified away from online ads to full-service campaigns that include e-mail marketing, research, and data.
CyberShop	Moved to New Jersey. Sold cybershop.com domain name and customer list to e-Commerce Solutions for $100,000 cash and $900,000 in stock. Changed name to Grove Strategic Ventures in February 2000 and became an incubator.
RareMedium	Ceased operations in third quarter of 2001.
24/7 Media	Acquired Real Media—a struggling private firm—for $2 million in stock and changed name to 24/7 Real Media in October 2001.
EarthWeb	Sold most of its online content sites and rights to EarthWeb trademark and focused on IT career solutions (online employment site). Sold rights to EarthWeb trademark to Internet.com in June 2001 and changed name to Dice, Inc.
theglobe.com	Sold most business properties and closed online community site in August 2001. Considering going into digital telephony. Moved to Florida where it operated an online game site.
Multex.com	Acquired by Reuters for $155 million in February 2003.
iVillage	Acquired by its main competitor, Women.com, in April 2001 from Hearst for $27 million in stock.
about.com	Acquired for $690 million by Primedia in early 2001.
iTurf	Acquired by dELiA*s, a catalog and retail store in November 2000.
Razorfish	Acquired by SBI and Company for $8.2 million (@ $1.70 a share) in November 2002.
Applied Theory	Filed for Chapter 11 bankruptcy protection in April 2002. Sold its network business to FASTNET Corp. and its managed hosting services business to Clear Blue Technologies.
Mapquest.com	Acquired by AOL in June 2000 in stock trade (@ 0.31558 of AOL stock per 1 Mapquest.com stock).

(continued)

APPENDIX D Continued

Firm	Fate of Company
Media Metrix	Acquired Jupiter Communications in trade of stock valued at $414 million to form Jupiter Media Metrix. Media Metrix unit closed in June 2002 and assets sold.
theStreet.com	On July 18, 2003, it announced that it had achieved its first positive cash flow during the second quarter of 2003.
Alloy Online	Makes seven acquisitions including all Kumpi. Marketing in May 2003 for $15.6 million.
Barnes&Noble.com	Bertelsmann sells its 36.8 percent stake to Barnes & Noble for $164 million ($2.80 a share) on July 30, 2003.
Juno Online	Acquired in stock trade by NetZero (another free Internet access provider) in June 2001 to form United Online. The exchange price was 1 share of Juno for 1.785 shares of NetZero.
StarMedia	Sold online assets for $8 million to Eres Mas Interactive (Spain) in July 2002. Focuses on "mobile solutions" (e.g., wireless), changed name to CycleLogic and moved HQ to Miami.
InterWorld	Foreclosed in May 2002 by its majority stakeholder, JNet Enterprise Corp. (a holding company that was formerly Jackpot Enterprises, a Nevada servicer of gambling machines). JNet, delisted from NYSE five days later, was seeking a strategic investor or a buyer for Interworld, or considering a shutdown.
Wit Capital Group	Merged with Soundview—a technology company—in January 2001 and changed name to Wit Soundview Group. In August 2001 changed name to Soundview Technology Group, Inc. and moved HQ to Greenwich, CT.
Net Creations	Acquired in April 2001 by Nickel Acquisitions, an affiliate of SEAT Pagine Gialle (owned by Telecom Italy). Nickel Acquisitions paid $109.1 million.
Big Star Ent.	Ceased operations in June 2001. As of August 2003 considered whether to redeploy remaining case assets in a new business venture or liquidate its assets.
Jupiter Communications	Acquired by Media Metrix in trade of stock valued at $414 million to form Jupiter Media Metrix. Media Metrix unit assets sold and unit closed in June 2002. After FTC opposed proposed acquisition by NetRatings for $71.2 million in February 2002, Jupiter sold online operations for $2 million and its patents for computer tracking to NetRating for $15 million. Also sold Jupiter Research and Jupiter Events to INF Media Group for $250,000 and ceased operations on July 31, 2002.

(continued)

APPENDIX D Continued

Firm	Fate of Company
Predictive Systems	Acquired by International Network Services of Santa Clara, CA, on June 19, 2003, for $0.46 a share.
Deltathree.com	Stock price was less than $1 a share for first half of 2003.
The Knot Inc.	Delisted from NASDAQ in August 2001. In February 2002 May Department Stores bought a 20 percent stake for $5 million.
Agency.com	Acquired by Seneca Investments in October 2001 at $3.35 a share for an estimated total of $147 million. Seneca was a new company formed by Omincon (a holding company in advertising that owned 65 percent of Agency.com) and Pegasus Capital (a private investment firm).
eSpeed	Most New York staff and top executives killed in World Trade Center attacks.
Streamedia Com.	Revenue-earning operations ended in July 2001. Changed name to XXIS Communications Corp. and moved HQ to Fredericksburg, VA. Merged with HOA Networks Corp. in January 2002.
Register.com	In early 2003 rejects 2 take-over offers: one at $230 million ($4.95 a share), a second at $204 million ($5.50 a share). In response to shareholder anger at its anti-take-over policy the firm agrees in July 2003 to distribute $120 million in dividends or share repurchases.
LivePerson Inc.	Having been delisted by NASDAQ, the firm met requirement to be listed in May 2003.
Opus 360	Exchanged 80 percent of its stock in November 2001 to acquire Artemis International (a subsidiary of Proha Plc of Finland) and a 20 percent share in two other Proha subsidiaries. Changed name to Artemis Information.

Sources: Registrations for Company Stock Offerings and Annual Reports.

NOTES

CHAPTER 1

1. Vanessa Grigoriadis, "Silicon Alley 10003," *New York Magazine*, 6 March 2000, p. 30.
2. Andy Pratt, "Sticky Places? A Comment on the Making of 'New Media' Spaces," working paper for Global II, A Workshop in Media and Communications, London School of Economics, 2000.
3. Sharon Zukin, *Loft Living* (New Brunswick, NJ: Rutgers University Press, 1982); Robert Fitch, *The Assassination of New York* (London: Verso, 1993).
4. PricewaterhouseCoopers, *3rd New York New Media Industry Survey* (New York, 2000), p. 34. Producer services led the recovery between 1977 and 1989, adding over 270,000 jobs to the city economy. Securities and business services accounted for nearly 180,000 jobs alone. Matthew Drennan, "The Decline and Rise of the New York Economy," in Manuel Castells and John Mollenkopf (eds.), *Dual City* (New York: Russell Sage Foundation, 1991), p. 35.
5. Jennifer Farley, "Take Two: Incubating Ideas and Accelerating Growth," *AlleyCat News*, January 2001, p. 76.
6. Employment in New York dropped by nearly 400,000 jobs between 1989 and 1993. The unemployment rate soared to 10 percent at the nadir and remained in the vicinity of 8 percent until the middle of the 1990s. Larry Kanter and Judith Messina, "Unexpected Riches Remake the City," *Crain's New York Business*, 29 November 1999, pp. 28, 30, 32; Steve Malanga, "New Economy Propels City Economy to Record Year," *Crain's New York Business*, 13 December 1999, pp. 1, 52. As of 1994 vacancies in commercial real estate still averaged between 15 and 20 percent in Lower Manhattan. Uddy Ward, "Special Report: Commercial Real Estate," *Crain's New York Business*, 17 January 2000, pp. 42, 48, 50.
7. Zukin, *Loft Living*.
8. In the "actor-network" approach authors such as Bruno Latour and Michel Callon see the making of technological systems to involve a weaving together of networks of diverse human actors and nonhuman elements. Bruno Lator, *We Have Never Been Modern* (Cambridge, MA: Harvard University Press, 1993); Michel Callon, "Some Elements of a Sociology of Translation," in John Law (ed.), *Power, Action and Belief* (London: Routledge & Kegan Paul, 1986), pp. 196–229. In this view, entrepreneurs are network-builders who frame technological solutions and muster material supports to enact them. Network-building revolves around the efforts of entrepreneurs to enroll various social actors in the enterprise and to reposition them vis-à-vis each other and assorted devices, materials, and processes. For their part, entrepreneurs must pragmatically revise their schemes as they align and realign

social actors and devices. Moreover, the path of network development reflects the relative power of the participants. In fact, entrepreneurs may find that "their" project has been taken over by a more powerful actor. For example, Thomas Edison lost control over the electric industry to one of his financial partners—J. P. Morgan. Mark Granovetter and Patrick McGuire, "Thomas Edison and the Social Construction of the Early Electricity Industry in America," in Richard Swedberg (ed.), *Explorations in Economic Sociology* (New York: Russell Sage Foundation, 1993), pp. 213–48. In our era, founders of start-ups may be ousted from executive positions by their financial partners—venture capitalists.

9. Pratt, "Sticky Places?" p. 9.

10. At the time of this writing there is much speculation about how elements of advanced technological systems might be used against American cities—for example, that urban infrastructures such as bridges, tunnels, and subways, like skyscrapers, might be turned into death-traps or that devices of mass destruction, such as suitcase nuclear bombs or weaponized germs, might be detached from the crumbling military-industrial complex of the former Soviet Union. One fears a drawn-out conflict with an international network of terrorists whose repertoire may feature a Jihad versus the Manhattans of the world. Moreover, this startlingly powerful tactic may well become part of the repertoire for terrorists of all stripes who might want to strike a blow at the United States—a possible unintended consequence or "blowback" of America's projection of military power throughout the world. Chalmers Johnson, *Blowback: The Costs and Consequences of American Empire* (New York: Henry Holt and Company, 2000).

11. Peter Coy, "The Center Must Hold," *BusinessWeek*, 22 October 2001, p. 108.

12. Ibid., p. 104.

13. Robert Shiller, *Irrational Exhuberance* (Princeton, NJ: Princeton University Press, 2000); Thomas Frank, *One Market Under God* (New York: Doubleday, 2000).

14. Nicholas Negroponte, *Being Digital* (New York: Vintage, 1995); Kevin Kelly, *Out of Control: The New Biology of Machines, Social Systems and the Economic World* (Reading, MA: Perseus, 1994); George Gilder, *Microcosm: The Quantum Revolution in Economics and Technology* (New York: Simon & Schuster, 1989).

15. Allen J. Scott, *The Cultural Economy of Cities: Essays on the Geography of Image-Producing Industries* (London: Sage, 2000), p. 208.

16. Joel Kotkin, *The New Geography: How the Digital Revolution Is Reshaping the American Landscape* (New York: Random House, 2000), p. 113.

17. Ibid., pp. 113, 130.

18. Richard Florida, *The Rise of the Creative Class* (New York: Basic, 2002), p. 55.

19. Kotkin, *The New Geography*.

20. My typology resembles Kotkin's in some respects. However, I disagree with his claim that computer industry enclaves create the plumbing for the Internet while new media districts produce the "content." My view of the new media district role draws heavily on economic sociology. Economic sociologists propose that markets are held together by cognitive frameworks and cultural conventions that help consumers decide which products are comparable and help firms identify who competitors are—and by networks that aid in the making of these shared meanings. For example, see Neil Fligstein, "Markets as Politics," *American Sociological Review*, 61 (1996): 656–73; also see Bruce Carruthers and Brian Uzzi, "Economic Sociology in the New Millennium," *Contemporary Sociology*, 29 (2000): 486–94.

21. Kotkin, *The New Geography*, p. 130.

22. Paul Hirsch, "Processing Fads and Fashions," *American Journal of Sociology*, 77 (1972): 639–59.

23. Latour, *We Have Never Been Modern*, p. 117.

24. Ibid.

25. R. B. Helfgott, "Women's and Children's Apparel," in M. Hall (ed.), *Made in New York* (Cambridge, MA: Harvard University Press, 1959), p. 63. Also see the account of the Lower Manhattan Garment District provided by Allen J. Scott, *Metropolis* (Berkeley: University of California Press, 1988), pp. 73–79.

26. Sharon Zukin, *Landscapes of Power: From Detroit to Disney World* (Berkeley: University of California Press, 1991).

27. Michael Storper, *The Regional World: Territorial Development in a Global Economy* (New York: The Guilford Press, 1997); Allen J. Scott, *The Cultural Economy of Cities*.

28. Pratt, "Sticky Places?" p. 12.
29. Monique Girard and David Stark, "Distributing Intelligence and Organizing Diversity in New Media Projects," *Environment and Planning A* 34 (forthcoming).
30. Pratt, "Sticky Places?" p. 12.
31. See Annalee Saxenian, *Regional Advantage: Culture and Competition in Silicon Valley and Route 128* (Cambridge, MA: Harvard University Press, 1994).
32. Matthew Zook, "Regional Systems of Financing." Paper presented at the Global Networks, Innovation, and Development Strategy Conference, University of California, at Santa Cruz, Santa Cruz, CA, 11–13 November 1999.
33. Wolf Heydebrand and Annalisa Miron, "Constructing Innovativeness in New Media Start-up Firms," *Environment and Planning A*, 34 (forthcoming).
34. Nigel Thrift, "It's the Romance, Not the Finance, that Makes the Business Worth Pursuing," *Economy and Society*, 30 (2001): 412–32.
35. Ibid., pp. 418–19.
36. Ibid.
37. Bennett Harrison, *Lean and Mean* (New York: Basic Books, 1994), p. 112.
38. Scott, *The Cultural Economy of Cities*.
39. There is a burgeoning literature on global cities. Sources comparing New York to other global cities include Janet Abu-Lughod, *New York, Chicago, Los Angeles: America's Global Cities* (Minneapolis: University of Minnesota Press, 1999); Richard Child Hill and J. W. Kim, "Global Cities and Developmental States," *Urban Studies*, 37 (2000): 2167–95; and Saskia Sassen, *The Global City: New York, London, Tokyo* (Princeton, NJ: Princeton University Press, 1991).
40. An example of the way in which these institutional differences matter can be seen in the way in which a city helps coordinate and control global businesses. In New York the role is played by networks of producer services; in Tokyo the role is played by policy networks anchored by state bureaus. Richard Child Hill and Kuniko Fujita, "The Nested City," *Urban Studies*, 40 (2003): 207–18.
41. Heydebrand and Miron, "Constructing Innovativeness in New Media Start-up Firms": Susan Christopherson, "Why Do National Labor Market Practices Continue to Diverge in the Global Economy? The 'Missing Link' of Investment Rules," *Economic Geography*, 78, 1 (2002): 1–20; Michael Indergaard, "The Webs They Weave: Malaysia's Multimedia Super Corridor and New York City's Silicon Alley," *Urban Studies*, 40 (2003): 379–401.
42. Kuniko Fujita, "Neo-Industrial Tokyo," *Urban Studies*, 40 (2003): 265.
43. Hans-Joachim Braczy, Gerhard Fuchs, and Hans-Georg Wolf (eds.), *Multimedia and Regional Economic Restructuring* (London: Routledge, 1999).
44. Pim den Hertog, Erik Bronner, and Sven Malther, "Innovation in an Adolescent Cluster: The Case of the Dutch Multimedia Cluster." (Utrecht, The Netherlands: Centre for Science and Policy/Dialogic, 2000).
45. Indergaard, "The Webs They Weave," p. 397.

CHAPTER 2

1. Mark Weiss, "Idealism and the Internet: A New Business Model," *@NY*, 17 July 1998, p. 2.
2. Casey Hait and Stephen Weiss, *Digital Hustlers* (New York: Regan Books, 2001), p. 102.
3. Thomas Hirschfield, "The Coming Showdown in Media City," *City Journal*, 7, 1 (1997): 3.
4. During the late 1990s, major consulting companies could bill corporations up to $1,500 an hour for rank-and-file consultants and $5,000 for partners. Melanie Warner, "Management Consulting: The Incredible Shrinking Consultant," *Fortune.com*, 12 May 2003, p. 2.
5. Kevin Phillips, "The Cycles of Financial Scandal," *New York Times*, 17 July 2002, p. 19.
6. Mark Stahlman, "How 'Bout Some Context, Please—Mark Stahlman's Response." A *interesting-people.org* posting on 13 February 1996. Some other Silicon Alley notables have expressed similar sentiment. Bob Stein, the founder of Voyager, remarked, "Instead of having nice homes, cities that work, and clean subways, the middle class is going to get Virtual World and live in their computers." Frank Owens, "Let Them Eat Software," *Village Voice*, 6 February 1996, p. 32.
7. Vanessa Grigoriadis, "Silicon Alley 10003," *New York Magazine*, 6 March 2000, p. 31.

8. Michael Krantz, "The Great Manhattan Geek Rush," *New York Magazine*, 13 November 1995, pp. 35–42.
9. Hait and Weiss, *Digital Hustlers*, p. 69. An Urban Desires archive on the Internet showcases all the issues published from 1994 to 1997.
10. Andrew Ross, "The Great Wired Way," posting on *medialounge.net*, 12 May 1997, p. 1.
11. Steve Johnson, "Web Editor Argues: Believe the Hype," *@NY*, 1997, p. 2.
12. Tom Watson, "It's Services Stupid. Realtime Replaces Branding," *@NY*, November 1997, p. 3.
13. J. Cherkovas, "New York's New Media's Ground Zero," *@NY*, 12 April 1996, p. 2.
14. Ibid., p. 1.
15. Hait and Weiss, *Digital Hustlers*, p. 65.
16. Interview, July 1998.
17. Hait and Weiss, *Digital Hustlers*, p. 70.
18. Krantz, "The Great Manhattan Geek Rush," p. 37.
19. Jason McCabe Calacanis, "The Story of Pseudo," *Silicon Alley Reporter*, 2, 11 (1998): 38. Also see T. Gabriel, "Where Silicon Alley Artists Go to Download," *New York Times*, 8 October 1995, p. 52.
20. Owens, "Let Them Eat Software."
21. David W. Chen, "For New Media, an Old-Time Forum," *New York Times*, 1 May 1997, Section B, p. 10; Amy Harmon, "Trying to Put Soul Back Into Silicon Alley," *New York Times*, 19 October 1997, p. 4.
22. Jason Chervokas, "How New York Has Changed," *@NY*, 5 September 1997, p.2.
23. Krantz, "The Great Manhattan Geek Rush," p. 42.
24. B. Pulley, "New York Striving to Become Technology's Creative Center," *New York Times*, 13 February 1995, Section A, p. 1; Section B, p. 2.
25. Interview, July 1998.
26. Interview, March 2002.
27. Shira J. Base, "Site Developers Case Wider Net," *Crain's New York Business*, 13 April 1998, p. 24.
28. Ian Fisher, "The Human Face of New York's Web World," *New York Times*, 8 August 1996, Section B, p. 1.
29. Austin Bunn, "Upstart Startups," *Village Voice*, 11 November 1997, p. 40.
30. Interview, July 1998.
31. Ibid.
32. Interview, November 1998.
33. Ruth Davis, "Silicon Survivors," *New York Magazine*, 20 April 1998, pp. 34–35.
34. Jason Chervokas and Tom Watson, "Silicon Alley Trades Attitude for Maturity," *CyberTimes*, 23 September 1996, p. 2.
35. Krantz, "The Great Manhattan Geek Rush," p. 41.
36. Davis, "Silicon Survivors"; Tom Watson, "The Web Portal that Never Was," *@NY*, 23 October 1998.
37. Interview, November 1998.
38. Krantz, "The Great Manhattan Geek Rush," p. 42.
39. John Motavalli, "AOL Executive Chides Content Developers," *ZDNN*, 19 June 1997, p. 1.
40. Interview, July 1998.
41. Ibid.
42. Ibid.
43. Ibid.
44. Ibid.
45. Ibid.
46. Fred Wilson, Comments at "The State of the New Media," a panel sponsored by the New York New Media Association, New York, 4 February 1999.
47. Interview, July 1998.
48. Jason Chervokas, "The Good Guys Won the Battle but Stand to Lose the War," *@NY*, 19 February 1999, p. 1.
49. Interview, July 1998.
50. Chan Suh, Comments at "The State of the New York New Media," a panel sponsored by the New York New Media Association, New York, 4 February 1999.
51. Steve Levy, ibid.

52. Fred Wilson, ibid.
53. B. Pulley, "New York Striving to Become Technology's Creative Center," *New York Times*, 13 February 1995, Section A, p. 1; Section B, p. 2.
54. The Group of 35, *Group of 35 Final Report: Preparing for the Future: A Commercial Development Strategy for New York City*, 2001, New York.
55. Chris Sandlund, "Desire to Please Turning Around WTC," *Crain's New York Business*, 16 October 2000, p. 68.
56. Joshua Macht, "It Takes a Cyber Village," *Inc. Tech*, 4 (1997): 79–94.
57. Claudia Deutsch, "Leasing Real Space to Denizens of Cyberspace," *New York Times*, 26 May 1996, Real Estate Section, p. 7.
58. V. Block, "Rising Firm Tally Expands Geography of Silicon Alley," *Crain's New York Business*, 24 November 1997, pp. 36, 37.
59. "Nuturing the New Media Entrants," Commercial Real Estate Advertisement, *New York Times*, 25 March 1997, Section D, p. 25.
60. Macht, "It Takes a Cyber Village," p. 80.
61. Warren St. John, "Media Mogul," *Wired.com*, July 1999, pp. 1–6.
62. Hait and Weiss, *Digital Hustlers*, p. 101.
63. Ibid., p. 102.
64. St. John, "Media Mogul," p. 2.
65. Interview, July 1998.
66. Hait and Weiss, *Digital Hustlers*, p. 21.
67. Steve Lohr, "New York Area is Forging Ahead in New Media," *New York Times*, 15 April 1996, Section D, pp. 1, 4; "New York's Dynamic New Media," *New York Times*, 16 April 1996, p. 20; Jason Chervokas and Tom Watson, "Report Gives City's New Media New Credibility," *CyberTimes*, 15 April 1996, pp. 1–4.
68. "New York's Dynamic New Media," *New York Times*, p. 20.
69. Almost none of my students at St. John's University in Queens had ever heard of Silicon Alley. A dean of mine who knew I was researching Silicon Alley asked if it was all in one building. Obviously his source was the PR for the NYITC.
70. Interview, September 2002.
71. Ibid.
72. Hait and Weiss, *Digital Hustlers*, pp. 106–7.
73. Interview, July 1998.
74. Warren St. John, "Brattitude Adjustment," *Wired.com*, September 2000, p. 3.
75. B. Warner, "Silicon Alley's Cool Fish," *thestandard.com*, 15 February 1999, pp. 2–3.
76. St. John, "Brattitude Adjustment."
77. Ibid.
78. Lisa Napoli and Saul Hansell, "For Silicon Alley, a Time to Rise and Shine," *New York Times*, 29 March 1999, p. 4.
79. Randall Rothenbery, "An Advertising Power, but Just What Does DoubleClick Do?" *New York Times*, 22 September 1999, E-Commerce Section, p. 14.
80. Ibid.
81. Ibid.
82. Barry Salzman, "The Web as a Global Medium," address at Silicon Alley Uptown conference, Columbia University Business School, New York, 17 November 2000.
83. J. Schwarz, "Trade Commission Drops Inquiry of DoubleClick," *New York Times*, 23 January 2001, Section C, p. 5.
84. Judith Messina, "Kevin O'Connor and the Mouse that Roared," *Crain's New York Business*, 15 May 2000, pp. 30, 32; Rothenbery, "An Advertising Power, but Just What Does DoubleClick Do?"
85. Lisa Napoli, "A Focus on Women at iVillage," *New York Times*, 3 August 1998, Section D, p. 6.
86. G. Gould, "Alley Girl: IVillage's Candice Carpenter on the Power of the Woman's Brand and How It May Change Silicon Alley," *Silicon Alley Reporter*, September 1998, p. 52.
87. Larry Kanter and Judith Messina, "Millionaires of Silicon Alley," *Crain's New York Business*, 29 November 1999.
88. Jason McCabe Calacanis, "Star Gazing; SAR Talks Business with StarMedia's Million-Dollar Man," *Silicon Alley Reporter*, 3, 8 (1999): 130.

89. Calacanis, "Star Gazing," p. 128.
90. Jennifer Rich, "StarMedia Faces New Challenges in Latin America," *New York Times*, 29 May 2000, pp. 34–35.

CHAPTER 3

1. Interview, November 1998.
2. David Chen, "Now in New York: Angels that Rescue Companies," *New York Times*, 2 July 1997.
3. Amy Harmon, "Stocks Drive a Rush to Riches in Manhattan's Silicon Alley," *New York Times*, 31 May 1999, p. B6.
4. Jeff Madrick, "Devotion to Free-Market, Laissez-Faire Dogma Makes for Ineffectual Policy," *New York Times*, 5 September 2000, p. C2.
5. H. Rowen, "Serendipity or Strategy: How Technology and Markets Came to Favor Silicon Valley," in C. Lee, W. Miller, M. G. Hancock, and H. Rowen (eds.), in *The Silicon Valley Edge* (Stanford, CA: Stanford University Press, 2000), p. 189.
6. Hengyi Feng, Julie Froud, Sukhdev Johal, Colin Haslam, and Karel Williams, "A New Business Model? The Capital Market and the New Economy," *Economy and Society*, 30 (2002): 486.
7. Neil Fligstein, *The Architecture of Markets: An Economic Sociology of Twenty-First Century Capitalist Societies* (Princeton, NJ: Princeton University Press, 2001), p. 227.
8. David Chen, "Venture Capital Showing Faith in Internet's Future," *New York Times*, 27 May 1997.
9. John Motavalli, *Bamboozled at the Revolution: How Big Media Lost Billions in the Battle for the Internet* (New York: Viking, 2002), p. 304.
10. Annalee Saxenian, *Regional Advantage* (Cambridge, MA: Harvard University Press, 1994); Martin Kenney and Richard Florida, "Venture Capital in Silicon Valley," in Martin Kenney (ed.), *Understanding Silicon Valley* (Stanford, CA: Stanford University Press, 2000), pp. 98–123.
11. Vivianna Zelizor argues that networks are "circuits of restricted exchange" when actors make distinctive use of money. Even in the case of legal tender people distinguish between bribes, donations, honorariums, tips, damages, pin money (and venture capital). They often make distinctive use of money when undertaking delicate or difficult matters such as creating ties, controlling others or dealing with risk. See Vivianna Zelizor, *The Social Meaning of Money* (New York: Basic Books, 1994).
12. Doug Mintz, "Behind the Venture Capital," *Silicon Alley Reporter*, 47 (2001): 17.
13. Chen, "Venture Capital Showing Faith in Internet's Future."
14. Lore Croghan, "Silicon Valley Bank Eyeing City's New Media Firms," *Crain's New York Business*, 3 February 1997.
15. Jason Calacanis, "Well Done," *Silicon Alley Reporter*, 26 (1999): 92.
16. Interview, July 1998.
17. Interview, July 1998.
18. Jason Chervokas, "The New Boys Network," *The Industry Standard*, 15 June 1998.
19. "Fred Wilson: New Media Money Man," *Crain's New York Business*, 31 March 1997; Chervokas, "The New Boys Network," p.32.
20. Chervokas, "The New Boys Network," p. 32.
21. Interview, July 1998.
22. Judith Messina, "Fund Gives Youngest Tech Firms Introduction to NY Billionaires," *Crain's New York Business*, 28 September 1998, p. 4.
23. Chervokas, "The New Boys Network," p. 32.
24. Jon Birger, "Chase's New Media Bonanza," *Crain's New York Business*, 21 June 1999, p. 56.
25. David Chen, "Virtual Pitch, but Real Jobs on the Line," *CyberTimes*, 16 June 1997, p.3.
26. Lynda Radosevich, "Start-up Star Warns Entrenched Companies to Retool or Be Surpassed," *InfoWorld Electric*, 23 February 1999, p. 1.
27. Mark Gimein, "Around the Globe, New Stock Market Mania," *The Industry Standard*, 28 December 1998, p. 40.
28. Jason Chervokas, "Looking Beyond the Madness," *@NY*, 13 November 1998, p. 1.
29. Gimein, "Around the Globe, New Stock Market Mania," p. 40.

30. Interview, July 1998.
31. David Ball, "Unearthing an IPO Success," *Silicon Alley Reporter*, 22 (1999): 46.
32. For a discussion of the symbolic economy of cities see Sharon Zukin, *Landscapes of Power* (Berkeley: University of California Press, 1991). For a classic sociological account of the cultural industries see Paul Hirsch, "Processing Fads and Fashions," *American Journal of Sociology*, 77 (1972): 639–59. I was also inspired by Andre Shleifer (Harvard) and Nick Barberis (University of Chicago) who are studying investment "styles." See Mark Hulbert, "The Value-Stock Advantage May Be Just a Mirage," *New York Times*, 21 July 2002, p. 8.
33. Casey Hait and Stephen Weiss, *Digital Hustlers* (New York: Regan Books, 2001), p. 45.
34. Andy Pelander, "Show Me the Money," *Silicon Alley Reporter*, 32 (1999): 72.
35. Ball, "Unearthing an IPO Success," p. 44.
36. Ibid.
37. Hait and Weiss, *Digital Hustlers*, p. 142.
38. Ball, "Unearthing an IPO Success," p. 48.
39. Andy Pelander, "The Bridge to IPO," *Silicon Alley Reporter*, 32 (1999): 108.
40. Judith Messina, "Silicon CFOs," *Crain's New York Business*, 24 March 1997, p. 28.
41. Andy Pelander, "Accounting for Dot-Coms," *Silicon Alley Reporter*, 32 (1999): 96.
42. Marilyn Alva, "Charging Silicon Alley," *Crain's New York Business*, 12 October 1998, p. 29.
43. Ibid. p. 30.
44. Marilyn Alva, "Internet Firms Count on Big 6 for Seal of Approval, *Crain's New York Business*, 9 June 1997, p. 24.
45. Marilyn Alva, "Taking Risks on Unknown Pays Off with Stock Offering," *Crain's New York Business*, 12 October 1998, p. 32.
46. "The Public Record," *AlleyCat News*, February 2001, p. 76.
47. Mark Gimein, "How Morgan and Goldman Caught a Cold," *The Industry Standard*, 2 November 1998, p. 20.
48. Pelander, "The Bridge to IPO," p. 106.
49. Ibid., p. 108.
50. Gimein, "How Morgan and Goldman Caught a Cold," p. 20.
51. Stephen Gandell, "Merrill Lynch Gets Cut Out of Tech IPO Boom," *Crain's New York Business*, 24 April 2000, pp. 1, 57.
52. Joseph Kahn, "Wall St. Is Flush with Cash but also Green with Envy," *New York Times*, 14 December 1999, p. 12.
53. Marcia Vickers and Gary Weiss, "Wall Street's Hype Machine," *BusinessWeek*, 3 April 2000, p. 114.
54. Ibid., p. 120.
55. Eric Dinallo, Assistant Attorney General, State of New York, *Affidavit in Support of Application for an Order Persuant to General Business Law Section 354 with Regard to the Acts and Practices of Merrill Lynch & Co, Inc., Henry Blodget et al.*, 8 April 2002, p. 24.
56. E. S. Browning and Grey Ip, "Here Are Six Myths that Drove the Boom in Technology Stocks," *TheWallStreetJournal.com*, 16 October 2000, p. 5.
57. Vickers and Weiss, "Wall Street's Hype Machine," p. 122.
58. Dinallo, *Affidavit*, p. 21.
59. Ibid., p. 12.
60. Ibid., p.13.
61. Interview, March 2001.
62. PricewaterhouseCoopers, *3rd New York New Media Survey* (New York, 2000), p. 25.
63. "1999: The Year in Silicon Alley Stocks," *At New York*, 7 January 2000, p. 1.
64. Tom Watson, "Billions Flowed into Silicon Alley, as Internet Industry Grew Up in 1999, *At New York*, 6 January 2000, p. 1.
65. "Resource: Silicon Alley IPOs for '99," *At New York*, 6 January 2000; "The Public Record," pp. 78–83.
66. David Chen, "Venture Capital Discovers New York's New Techology," *New York Times*, 5 February; PricewaterhouseCoopers, *3rd New York New Media Survey* (New York, 2000).
67. Ken Li, "Urge to Merge Pervades Silicon Alley," *TheStandard.com*, 16 August 1999, p. 1.
68. PricewaterhouseCoopers, *3rd New York New Media Survey*.
69. "AlleyCat Investor Scorecard," *AlleyCat News*, February 2001, pp. 86–94.
70. John Tierney, "In E-World, Capital Is Where Its @," *New York Times*, 3 May 2000, p. 1.

71. Jerry Colonna, "For Internet Stocks, the Fall of Overvalued Companies Can Hurt Strong Companies," *New York Times*, 1 June 1998, p. 25.
72. Interview, July 1998.
73. Saul Hansell, "Gold Rush in Silicon Alley," *New York Times*, 7 February 2000, p. 13.
74. Doug Mintz, "Flatiron's Future," *Silicon Alley Reporter*, 42 (2001): 28.
75. Hansell, "Gold Rush in Silicon Alley," p. C13.
76. Mark Walsh, "Venture Capital Investors Crowd Internet Gateway," *Crain's New York Business*, 6 November 2000, pp. 63, 66; Hansell, "Gold Rush in Silicon Alley," pp. C1, 13.
77. Rafat Ali, "Make Sure to Take an Umbrella," *Silicon Alley Daily*, 28 November 2001, p. 4.
78. Hansell, "Gold Rush in Silicon Alley," p. C13.
79. Pelander, "Show Me the Money," p. 70.
80. Jason Chervokas, "The Good Guys Won the Battle but Stand to Lose the War," @NY, 19 February 1999, p. 2; Jason Calacanis, "The Internet 2.0 Manifesto," *Silicon Alley Daily*, 13 November 2000, p. 3.
81. Lisa Napoli and Saul Hansell, "For Silicon Alley, a Time to Rise and Shine," *New York Times*, 29 March 1999, p. C4.
82. Hansell, "Gold Rush in Silicon Alley," p. C13.
83. Napoli and Hansell, "For Silicon Alley, a Time to Rise and Shine," p. C4.
84. Larry Kanter and Judith Messina, "Unexpected Riches Remake the City," *Crain's New York Business*, 29 November 1999, p. 47.
85. Jason Calacanis, "The Force of the Slacker Generation," *Silicon Alley Reporter*, 31 (1999): 20.

Chapter 4

1. From Wolf Heydebrand and Annalisa Miron, "Constructing Innovativeness in New Media Start-up Firms," *Environment and Planning A*, 34 (forthcoming).
2. Port Authority of New York and New Jersey, "World Trade Center Is Hot New Address on Silion Alley, as Sun Microsystems Leases Two Floors in 2 WTC." Press release, World Trade Center, 4 February 1999.
3. C. J. Hughes, "Chinatown by Bus: More Silicon, Fewer Garments," *Silicon Alley Daily*, 9 December 2000, p. 9.
4. Port Authority of New York and New Jersey, ibid.
5. Andy Pratt, "New Media," *Geoforum*, 31 (2000): 425–36; Monique Girard and David Stark, "Distributing Intelligence and Organizing Diversity in New Media Projects," working paper, Institute for Social and Economic Research and Policy, Columbia University, 2001; Rosemary Batt, Susan Christopherson, Ned Rightor, and Van Jaarsveld, *Net Working: Work Patterns and Workforce Policies for the New Media Industry* (Washington, DC: Economic Policy Institute, 2001); Heydebrand and Miron, "Constructing Innovativeness in New Media Start-up Firms."
6. Allen J. Scott, "From Silicon Valley to Hollywood," in Hans-Joachim Braczy, Philip Cooke, and Martin Heidenreich (eds.), *National Innovation Systems* (London: UCL Press, 1998), pp. 136–62; Andy Pratt, "Sticky Places?" A Comment on the Making of 'New Media' Spaces," working paper for Global II, A Workshop in Media and Communications, London School of Economics, 2000; Ann-Katrin Backlund and Ake Sandberg, "New Media Industry Development," *Regional Studies*, 36 (2002): pp. 87–91.
7. Heydebrand and Miron, "Constructing Innovativeness in New Media Start-up Firms," pp. 28–29.
8. Nigel Thrift, "Its the Romance, Not the Finance, that Makes the Business Worth Pursuing," *Economy and Society*, 30 (2001): 412–32.
9. Paul DiMaggio, "Conclusion: The Future of Business Organization and Paradoxes of Change," in Paul DiMaggio (ed.), *The Twenty-First Century Firm* (Princeton, NJ: Princeton University Press, 2001), pp. 210–244; Walter Powell, "The Capitalist Firm in the Twenty-First Century," in DiMaggio (ed.), *The Twenty-First Century Firm*, pp. 33–68.
10. Craig Johnson, "Advising the New Economy: The Role of Lawyers," in C. Lee, W. Miller, M. G. Hancock, and J. Rowen (eds.), *The Silicon Valley Edge* (Stanford, CA: Stanford University Press, 2000), pp. 325–41; Mark Suchman, "Dealmakers and Counselors: Law Firms as Intermediaries in the Development of Silicon Valley," in Martin Kenney (ed.), *Understanding Silicon Valley* (Stanford, CA: Stanford University Press, 2000), pp. 71–97.

11. Francesca Poletta, "It Was Like a Fever . . . " Narrative and Identity in Social Protest," *Social Problems*, 45 (May 1998): 137–59.

12. Larry Kanter and Judith Messina, "New Media Lifts New York Economy," *Crain's New York Business*, 15 May 2000, p. 129.

13. Alair Townsend, "With Right Leaders, City's Latest Boom Won't Be Doomed," *Crain's New York Business*, 15 May 2000, p. 99.

14. Larry Kanter and Judith Messina, "Power Alley," *Crain's New York Business*, 29 November 1999, pp. 27, 30.

15. Steve Malanga, "New Economy Propels City to Record Year," *Crain's New York Business*, 13 December 1999, pp. 1, 52.

16. Larry Kanter and Judith Messina, "Unexpected Richs Remake the City," *Crain's New York Business*, 29 November 1999, p. 30.

17. PricewaterhouseCoopers, *3rd New York New Media Survey* (New York, 2000), p. 11.

18. Ibid., p. 37.

19. Townsend, "With Right Leaders," p. 99.

20. Rae D. Rosen and Reagan Murray, "Opening Doors: Access to the Global Market for Financial Sectors," in Margaret Crahan and Alberto Vourvoulias-Bush (eds.), *The City and the World* (New York: Council on Foreign Relations, 1997), pp. 39–50.

21. David Kirkpatrick, "Street Addict," *New York*, 1 May 2000, p. 36.

22. "Market Facts 2000," *Crain's New York*, 3 July 2000, pp. 24–26.

23. Kirkpatrick, "Street Addict," p. 36.

24. Jason Bram and James Orr, "Can New York City Book on Wall Street?" *Current Issues in Economics and Finance: Second District Highlights. Federal Reserve Bank of New York*, 5, 11 (July 1999): 1–2; the data on tax revenue is from Carol O'Cleireacain, "The Private Economy and the Public Budget of New York City," in Crahan and Vourvoulias-Bush (eds.), *The City and the World*, p. 31.

25. Jason Bram and Mike DeMott, "New York City's New-Media Boom: Real or Virtual?" *Current Issues in Economics and Finance: Second District Highlights. Federal Reserve Bank of New York*, 4, 10 (October 1998): 1–4.

26. "Biggest Stakes in Silicon Alley," *Crain's New York Business*, 29 November 1999, p. 47.

27. Razorfish, *Prospectus for Inital Public Offering*, 1999, p. 41.

28. Razorfish, *Annual Report for Fiscal Year 1999*, 2000.

29. Razorfish, *Annual Report for Fiscal Year 2001*, 2002.

30. DoubleClick, *Annual Report for Fiscal Year 1999*, 2000, pp. 6–7.

31. "Biggest Stakes in Silicon Alley," *Crain's New York Business*, 29 November 1999, pp. 46–47.

32. iVillage, *Annual Report for Fiscal Year 1999*, 2000, p. 3.

33. Matthew Flamm, Fredrick Gabriel, and Faye Brockman, "Millionaires of Silicon Alley," *Crain's New York Business*, 29 November 1999.

34. StarMedia, *Annual Report for Fiscal Year 1999*, 2000, pp. 6–7.

35. Ibid., StarMedia, *Annual Report for Fiscal Year 2001*, 2002.

36. StarMedia, *Annual Report for Fiscal Year 1999*, 2000, p. 4.

37. Batt et al., *Net Working*, p. 46.

38. Girard and Stark, "Distributing Intelligence and Organizing Diversity in New Media Projects"; Heydebrand and Miron, "Constructing Innovativeness in New Media Start-up Firms."

39. Girard and Stark, "Distributing Intelligence and Organizing Diversity in New Media Projects," pp. 11, 13, 19.

40. Heydebrand and Miron, "Constructing Innovativeness in New Media Start-up Firms," pp. 19–27.

41. Batt et al., *Net Working*, pp. 6–8.

42. The Cornell group conducted a website survey of members in five associations including NYNMA, Webgrrls, and WWWAC. Members of the associations were asked to respond to a March 1999 survey. The number who responded was 335, which represented a response rate of 5 percent. Batt et al., *Net Working*, p. 54.

43. Batt et al., *Net Working*, pp. 8–13.

44. Ibid., pp. 24–39.

45. Thrift, "Its the Romance, Not the Finance, that Makes the Business Worth Pursuing," pp. 418–21.

46. Interview, July 1998.

47. Jennifer Epel, "I Like the Nightlife, Baby," *Silicon Alley Reporter*, 4 (2000): 122.
48. John Motavalli, *Bamboozled at the Revolution* (New York: Viking, 2002), pp. 236–37.
49. Razorfish spent $10,000 to throw a similar May Day party in 1997 that became known in local lore as "The Party." Bernhard Warner, "Silicon Alley's Cool Fish," *theStandard.com*, 15 February 1999, pp. 1–6.
50. Two interviews, September 2002.
51. Ginn Neff, Elizabeth Wissinger, and Sharm Zukin, 2000, " 'Cool' Jobs in 'Hot' Industries." Unpublished ms., New York: Program in Sociology, Graduate Center of the City University of New York; Pratt, "New Media."
52. Nina Munk, "The Price of Freedom," *New York Times Magazine*, 5 March 2000, p. 51.
53. The author of the *Fast Company* story, Daniel Pink (a former speechwriter for Al Gore) had dedicated himself to spreading the Free Agent gospel. He states that it's all "about emotions, feelings, lifestyle, family. . . . Work has become almost a secular religion; people are trying to self-actualize through work. . . . It's easier when you're on your own." Munk, "The Price of Freedom," p. 52.
54. Judith Dobrzynski, "Online Pioneers: The Buzz Never Stops," *New York Times*, 21 November 1999, Section 3, p. 14.
55. G. Gould, "Alley Girl," *Silicon Alley Reporter* (September 1998): 52.
56. Kanter and Messina, "Unexpected Richs Remake the City," p. 30.
57. Interview, July 1998.
58. Tom Watson, "The Geek's Ultimate Revenge," *@NY*, 13 August 1999, pp. 1–2.
59. Judith Messina, "Software Pitchmen Strong Believers in New York's Burgeoning Sector," *Crain's New York Business*, 5 February 1996, p. 1.
60. Larry Kanter and Judith Messina, "Many Industries Bet Future on New Media," *Crain's New York Business*, 29 November 1999, p. 30.
61. Heydebrand and Miron, "Constructing Innovativeness in New Media Start-up Firms," p. 22.
62. Kanter and Messina, "Many Industries Bet Future on New Media," p. 34.
63. M. Baer, "The New Economy's Currency Is Stock, Stock, Stock," *New York Times*, 29 March 2000, p. 12.
64. Richard Sennett, *The Corrosion of Character* (New York: Norton, 1998), p. 81.
65. Ibid., p. 139.
66. Heydebrand and Miron, "Constructing Innovativeness in New Media Start-up Firms," p. 23.
67. Alan Cohen, "Law Firms Woo Silicon Alley Start-ups," *New York Law Journal*, 14 June 1999, pp. 1–5.
68. Ibid., pp. 1–3.
69. Charles Keenan, "Law Firm Scores Technical Knockout," *Crain's New York Business*, 4 September 2000, p. 16.
70. M. Baer, "The New Economy's Currency Is Stock, Stock, Stock," p. 12.
71. Flamm, Gabriel, and Brockman, "Millionaires of Silicon Alley," p. 49.
72. Michelle Leder, "Internet Ad Blitz Booms, Reshaping NY Landscape," *Crain's New York Business*, 6 March 2000, p. 36.
73. Larry Kanter and Judith Messian, "Nightlife, Culture Explores Geek Chic," *Crain's New York Business*, 29 November 1999, p. 42.
74. Thrift, "It's the Romance, Not the Finance, that Makes the Business Worth Pursuing," p. 417.
75. Kanter and Messina, "Many Industries Bet Future on New Media," p. 36.
76. Lore Croghan, "Silicon Alley Style," *Crain's New York Business*, 3 February 2000, p. 58.
77. The Group of 35, *Group of 35 Final Report: Preparing for the Future: A Commercial Development Strategy for New York City* (2001).
78. Sarah Bernard, "Gotham Expansion Teams," *New York Magazine*, 12 June 2000, p. 14.
79. Leo Jacobson, "Back to the Garage: Sen. Chuck Schumer and His Group of 35 Tackle the City's Space Crunch," *Silicon Alley Reporter*, 4 (2000): 70, 148.
80. J. Chiu, "Space Grabbers," *Crain's New York Business*, 7 August 2000, pp. 1, 54.
81. Randal Archibad, "A Silicon Alley Street Fair, Until a Virtual One Comes Along," *New York Times*, 22 May 2000, p. 1.
82. Kanter and Messina, "Unexpected Richs Remake the City," p. 30.
83. John Holusha, "Commercial Real Estate; Industrial Center is Reborn as Offices," *New York Times*, 11 October 2000, Section B, p. 8.
84. Lore Croghan, "Jupiter Signs 15-Year Lease; First to Pick Astor Place," *Crain's New York Business*, 20 March 2000, p. 4.

85. Ellen Rand, "Commercial Real Estate High Tech Touch," Special Advertisement, *New York Times*, 21 March 2000, p. 8.

86. Laurie Aron, "Downtown Re-emerges as Office Mecca," *Crain's New York Business*, 17 January 2000, p. 28; Lore Croghan, "Downtown Catches Midtown Office Fever," *Crain's New York Business*, 10 July 2000, pp. 3, 26.

87. Karen Angel, "Who Needs Square Footage? Tenants Seek Net Connections," *Crain's New York Business*, 16 August 1999, p. 29.

88. Rand, "Commercial Real Estate High Tech Touch," p. 9.

89. Judith Messina, "Telecoms Get in on, and Wire, the Ground Floor," *Crain's New York Business*, 17 January 2000, p. 30.

90. The Group of 35, *Group of 35 Final Report.*

91. Lore Croghan, "Web Host Expands to NYC as AT&T Site Goes Dot-Com," *Crain's New York Business*, 28 August 2000, p. 11.

92. Lore Croghan, "Taking Calls for a New Telco Hotel," *Crain's New York Business*, 25 September 2000, p. 46.

93. John Holusha, "Dot-Coms Accounted for 25% of First-quarter Leases," *New York Times*, 23 April 2000, p. 4.

94. Laurie Aron, "Web, Retail Surge Earns Full House for Midtown South, *Crain's New York Business*, 17 January 2000, pp. 26, 48; D. Anderson, "The Race for Office Space," *TheStandard.com*, 11 January 2000, pp. 1–3.

95. Mark Walsh, "Companies Parking in Alley Confront Cyberspace Jam," *Crain's New York Business*, 14 September 1998, p. 47.

96. Baer, "The New Economy's Currency Is Stock, Stock, Stock," p. 12.

97. Anderson, "The Race for Office Space," pp. 1–3.

98. Rand, "Commercial Real Estate High Tech Touch," p. 2.

99. Stefani Eads, "Selling Their Souls to Be in Silicon Alley," *Businessweek.com*, 24 April 2000, pp. 1–3; Aron, "Web, Retail Surge Earns Full House for Midtown South," pp. 26, 48.

100. Claude Solnik, "Famed Architects Exert Their Outside Influence," *Crain's New York Business*, 15 January 2001, p. 26.

101. Lorraine Kreahling, "Name Your Price," *Crain's New York Business*, 15 January 2001, p. 24.

102. M. Flamm, "A Booming Economy Remakes Manhattan," *Crain's New York Business*, 17 January 2000, p. 24; Anderson, "The Race for Office Space," p. 2; Kreahling, "Name Your Price," p. 24.

103. Rand, "Commercial Real Estate High Tech Touch."

104. Lorraine Kreahling, "New Media Firms' Space Program," *Crain's New York Business*, 18 October 1999, pp. 41, 54.

105. Michael McDonald, "Chinatown Loses Its Edge," *Crain's New York Business*, 19 June 2000, p. 1.

106. U. Ward, "Special Report: Commercial Real Estate," *Crain's New York Business*, 17 January 2000, pp. 42, 48, 50.

107. Aron, "Downtown Re-emerges as Office Mecca," p. 28.

108. Kanter and Messina, "Unexpected Richs Remake the City," p. 28; Aron, "Downtown Re-emerges as Office Mecca," p. 28.

109. Bernard, "Gotham Expansion Teams," p. 14.

110. S. Boss, "Free Trade, High Rents Hang Garment Makers Out to Dry," *Crain's New York Business*, 13 March 2000; Tom Fredrickson, "Garment Area Jobs Stripped," *Crain's New York Business*, 25 March 2001, pp. 1, 45.

111. John Holusha, "A Developer Puts a Bet on the Meatpacking District," *New York Times*, 16 July 2000, p. 9.

112. D. Dunlap, "For Once-Gritty Tribeca, a Golden Glow," *New York Times*, 30 July 2000, Section 11, pp. 1, 8.

113. Lisa Goff, "Tenants' Tastes Remap Manhattan: New Borders Reflect Changing Hot Spots," *Crain's New York Business*, 16 October 2000, pp. 63–64.

114. John Holusha, "An Upcycle Just Keeps Rolling," *New York Times*, 24 September 2000, pp. 1, 6.

115. Peter Malbin, "Trinity Real Estate," *Crain's New York Business*, 15 January 2001, p. 50.

116. McDonald, "Chinatown Loses Its Edge," pp. 1, 54.

117. Bernard, "Gotham Expansion Teams," p. 14.

118. Aron, "Downtown Re-emerges as Office Mecca," p. 28.

119. Eads, "Selling Their Souls to Be in Silicon Alley," p. 2.

120. Jacobson, "Back to the Garage," p. 146.

121. Michelle Leder, "Newmark & Co.," *Crain's New York Business*, 15 January 2001, p. 48.
122. Manuel Castells, *The Rise of the Network Society* (Oxford: Blackwell, 1996).

CHAPTER 5

1. Bruce Bernstein, "Silicon Alley's Albany Agenda: Expand the Technology Boom," *@NY*, 4 June 1999, p. 1.
2. Upper Manhattan Empowerment Center Development Corporation, "HIWAY 125" Paves the Way for New Technology Zone & Welcomes Urban Box Office Network to Harlem," press release, 19 April 2000, p. 1.
3. Ibid.
4. C. J. Hughes, "Bronx Online," *Silicon Alley Daily*, 25 January 2001, pp. 2–5.
5. For the population composition of New York in 2000, see New York City Department of Planning website, dated 20 August 2001; for the numbers on new media workers see PricewaterhouseCoopers, *3rd New York New Media Survey* (New York, 2000), p. 26.
6. Jason Chervokas, "The New Boys' Network," *The Industry Standard*, 15 June 1998.
7. "Urban Box Office Founder Dies," *At New York*, 16 February 2000, pp. 1–2.
8. Office of the Comptroller, City of New York, *The NYC Software/IT Industry: How NYC Can Compete More Effectively in Information Technology* (April 1999).
9. Jason Chervokas, "Why Silicon Alley Isn't a Neighborhood, It's a Region," *At New York*, 12 March 2000, p. 2.
10. Judith Messina, "How to Boost High Tech in NY Area? It's Academic," *Crain's New York Business*, 11 January 1999, p. 13.
11. Ibid., pp. 13–14.
12. For a broad sampling of the literature on innovative regions see Allen J. Scott, *Regions and the World Economy* (Oxford: Oxford University Press, 2000); Michael Storper, *The Regional World: Territorial Development in a Global Economy* (New York: Guilford Press, 1997); Paul Krugman, *Geography and Trade* (Cambridge, MA: MIT Press, 1991); and Hans-Joachim Braczy, Philip Cooke and Martin Heidenreich (eds.), *Regional Innovation Systems* (London: UCL Press, 1998).
13. Annalee Saxenian, *Regional Advantage* (Cambridge, MA: Harvard University Press, 1994).
14. See H. Savitch and R. Vogel (eds.), *Regional Politics* (Thousand Oaks, CA: Sage, 1996); and Michael Indergaard, "Beyond the Region," *Urban Affairs Review*, 34 (1998): 241–62.
15. Manuel Castells and Peter Hall, *Technopoles of the World* (London: Routledge, 1994); and Ann Markusen, Young-Sook Lee, and Sean DiGiovanna (eds.), *Second Tier Cities* (Minneapolis: University of Minnesota Press, 1999).
16. See John Allen, Doreen Massey, and Allan Cochrane, *Rethinking the Region* (London: Routledge, 1998).
17. PricewaterhouseCoopers, *3rd New York New Media Survey* (New York, 2000).
18. A second data set collected by the American Electronics Association for a somewhat different mix of high tech sectors confirmed that the concentration of "technology" workers extended into the city's suburbs and its neighbor across the Hudson River—New Jersey. As of 1998 some 115,900 technology workers were located in New York and its in-state suburbs, while some 41,300 were located in the six New Jersey counties adjacent to New York City. In all, some 135,000 technology workers were present in New Jersey (American Electronics Association, 2000).
19. Office of the Comptroller, *The NYC Software/IT Industry*, p. ix.
20. "City Comptroller Calls for Incubators, Office of Technology," *@NY*, 23 April 1999, p. 1.
21. Bernstein, "Silicon Alley's Albany Agenda," p. 1.
22. Judith Messina, "For Job, Push Enter: New Media Firms Promise Entry-level Positions, Ask City to Shift Focus from Big Firm Goodies," *Crain's New York Business*, 25 September 1995, pp. 3, 37.
23. The other members included the Environmental Business Association of New York, the New York Biotechnology Association, the New York Photonics Development Corp., and a Long Island technology association. Judith Messina, "Feisty High Tech Coalition Emerging," *Crain's New York Business*, 10 March 1997, pp. 3, 33.

24. Interview, July 1998.
25. Interview, July 1998.
26. "Pataki Must Help High Growth Firms," *Crain's New York Business*, 17 March 1997, p. 8.
27. "Vallone Proposes Help for Tech Firms," *Crain's New York Business*, 10 November 1997, p. 12.
28. Charles Millard, "How New York City is Working to Give a Leg Up to Silicon Alley," *@NY*, 26 February 1999, pp. 1–2.
29. Bernhard Warner, "New York Offers Aid to Keep Net Firms," *The Standard.com*, 22 June 1999, pp. 1–3.
30. Steve Malanga, "Horse Trading for City Jobs," *Crain's New York Business*, 8 February 1999, p. 9.
31. Bernstein, "Silicon Alley's Albany Agenda," p. 1.
32. Christine Gordon, "You Take Manhattan: Will Net Companies Adopt 'Other' Boroughs," *At New York*, 21 February 2000, p. 2.
33. Bernstein, "Silicon Alley's Albany Agenda," pp. 1–2.
34. There was one site each in Staten Island ("SI Hub"); Manhattan ("HIWay125," Harlem); Queens ("CyberCity@LIC," Long Island City); and Bronx ("BronxSmart"). There were four sites in Brooklyn: (1) "Downtown Brooklyn Connected," a zone from DUMBO to Metro Tech Center; (2) the "Brooklyn Information Technology Center" (Bush Terminal); (3) "Silicon Harbor" (Red Hook); and (4) the Brooklyn Navy Yard.
35. Steve Malagna, "Leap of Faith for Landlords," *Crain's New York Business*, 22 May 2000, p. 9.
36. Ellen Rand, "Commercial Real Estate High Tech Touch," Special Advertisement *New York Times*, 21 March 2000, p. 8.
37. Gordon, "You Take Manhattan: Will Net Companies Adopt 'Other' Boroughs," p. 2.
38. The Group of 35, *Group of 35 Final Report*, 2001.
39. Leo Jacobson, "Back to the Garage: Sen. Chuck Schumer and His Group of 35 Tackle the City's Space Crunch," *Silicon Alley Reporter*, 4 (2000): 70.
40. Ibid.
41. P. Lentz, "Pursuing West Side Glory," *Crain's New York Business*, 18 September 2000, pp. 1, 52.
42. Jacobson, "Back to the Garage."
43. The city's total investment in the fund was only $10 million but its shares in 24/7 were worth $38 million and its holdings in Multex were also worth $38 million as of April 1999; it apparently received very good professional advice (as institutional investors often do) with regard to a third prospect—the Mining Co. (later known as about.com). The city's $3 million contribution in the last round of investment before the firm's IPO, ended up being worth $43 million. James Ledbetter, "New York Places a Little Internet Wager," *The Standard.com*, 30 April 1999, pp. 1–2.
44. Mark Walsh, "State Tech Dollars Won't Flow to City," *Crain's New York Business*, 17 July 2000, p. 46.
45. Terry Pristin, "New York City Partnership and Chamber of Commerce Names New Head," *New York Times*, 8 December 2000, p. 14.
46. Laurie Joan Aron, "The Right Stuff: Aiming to Create Jobs, Lift Distressed Areas, Investment Fund Takes Odd Risks that Often Pay Off," *Crain's New York Business*, 14 May 2001, pp. 23, 28.
47. Michael McDonald, "Kravis City Fund Ends Manufacturing Push," *Crain's New York Business*, 17 April 2000, pp. 1, 81.
48. Ericsson Cyberlab, "The New York City Investment Fund and the New York New Media & Technology Community," *Cyberlab-ny.ericsson.com*, no date, pp. 1–2.
49. Judith Messina, "Colleges Spend on Teaching Tech," *Crain's New York Business*, 22 November 1999, p. 44.
50. Polytechic and five colleges also formed the Knowledge Workers Education Alliance. Their goal was to funnel graduates of the liberal arts undergraduate programs at the smaller colleges to a Polytechnic program offering a one-year master's degree in computer science. Judith Messina, "Colleges Spend on Teaching Tech," p. 1.
51. Amy Harmon, "Stocks Drive a Rush to Riches in Manhattan's Silicon Alley," *New York Times*, 31 May 1999, Section B, p. 6.
52. Mark Walsh, "NYU: Private University in Public Market," *Crain's New York Business*, 24 January 2000.
53. Jennifer Farley, "Take Two: Incubation Ideas and Accelerating Growth," *AlleyCat News*, January 2001, pp. 74–76.

54. The two venture capital firms each contributed $500,000—and their CEOs became managing partners of the New York Telemedia Accelerator—while NYCIF provided $500,000 and a $2.5 million line of credit. The venture pays the college below-market rent of $10 a square foot. Karen Arenson, "Community College Offers a Nest for Digital Ventures," *New York Times*, 22 April 1999, Section B, p. 9.

55. Farley, "Take Two: Incubation Ideas and Accelerating Growth," p. 76.

56. Charles Keenan, "CUNY Learns Lesson in Linking to Business," *Crain's New York Business*, 7 August 2000, p. 24.

57. Antonio Perez, letter to the editor, *New York Times*, 27 May 2000, p. 14.

58. Keenan, "CUNY Learns Lesson in Linking to Business," p. 24.

59. "Flatiron Launches Venture Philanthropy Funds," *At New York*, 3 April 2000, p. 1.

60. Ibid.

61. Fred Wilson remarked, "We will take board seats and we will measure these groups the way we measure deals: did they achieve their business plans for the year?" Saul Hansell, "The Nouveaux Riches of the Internet Take a New Approach to Charity, with the Accent on Web Education and Start-ups," *New York Times*, 3 April 2000, p. 4.

62. Ibid.

63. Ibid.

64. Ibid.

65. Max Weber, *The Protestant Ethic and the Spirit of Capitalism* (New York: Scribners, 1958).

66. Manuel Castells, *The Rise of the Network Society* (Oxford: Blackwell, 1996).

67. Jennifer Epel, "I Like the Nightlife, Baby," *Silicon Alley Reporter*, 4 (2000): 122.

68. For the classic treatment on free market ideology see Karl Polanyi, *The Great Transformation* (Boston: Beacon Press, 1944); regarding millennialism and faith in technology see David Noble, "The Religion of Technology: The Myth of a Masculine Millennium," *Progress Without People* (Toronto: Between the Lines Press, 1996), pp. 127–42.

69. Michael Deaver, "Reagan Democrats: Gone but Not Forgotten," *New York Times*, 22 February 2000, p. 23.

70. P. Henning, "Charles Darwin Meet Adam Smith, *Red Herring*, September 2000, pp. 229–30.

71. Judith H. Dobrzynski, "Online Pioneers: The Buzz Never Stops," *New York Times*, 21 November 1999, Section 3, p. 1.

72. Amy Harmon, "Stocks Drive a Rush to Riches in Manhattan's Silicon Alley," *New York Times*, 31 May 1999, Section B, p. 6.

73. Dobrzynski, "Online Pioneers: The Buzz Never Stops," p. 14.

74. Leo Jacobson, "Republican Senate-Hopeful Rick Lazio Has Friends in Silicon Alley After All," *Silicon Alley Daily*, 21 September 2000, p. 4.

75. See Daniel Gross, *Bull Run: Wall Street, the Democrats, and the New Politics of Personal Finance* (New York: Public Affairs, 2000).

76. David Kirkpatrick, "Street Addict," *New York Magazine*, 1 May 2000, p. 35.

77. John Tierney, "@ Wits' End and in a Mood to Taunt," *New York Times*, 5 February 2000, Section B, p. 1.

CHAPTER 6

1. Lore Croghan, "Jupiter Signs 15-year Lease," *Crain's New York Business*, 20 March 2000, p. 4.

2. "Dot-Com Crash, or Fender Bender," *Crain's New York Business*, 24 July 2000, p. 8.

3. "AOL/Time Warner," *Silicon Alley Reporter* (January 2001): 29.

4. Mark Walsh, "Time, AOL Deal Brings Merger Frenzy to Alley," *Crain's New York Business*, 17 January 2000, pp. 1, 69.

5. James Ledbetter, "A New Media World Order," *Thestandard.com*, 14 January 2000, p. 1.

6. Ibid.

7. Ibid., pp. 2–3.

8. For example, see Paul DiMaggio, "Endogenizing 'Animal Spirits' ": Toward a Sociology of Collective Response to Uncertainty and Risk," in Mauro Guillén et al. (eds.), *The New Economic Sociology* (New York: Russell Sage Foundation, 2002), pp. 79–100; W. R. Scott, *Institutions and Organizations* (Thousand Oaks, CA: Sage, 1995); Walter Powell and Paul DiMaggio (eds.), *The New Institutionalism in Organizational Analysis* (Chicago and London: University of Chicago Press, 1991).

9. Paul DiMaggio, "Endogenizing 'Animal Spirits.'"
10. Michael Piore, *Beyond Individualism* (Cambridge, MA: Harvard University Press, 1995), pp. 137–39.
11. Randall Collins, "On the Microfoundations of Macrosociology," *American Journal of Sociology* 86 (1981): 984–1014.
12. Judy Temes, "Burned Offerings: Weak Market Hits IPOs," *Crain's New York Business*, 14 April 1997, p. 12.
13. Tom Watson, "Will Stock Dive Finally Kill Net Hype Once and for All?" *@NY*, 1 January 1998, p. 1.
14. Jon Birger and Judith Messina, "Up in Smoke," *Crain's New York Business*, 16 November 1998, pp. 51–52.
15. Ibid., p. 53.
16. Alice O'Rourke, letter to the editor, *Crain's New York Business*, 7 December 1998, p. 8.
17. Carl Weisbrod, letter to the editor, *Crain's New York Business*, 30 November 1998, p. 8.
18. Judith H. Dobrzynski, "Online Pioneers: The Buzz Never Stops," *New York Times*, 21 November 1999, Section 3, p. 14.
19. Andrew Ross, *No-Collar: The Humane Workplace and Its Hidden Costs* (New York: Basic Books, 2003), p. 74.
20. Monique Girard and David Stark, "Distributing Intelligence and Organizing Diversity in New Media Projects," working paper, Institute for Social and Economy Research and Policy, Columbia University, 2001.
21. Wolf Heydebrand and Annalisa Miron, "Constructing Innovativeness in New Media Start-up Firms," *Environment and Planning* A, 34 (forthcoming).
22. Rosemary Batt, Susan Christopherson, Ned Rightor, and Van Jaarsveld, *Net Working: Work Patterns and Workforce Policies for the New Media Industry* (Washington, DC: Economic Policy Institute, 2001), 39.
23. Interview, September 2002.
24. Ibid.
25. Ibid.
26. Ibid.
27. Ibid.
28. Interview, March 2001.
29. Interview, September 2002.
30. Dan Mitchell, "Profit or Persish," *The Industry Standard*, 24 January 2000, pp. 208, 213.
31. Gretchen Morgenson, "If You Think Last Week Was Wild . . . ," *New York Times*, 19 March 2000, Section 3, p. 1.
32. Floyd Norris, "NASDAQ Market at 5,000: Redefining Market Volatility," *New York Times*, 10 March 2000, p. 10.
33. Ibid.
34. David Lipschultz, "A Simple Case of Supply and Demand," *Red Herring* (May 2000): 426–34.
35. Dan Mitchell, "Profit or Perish," p. 213.
36. Morgenson, "If You Think Last Week Was Wild . . ."
37. Ibid.
38. Paul Krugman, "The Ponzi Paradigm," *New York Times*, 12 March 2000, p. 15.
39. Jerry Useem, "New Ethics or No Ethics," *Fortune*, 20 March 2000, pp. 82–86.
40. Marcia Vickers and Gary Weiss, "The Wall Street Hype Machine," *BusinessWeek*, 3 April 2000, pp. 114–26.
41. Gretchen Morgenson, "Getting Reacquainted With Risk," *New York Times*, 9 April 2000, Section 3, pp. 1, 7.
42. "Spring Fever," *New York Times*, 18 April 2000, Section C, p. 16.
43. Eric J. Savitz, "Has the Nasdaq Hit Bottom?" *The Industry Standard*, 19 March 2001, p. 36.
44. Steve Lohr, "Technology Sell-Off May Bring Shakeout of Dot-Com Concerns," *New York Times*, 17 April 2000, p. 17.
45. Tom Watson, "Special Report: The End of Nasdaq Welfare," *At New York*, 17 April 2000, p. 1.
46. Matt Richel, "www.layoffs.com: Internet Work Force Has Its First Brush with Downsizing," *New York Times*, 22 June 2000, p. 12.
47. Alexia Vargas, "Falling Dot.coms Confront Delisting," *Crain's New York Business*, 10 July 2000, p. 3.

48. Lark Park, "Out on the Venture Plateau," *The Industry Standard*, 13 Novemeber 2000, p. 77.
49. Mark Walsh, "Venture Season Is Hot, Even as Stocks Cool," *Crain's New York Business*, 21 August 2000, p. 34.
50. Mark Walsh, "Profits of Boom," *Crain's New York Business*, 21 August 2000, p. 39.
51. PricewaterhouseCoopers, *New York New Media Survey: Climate Study*, January 2001.
52. Walsh, "Profits of Boom," p. 39.
53. Mark Walsh, "Venture Funds Seek Greener Pastures," *Crain's New York Business*, 13 November 2000, p. 68.
54. Laurie Joan Aron, "Return of the Killer Ap," *Crain's New York Business*, 26 March 2001, p. 23.
55. Simon Romero, "Wireless Internet Casts Its Shadow, and Substance, in New York," *New York Times*, 21 August 2000, p. 1.
56. Richel, "www.layoffs.com: Internet Work Force Has Its First Brush with Downsizing," p. 12.
57. Alexia Vargas, "Alley-ites Find Life After Layoffs," *Crain's New York Business*, 24 July 2000, p. 1.
58. Lisa Ammerman, "The Pink Slip Holiday Tribute Bash," *Silicon Alley Daily*, 21 December 2000, pp. 5–6.
59. "Readers Respond to Pseudo Shutdown," *Silicon Alley Daily*, 21 September 2000, p. 7.
60. Stacy Cowley, "Six-year-old Pseudo Exhausts Its Cash Supply and Shuts Down," *Silicon Alley Daily*, 19 September 2000, p. 2.
61. "Pseudo's (Former) CFO David Bohrman: The Sinking of Pseudo," *Silicon Alley Daily*, 26 September 2000, p. 2.
62. Erin Joyce, "Overserved Media Market: MTVi's Layoffs Only the Start," *At New York*, 28 September 2000, p. 1.
63. Charles LeDuff, "What a Long, Strange Trip: Pseudo.com to Dot-Nowhere," *New York Times*, 27 October 2000, p. 10.
64. Steve Baldwin, "The Fire This Time," Disobey.com, 2 July 2000, p. 1.
65. "Disgusted," Disobey.com, 3 August 2000, p. 6.
66. Mike Rinzel, "The Dot-Com Fallout: How Baby Boomers Screwed Gen X," *Silicon Alley Daily*, 9 November 2000, p. 4.
67. Michael Indergaard, "Innovation, Speculation, and Urban Development: The New Media Market Brokers of New York City," in Kevin Fox Gotham (ed.), *Research in Urban Sociology. Volume 6: Critical Perspectives on Urban Redevelopment* (Oxford: JAI Press, 2001), p. 138.
68. Vargas, "Falling Dot.coms Confront Delisting," pp. 3, 31.
69. The number is based on firm filings to the SEC.
70. Mark Walsh, "Head Resident of iVillage," *Crain's New York Business*, 5 June 2000, p. 2.
71. Hearst purchased $20 million in stock in iVillage and provided a nice wedding present: an agreement to purchase some $15 million to $20 million in ads and other services from iVillage over a three-year period. Jill Hunter, "And Then There Was One: iVillage Buys Competitor Women.com," *Silicon Alley Daily*, 6 February 2001, pp. 4–5.
72. Lisa Ammerman, "Post-Women.com Merger, iVillage to Cut 50 Percent of Its Staff," *Silicon Alley Daily*, 22 June 2001, pp. 5–6.
73. Dakota Smith, "StarMedia Cuts 125 Staffers," *Silicon Alley Daily*, 14 September 2000, pp. 2–3.
74. Mark Walsh, "Crunch Leaves Alley Firms Few Choices," *Crain's New York Business*, 26 February 2001, p. 42.
75. Brian Morrissey, "StarMedia CEO Shuffle: Narciso Replaces Espuelas," *Silicon Alley Daily*, 8 August 2001, pp. 3–4.
76. "DoubleClick Acquires @plan in $120 Million Deal," *Silicon Alley Daily*, 25 September 2000, p. 8.
77. Chris Gaitler, "DoubleClick in Layoffs as Online Advertising Slackens," *New York Times*, 5 December 2000, Section C, p. 4.
78. Brian Morrissey, "DoubleClick Turns to E-Mail to Weather Online Ad Storm," *Silicon Alley Daily*, 11 July 2001, pp. 2–3.
79. "Consultant, Heal Thyself," *Economist*, 9 December 2000, p. 74.
80. Andrew Ross, *No-Collar*, p. 85.
81. Ibid., pp. 210–11.
82. Brian Morrissey, "Honey, I Shrunk the Fish: Razorfish Gets Smaller," *Silicon Alley Daily*, 15 August 2001, p. 5.
83. Mark Walsh, "Everything Old Is New Again," *Crain's New York Business*, 3 July 2000, p. 3.
84. Michael O'Sullivan, Comments, panel on The Path to Profitability, Silicon Alley Uptown, Columbia University, 17 November 2000.

85. Andy Weissman, "Surviving the Alley," keynote address at Alley Talks, New York University, 2 March 2001.
86. Wenda Harris Millard, Comments, panel on State of the New York New Media 2001, New York New Media Association, New York, 30 January 2001.
87. Scott Kurnit, Comments, panel on State of the New York New Media, 2001.
88. Jerry Colonna, Comments, panel on State of the New York New Media, 2001.
89. Laurie Joan Aron, "IBM Makes Inroads in Silicon Alley," *Crain's New York Business*, 2 April 2001, p. 14.
90. "Primedia to Acquire About.com for $690 Million," *Silicon Alley Daily*, 30 October 1999, p. 1.
91. Mark Walsh, "Old Media, New Rush to E-Merge," *Crain's New York Business*, 6 November 2000, p. 3.
92. Kenneth Li, "Viacom Goes Super Sonic," *The Industry Standard*, 16 October 2000, p. 124.
93. Lisa Ammerman, "I Want My Synergy," *Silicon Alley Daily*, 26 March 2001, p. 4.
94. "AOL/Time Warner," *Silicon Alley Reporter* (January 2001): 29.
95. Jill Hunter, "In New Venture, Pseudo's Harris Bares Much More than His Soul," *Silicon Alley Daily*, 7 December 2000, pp. 1–4.
96. C. J. Hughes, "Convergence, Convergence," *Silicon Alley Daily*, 11 January 2001, p. 5.
97. C. J. Hughes, "CondeNet Sports a New Look," *Silicon Alley Daily*, 18 January 2001, p. 4.
98. C. J. Hughes, "Lobbying for Change," *Silicon Alley Daily*, 30 November 2000, p. 5–6.
99. "AOL/Time Warner," p. 29.

CHAPTER 7

1. Andrew Ross, *No-Collar: The Humane Workplace and Its Hidden Costs* (New York: Basic Books, 2003), p. 236.
2. Richard Florida, "People Who Can Rebuild a City," *New York Times*, 26 July 2002, p. 2.
3. Ethan Brown, "Generation Hexed," *New York Magazine*, 17 March 2003, p. 28.
4. Carl Swanson, "We Know What You Paid Last Summer," *New York Magazine*, 12 March 2001, p. 29.
5. "The Neighborhoods," *New York Magazine*, pp. 35–46.
6. Swanson, "We Know What You Paid Last Summer," p. 30.
7. "The Neighborhoods," pp. 35–46.
8. Charles Bagli, "Firms in Bidding War for Midtown Space," *New York Times*, November 30, 2000, Section B, p. 9.
9. Saskia Sassen, "How Downtown Can Stand Tall and Step Lively Again," *New York Times*, 26 January 2003, p. 35.
10. The source for these figures is a December 24, 2002, posting to an urban sociology listserve by Andrew Beveridge. He also reported that the Trade Center had its own zip code. The total in wages and salaries to the 34,000 workers in the complex amounted to $3.15 billion—an average of $93,000 each.
11. Neoliberal policies helped spur the globalization of the city's financial and producer services, and U.S. monetary polities, trade policies, and geopolitical maneuvering have boosted the ensemble's standing in the world economy. Richard Child Hill and J. W. Kim, "Global Cities and Developmental States," *Urban Studies*, 38 (2000): 2167–95. The roots of the growing interdependence between aggressive foreign policy and the financialization of the U.S. economy lay in the $3 trillion in trade deficits the United States has amassed since its manufacturing sector began to fall behind in the early 1980s; as a consequence, the United States had become the world's biggest borrower. This accelerated in the 1990s. While foreign investors held 20 percent of the federal debt to private interests in 1993, they held 40 percent in 2003. Niall Ferguson, "True Cost of Hegemony: Huge Debt," *New York Times*, 20 April 2003, Section 4, pp. 1, 5.
12. Naval War College, "Asian Energy Futures Event Report (1): Project Overview and Introduction," NWC.navy.mil, April 2001, pp. 1–11.
13. Ibid., p. 3.
14. Ibid., p. 6.
15. Ibid.
16. Chalmers Johnson, *Blowback: The Costs and Consequences of American Empire* (New York: Henry Holt, 2000); John Aruilla and David Ronfeldt, *Networks and Netwars* (Santa Monica, CA: Rand, 2001).

17. "ESpeed Moves Up Profits Date," *Silicon Alley Daily*, 1 February 2001, pp. 7–8.
18. This is my transcription of this report, which can be heard on the Silicon Alley Station website.
19. Brian Morrissey, *Silicon Alley Daily*, 12 September 2001, p. 6.
20. Leslie Eaton, "Economy Is Tough All Over, But in New York, It's Horrid," *New York Times*, 19 February 2003, Section B, p. 6.
21. New York City Partnership, *Working Together to Accelerate New York's Recovery: Update of the NYC Partnership's Economic Impact Analysis of the September 11th Attack on New York City*, 11 February 2002.
22. Charles R. Morris, "New York and Wall Street," *New York Times*, 11 May 2003, Weekend Section, p. 5.
23. Leslie Eaton, "Job Losses in New York City Since 9/11 Continue to Grow," *New York Times*, 14 March 2003, Section B, p. 3.
24. Katin Hetter, "Report: Attacks 'Wound' Many Industries," *Newsday.com*, 31 October 2000, p. 1.
25. Charles Bagli, "Insurer Considers Major Move to Downtown's Empty Office Spaces," *New York Times*, 7 March 2003, Section D, p. 4.
26. Kyle Shannon, Comments, panel on the State of the NYC Digital Economy, New School University, 8 November 2001.
27. Lore Croghan, "Disappearing Downtown," *Crain's New York Business*, 14 January 2002, p. 19.
28. Relief, Rebuilding, and Recovery Community Meeting, 3 October 2001.
29. "Media Roll-ups," *Silicon Alley Daily*, 18 January 2001.
30. Though Microsoft quickly backtracked on its short-lived plans to remake itself into a media company, it continues to explore multiple paths in hopes of gaining leverage via the Internet; News Corp. is developing leverage in the area of direct satellite service.
31. About.com contributed greatly to large losses for Primedia, including one of $278 million in the third quarter of 2001. Andrew Marks, "Revisiting a Vastly Changed Alley," *Crain's New York Business*, 26 November 2002, p. 20. Primedia ended up writing off $326 million on its about.com purchase. In April 2003, Kohlberg Kravis Roberts (KKR)—Primedia's main investor—pressured Primedia's CEO to resign and reportedly decided to put much of Primedia up for sale. It was thought that in the best case scenario KKR would end up with a net loss of $1 billion on its investment.
32. In late 2002 AOL Time Warner acknowledged that advertising revenue during the time that the merger was pending had been overstated by some $190 million—mostly at AOL; in April 2003 the company disclosed that the Securities and Exchange Commission was questioning an additional $400 million in revenue. A bevy of lawsuits by investors followed, claiming that the company had inflated its results by $1.7 billion and that top executives had disguised the deterioration of the business while they were dumping almost $1 billion of their own stock. David D. Kirkpatrick, "Lawsuits Say AOL Investors Were Mislead," *New York Times*, 15 April 2003, Section C, pp. 1, 13.
33. Randy Whitestone, "Flatiron Partners to Move in with J. P. Morgan to Save Money," *Bloomberg.com*, 14 May 2001, p. 1.
34. David Whitford, "Recalculating His Riches," *Fortune Small Business*, October 2001, p. 1.
35. Its venture capital unit (Chase Capital Partners), which had partnered with Flatiron Partners to invest in firms such as StarMedia and theStreet.com had become an albatross for the parent company—"the dead bird around its neck," in the words of an investment banker. Stephen Gandel, "Chase Fails to Capitalize on Unit, " *Crain's New York Business*, 13 November 2000, p. 12. Its $32 billion acquisition of J. P. Morgan in a bid to become a player in IPO underwriting was a dismal failure, and it sustained huge losses from loans to former New Economy wunderkind, Enron and Worldcom. Moreover, it was the target of lawsuits from angry investors due to its role in Enron deals. By September 2002, the bank's share price had fallen 61 percent from its August 2000 high (in comparison, a stock index for large banks had dropped 22 percent in the same period). Heike Wipperforth, "A Triple Play of Mistakes," *Crain's New York Business*, 23 September 2002, p. 53.
36. From 2000 to 2001 the number of advertising pages for *BusinessWeek*, *Fortune*, and *Forbes* as a group had fallen 37 percent. They fell another 25 percent between July 2001 and July 2002. Paul D. Colford, "Biz, Money Mags in Ad Crunch," *New York Daily News*, 3 September 2002, p. 1. By 2003 the ranks of New Economy magazines had been devastated by the closures of *The Industry Standard*, *Upside*, and *Red Herring*. CNBC, which had become the most-watched cable news source by mid-2000, reeled as its primetime audience dropped 43

percent between 2001 and 2002. CNBC decided to depart from the "sports" model of business news (each trading day is treated as a sporting event). Jim Rutenberg, "CNBC Official for Business News Resigns," *New York Times*, 8 August 2002, Section C, p. 4.

37. Ryan Naraine, "*Silicon Alley Reporter* Goes Under," *internetnews.com*, 8 October 2001, p. 1.

38. Amy Harmon, "Requiem for a Cheerleader: Silicon Alley Magazine Is Dead," *New York Times*, 8 October 2001, Section C, p. 9.

39. "Media Technology Firm Puts Itself Up for Sale," *Crain's New York Business*, 27 January 2003, pp. 1–2.

40. Lisa Fichenscher, "Abandoned in NY," *Crain's New York Business*, 20 May 2002, p. 26.

41. Ibid., p. 21.

42. Ibid., p. 26.

43. In response to a NYSIA preelection survey, Green and three other Democratic candidates all pledged broad programs of support for Silicon Alley; Michael Bloomberg did not respond. On September 7, 2001, NYSIA's head commented that the responses of the four Democrats "show that they're taking Silicon Alley seriously." C. J. Hughes, "Running Through the Alley: Candidates Log Their Tech Position," *Silicon Alley Daily*, 7 September 2001, p. 4.

44. Fichenscher, "Abandoned in NY," p. 26.

45. Ibid.

46. Lisa Fichenscher, "NY Tech Jobs Crash-Landing in NJ, Abroad," *Crain's New York Business*, 3 March 2003, p. 30.

47. Lisa Fichenscher, "Abandoned Alley," *Crain's New York Business*, 16 November 2001, p. 16.

48. Interview, September 2002.

49. Fichenscher, "NY Tech Jobs Crash-Landing in NJ, Abroad," pp. 1, 30.

50. Susan Stallin, "The Long, Humbling Quest for a Job in Technology," *New York Times*, 17 March 2002, Section 10, pp. 1, 3.

51. Anne Field, "When a Job Hunt Is Measured in Seasons or Even in Years," *New York Times*, 8 December 2002, Section 10, pp. 1, 3.

52. Michael Indergaard, "Retrainers as Labor Market Brokers: Remaking the Networks and Narratives of Downriver Detroit," *Social Problems*, 46, 1 (1999): 67–87; Vicki Smith, *Crossing the Great Divide* (Ithaca, NY: ILR Press, 2001).

53. Jonathan Mahler, "Commute to Nowhere," *New York Times Sunday Magazine*, April 13, 2003, p. 44.

54. Ibid., p. 75.

55. Smith, *Crossing the Great Divide*, p. 134.

56. Mahler, "Commute to Nowhere," p. 75

57. Ibid.

58. Brown, "Generation Hexed," p. 29.

59. Ibid., p.30.

60. Interview, September 2002.

61. Ibid.

62. Kyle Shannon, Comments, New York New Media Association Town Hall Meeting, Now What? 12 July 2001, New York; Marisa Bowe, Comments, New York New Media Association Town Hall Meeting, Now What? 12 July 2001, New York.

63. Kevin Werbach, Comments, New York New Media Association Town Hall Meeting.

64. Robert Friedman, Comments, New York New Media Association Town Hall Meeting.

65. Erin Joyce, "Rumors of Death of Silicon Alley," *At New York*, 16 November 2001, pp. 2–3.

66. Fichenscher, "Abandoned Alley," p. 16.

67. Ibid., pp. 15–16.

68. Denny Lee, "Silicon Alley: A Once-Evocative Name Falls Victim to the Bursting of the High-Tech Bubble," *New York Times*, 24 March 2002, p. 4.

69. A search of the *New York Times* archives for the period 1996 to 2001 produced 191 "hits" on the name; in 2002 there were only 12 while in 2003 (up to May 4) there were 2.

70. Erin Joyce, "A Pitch for the State of New Media, Software Summit," *At New York*, 1 March 2002, p. 3; Kathryn Wylde, Comments, panel on State of New York New Media 2002, 26 February 2002, New York; Alan Patricof, Comments, panel on State of New York New Media 2002, 26 February 2002, New York.

71. Sharon Zukin, *The Cultures of Cities* (Malden, MA: Blackwell, 1995); idem, *Loft Living* (New Brunswick, NJ: Rutgers University Press, 1982).

72. Nanette Byrnes, "The Future of the City," *BusinessWeek*, 1 October 2001, p. 52.
73. Tenants preapprove visitors by putting visitors' names into the computer. When visitors arrive they show their ID to a guard who pushes a button to send a message to the person being visited; the computer prints out a bar-coded security badge for the visitor that is programmed to limit the time of the visit and where in the building they can go. The badge allows a visitor to pass through electronic turnstyles and to use elevators that can access the floors the visitor is cleared for. If one overstays a visit he or she cannot go through any turnstyles or use any elevators. Edwin McDowell, "Advancing Technology Tightens Building Security," *New York Times*, 5 March 2003, Section C, p. 5.
74. At a Columbia University event in 2002 architects presented plans for the World Trade Center site that included mammoth buildings; during a break another academic—concerned that such sites would draw terrorists—asked me why technology could not be developed to put a bubble over Manhattan. This sort of rational fantasy flies in the face of a key lesson of the Trade Center—the risk in letting everything ride on one complex system.
75. The developer who heads the group that owns the site's ninety-nine–year lease claims that he has the right to rebuild two one hundred–story towers. And the New York–New Jersey Port Authority wants to replace most or all of the commercial space that was destroyed so that it can continue to charge full rent for the site ($120 million a year). Indeed, the Port Authority criteria in the design competition for the site required that 11 million square feet of commercial space be provided, forcing designs to feature high-rise towers. Charles Bagli, "A Memorial, Yes, but Battle Lines Form for Everything Else at Ground Zero," *New York Times*, 27 February 2003, Section B, p. 6; Edward Wyatt, "At Trade Center Site, A Wealth of Ideas," *New York Times*, 28 July 2002, pp. 25, 27.
76. Neil Scott Kleinman, "The Creative Engine: How Arts & Culture Is Fueling Economic Growth in New York City Neighborhoods," Center for an Urban Future, New York, 12 November 2002, p. 15.
77. Kathyrn Wylde, Comments, panel on State of New York New Media 2002, 26 February 2002, New York; Alan Patricof, Comments, panel on State of New York New Media 2002, 26 February 2002, New York.
78. Jennifer Steinhauer, "Mayor's Proposal Envisions Lower Manhattan as an Urban Hamlet," *New York Times*, 13 December 2002, pp. 1–2.
79. Kleinman, "The Creative Engine," p. 16.
80. Richard Florida, *The Rise of the Creative Class* (New York: Basic Books: 2002); Joel Kotkin, *The New Geography* (New York: Random House, 2000).
81. Joel Kotkin, "Saving Silicon Alley: The Key to Lower Manhattan's Future," *Techscapes* (2002): 1–4. It would be harder to find a more stark contrast between two areas in the United States. North Dakota is losing population because, like most of the Great Plains, it has suffered from a chronic crisis in the family farm economy due to the rise of corporate farming and the relaxation of barriers to low-cost foreign agricultural goods.
82. The firm's president reported that he cultivated a "creative" workplace, so as to draw local college students: "If we can get them exposed to the work culture and the creative environment . . . it's a pretty compelling argument to keep people here." John Lamb, "Creative Climate Might Be Cure," *Fargo Forum*, 29 December 2002, p. 1. Notice that his focus is on the appeal of the workplace as opposed to that of amenities—Florida's main policy emphasis.
83. Ibid.
84. A Minneapolis thinktank commented, "This is really a program that provides a subsidy to middle-class folks." Kotkin claims there is a need to break up a culture of dependency in the farmbelt that has been fostered by farm subsidies and Social Security. Patrick Springer, "Plan Offers Old Name, New Twist," *Fargo Forum*, 30 December 2002, p. 4.
85. Joel Kotkin, "New York State of Blind," Center for an Urban Future, New York, 13 May 2002, p. 2.
86. Ibid.
87. Richard Florida, "People Who Can Rebuild a City," *New York Times*, 26 July 2002, p. 21.
88. Mike Wallace, "New York, New Deal," in Michael Sorkin and Sharon Zukin (eds.), *After the World Trade Center: Rethinking New York City* (New York: Routledge, 2002), p. 210.
89. Ibid., p. 215.
90. Jane Jacobs, *The Nature of Economics* (New York: Modern Library, 2000); Frederick Hayek, *The Road to Serfdom* (Chicago: University of Chicago Press, 1994). Historian Eric Foner

notes that Hayek stressed the inferior capacity of central planning offices compared to "a spontaneous social order based on the free market" when it came to mobilizing "fragmented and partial knowledge scattered throughout society." Eric Foner, *The Story of American Freedom* (New York: W. W. Norton, 1998), p. 236.

91. The prominence of accounting tricks and fraud is evidenced by class action law suits against on the one hand firms, executives, and underwriters involved in over three hundred IPOs and on the other, corporate giants such as AOL Time Warner. Even in the case of Cisco—the model firm—much of its vaunted model turned out to hinge on its ability to exploit accounting loopholes regarding acquisitions.

92. Kevin Phillips, "The Cycles of Financial Scandal," *New York Times*, 17 July 2002, p. 19; also see idem, *Wealth and Democracy* (New York: Broadway Books, 2002). The example of the drawn out development of mass production's characteristic features is illustrative. While Henry Ford introduced his assembly line in 1913–14, it took thirty years to develop the full array of institutions that tamed and harnessed mass production to lift the majority of Americans out of poverty: The multidivisional corporation, segmented mass markets, New Deal labor law and social welfare mechanisms such as unemployment insurance, industrial unions, Keynesian demand management, regular wage increases matched to productivity increases, and health and pension benefits are some examples.

93. Miriam Kreinin Souccar, "Groups Urge Link of Arts, New York Economy," *Crain's New York Business*, 11 November 2002, p. 3.

94. Joel Kotkin, "Why Saving Silicon Alley Is Essential for New York," *WallStreetJournal.com*, 25 April 2002, p. 1.

95. In 2002 the State Assembly agreed to give the City University of New York $7.5 million to create a network of incubators at four community colleges. The incubators are to specialize in the areas of health care, high tech entertainment businesses like video games and design. The models for the incubators were developed by a group that included the New York City Partnership and NYSIA. Karen W. Arenson, "CUNY Getting Money to Nurture High-Tech Firms," *New York Times*, 17 October 2002. NYSIA also received a total of $4 million from the state and federal government to set up an Institute for Advanced Studies in Software and Information Techology. The R&D facility is expected to launch as many as fifty projects a year when it opens in 2004. "Feds Give $1 Million for Software Institute," *Crain's New York Business*, 17 March 2003, p. 2.

96. The New York City Partnership has helped form a consortium consisting of a dozen research institutions, businesses, investment firms, and city and state officials in order to push for the creation of a biotech hub in downtown Manhattan. In a second phase, the group envisions that a ring of commercial laboratories would be built by university campuses across the city to incubate start-up firms. Harold Varmus, "The DNA of a New Industry," *New York Times*, 24 September 2002, p. 27.

97. Jane Roh, "High (-Finance) Art: Arts Organization Thundergulch Seeks Synergy in the Alley," *Silicon Alley Reporter*, 5 (2001): 76.

98. Michael Hess, "Never-Ending Stories?" *AlleyCat News*, February 2001, p. 67.

99. The filmmaker remarks that local "indie" films are characterized by "the strong, uncompromising, personal vision of a director, minimal budgets, and a fetish for challenging forms, content, and style." Hess 2001, p. 56.

100. According to a curator, a number of photographers working after World War II were drawn to the notion of an open city as a metaphor for a place of "spontaneity and innovation, authenticity and artifice" that was "constantly forming new patterns." Sarah Boxer, "Photography Review: The Street Game Is to Be Distinctive Without Seeming to Work at It," *New York Times*, 5 July 2002, Section E, p. 34.

101. Cathy Lang Ho, "To the Rise of Techno-Decor," *New York Times*, 12 September 2002, Section F1, p. 2.

102. Julia Chaplin, "On Wall Street After Dark, A New Bohemia Beckons," *New York Times*, 18 August 2002, Section 9, p. 2.

103. Ibid.

104. Lang Ho, "To the Rise of Techno-Decor," p. 1.

105. Sir Peter Hall, *Cities in Civilization* (New York: Pantheon, 1998).

106. Lang Ho, "To the Rise of Techno-Decor," p. 9.

107. Ibid.

108. Ibid.
109. Ibid.
110. Kuniko Fujita, "Neo-Industrial Tokyo: Urban Development and Globalization in Japan's State-Centered Developmental Capitalism," *Urban Studies*, 40, 2 (2003): 249–82.
111. Chicago has set up four special manufacturing districts. The one on Goose Island, for example, demonstrates that manufacturing can prosper in the city if its district is protected from real estate speculators and gentrification; after Goose Island—which was surrounded by gentrifing neighborhoods—was made a district, the number of workers employed by industry there increased from one thousand to five thousand. Robert Sharoff, "Rebirth of a Chicago Industrial Area," *New York Times*, 26 March 2003, Section C, p. 4.
112. With regard to real estate specifically, urban researcher Susan Fainstein has documented that recent administrations in New York City have relied far too heavily "on the property industry as the vehicle for growth policy." Susan Fainstein, *The City Builders: Property Development in New York and London, 1980–2000*, 2nd ed. (Lawrence: University Press of Kansas, 2001), p. 219.
113. The notion of industrial politics was developed by Charles Sabel and has been applied by many authors to analyze industrial districts. See Charles Sabel, "Bootstrapping Reform: Rebuilding Firms, the Welfare State, and Unions," *Politics and Society*, 23 (1995): 5–48; Gary Herrigel, "Power and the Redefinition of Industrial Districts," in Gerhard Grabher (ed.), *The Embedded Firm* (London: Routledge & Kegan Paul, 1993), pp. 227–51; Ash Amin and Nigel Thrift, "Living in the Global," in Amin and Thrift (eds.), *Globalization, Institutions, and Regional Development in Europe* (New York: Oxford University Press, 1994), pp. 1–22.

INDEX